RED'S CC
A SHORT HISTORY OF MODERN PHILOSOPHY

This new edition of Roger Scruton's widely acclaimed *Short History* covers all the major thinkers in the Western tradition, from Descartes to Wittgenstein. It is an ideal introduction to philosophical history for all those with an interest in this fascinating subject.

In order to reflect recent debates and advances in scholarship and in response to the explosion of interest in the history of philosophy, Roger Scruton has substantially revised his book, while retaining the lucid and accessible style of the original version. He has also enlarged and updated the bibliography.

A Short History of Modern Philosophy will make excellent reading for anyone who would like to understand the principal ideas and arguments that have shaped modern philosophy.

Roger Scruton is well known as a writer, broadcaster and journalist. He has written numerous books, including *The Meaning of Conservatism*, *Sexual Desire* and *Xanthippic Dialogues*.

Related titles from Routledge:

Philosophy: The Basics
Nigel Warburton

Classical Modern Philosophers
Richard Schacht

The Continental Philosophy Reader
Edited by Richard Kearney and Mara Rainwater

A Dictionary of Philosophy
A. R. Lacey

Roger Scruton
A Short History of Modern Philosophy
From Descartes to Wittgenstein

Second edition

London and New York

First published in 1981 as
From Descartes to Wittgenstein
ARK edition 1984
Reprinted six times

Second revised and enlarged edition published 1995
by Routledge
11 New Fetter Lane, London EC4P 4EE

Simultaneously published in the USA and Canada
by Routledge
29 West 35th Street, New York, NY 10001

Reprinted in 1996

Typeset in Adobe Garamond by Keystroke, Jacaranda Lodge,
Wolverhampton

Printed and bound in Great Britain by Clays Ltd, St Ives PLC

British Library Cataloguing in Publication Data
A catalogue record for this book is available from the British Library.

Library of Congress Cataloguing in Publication Data
A catalogue record for this book has been requested.

ISBN 0–415–13327–0 (hbk)
ISBN 0–415–13035–2 (pbk)

CONTENTS

PREFACE TO THE FIRST EDITION

This book provides a synthetic vision of the history of modern philosophy, from an analytical perspective. It is necessarily selective, but I hope that I have identified the principal figures, and the principal intellectual pre-occupations, that have formed Western philosophy since Descartes. It is, I believe, fruitful to approach these matters from the standpoint of analytical philosophy, which in recent years has become interested in the history which it had ignored for so long, and has sought to re-establish its connections with the Western intellectual tradition. Areas which were of the greatest concern to historical philosophers – aesthetics, politics, theology, the theory of the emotions – had been for some years ill-served in English and American writings; moreover, an increasing narrowness of vision, an obsession with technique and competence, had tended to replace that broad sensitivity to the human condition which is the traditional attribute of the speculative philosopher. The renewed interest in philosophical history promises to remedy those defects, and already fields such as aesthetics and political philosophy are beginning to appear, if not central, at least not wholly marginal, to a mature philosophical under-standing.

I discuss analytical philosophy through the imaginative thought of its greatest exponent, Wittgenstein, and I have been obliged to pass over the many interesting, but perhaps overrated, achievements of the English and American thinkers for whom logic and language have equally been philosophy's first concern. My intention has been to give a perspective that is as broad as possible, and to show the underlying continuity of argument which recent achievements help us to perceive.

In the first chapter I explain why I confine my discussion for the most part to the leading figures of post-Renaissance philosophy, and why my methods differ from those of the historian of ideas. My concern is to describe the content of philosophical conclusions and arguments, and not the contexts in which they occurred or the influences which led to them. Those with an interest in the history of ideas will wish to go back over the ground covered by this book and to explore the historical conditions from which the arguments grew, and the currents of influence which led from Hobbes to Spinoza, from Malebranche to Berkeley, from Rousseau to Kant, and from Schopenhauer to Wittgenstein. The classifications of schools and arguments that I have adopted may then begin to appear, if not arbitrary, at least very much matters of philosophical convenience.

It is necessary to mention the peculiarities of the standpoint from which this book is written. Although it has taken time for analytical philosophy to emerge from its cultural isolation, it seems to me that the light that it has begun to cast on the history of philosophy is greater than any that was cast by the compendious surveys which appeared during the hundred years preceding its development. A new style of philosophical history has emerged, which attempts to discover arguments which might be put forward and accepted, not just at the time when they were first announced, but at any time. To ask whether it is possible *now* to believe what Leibniz wrote is to submit one's interpretation to a severe intellectual discipline. It becomes necessary to discover what Leibniz really meant by his conclusions, and what arguments justified, or might justify, his belief in them. It becomes necessary to translate the thought of previous philosophers from the jargon that might obscure its meaning, to remove from it all that is parochial and time-bound, and to present it in the idiom which modern people would use in the expression of their own most serious beliefs. In the bibliography to this work the reader will find references to recent studies in the history of philosophy which, while they may lack the range and the cultural sophistication of earlier studies, seem to me to have changed irreversibly the way in which philosophical history now appears, precisely by looking to the past for answers to present questions. Just as the discovery of the new logic enabled philosophers to understand the researches of medieval logicians for the first time, so has the new philosophy of language and mind made the arguments of Kant intelligible in a way that they were not intelligible to those whom Kant first influenced.

It should not be thought, however, that the analytical version of the history of philosophy bears no relation to the history of philosophy as it is seen by thinkers from other schools. The interpretation that I offer is one that would be acceptable, in its broad outlines, to many phenomenologists. Like the phenomenologists I see the main current in modern philosophy as springing from the Cartesian theory of the subject, and from the consequent divorce between subject and object, between the realm of certainty and the realm of doubt. I believe that this current runs through epistemology, metaphysics, ethics and political philosophy, throughout the period that I survey. I also believe that Wittgenstein's detailed demonstration of the untenability of the Cartesian vision has effectively brought a period of philosophical history to an end. However, the arguments of Wittgenstein to which I refer also, I believe, destroy the credibility of phenomenology.

Needless to say, because this book is as brief as I could make it, it can serve only as a guide; my task will have been accomplished if it helps the reader to understand and enjoy the works of the philosophers that I discuss.

Preface to the Second Edition

During the fifteen years since this book was first published, analytical philosophers have devoted much of their attention to philosophical history. Although the broad outlines of the subject remain the same, the details have inevitably changed. In certain cases – notably that of Hume – the traditional understanding of a philosopher's aims and arguments has been entirely revised. And thinkers whose work had been for many years dismissed, or passed over with a cursory and disapproving glance, have been rehabilitated – Fichte and Reid being prominent examples.

Although this recent scholarship lies beyond the scope of this short introduction, it has necessitated considerable revisions of the text and a much fuller bibliography than was provided in the first edition. It goes without saying that a short introduction is bound to be controversial. Nevertheless I have tried to represent accurately, and in the minimum space, what the great modern philosophers have thought, and to show why they are still important.

I have been greatly helped in preparing this second edition by comments and criticisms from friends, colleagues and students. I am particularly grateful to Fiona Ellis, whose scholarly expertise has saved me from many grievous errors.

Malmesbury, 1995

Introduction

1

HISTORY OF PHILOSOPHY AND HISTORY OF IDEAS

The subject matter of this work is 'modern' philosophy. In common with others I suppose that modern philosophy begins with Descartes, and that its most significant recent manifestation is to be found in the writings of Wittgenstein. I hope to give some ground for these assumptions, but my principal purpose will be to present the history of modern Western philosophy as briefly as the subject allows.

It is my intention that the contents of this book should be intelligible to those who have no specialised knowledge of contemporary analytical philosophy. It is unfortunately very difficult to describe the nature of philosophy in a small compass; the only satisfaction that an author can draw from the attempt to do so lies in the knowledge that an answer to the question 'What is philosophy?' is apt to seem persuasive only to the extent that it is brief. The more one ponders over the qualifications that any reasoned answer must contain, the more one is driven to the conclusion that this question is itself one of the principal subjects of philosophical thinking. It goes without saying that the description that I now give of the nature of philosophy will reflect the particular philosophical standpoint of which I feel persuaded, and its merit in the eyes of the reader must reside in the fact that it has recommended itself to a philosopher who is also a contemporary.

The nature of philosophy can be grasped through two contrasts: with science on the one hand, and with theology on the other. Simply speaking, science is the realm of empirical investigation; it stems from the attempt to understand the world as we perceive it, to predict and explain observable events and to formulate the 'laws of nature' (if there be any) according to which the course of human experience is to be explained. Now any science will generate a number of questions which lie beyond the reach of its own methods of enquiry, and which it will therefore prove powerless to solve. Consider the question, asked of some episode deemed remarkable, 'What caused that?' A scientific answer is likely to be formulated in terms of preceding events and conditions, together with certain laws or hypotheses, which connect the event to be explained with the events that explain it. But someone might ask the same question of those other events, and if the same kind of answer is given then, potentially at least, the series of causes could go on for ever, stretching backwards into infinite time. Perceiving the possibility of this, one might be prompted to ask the further question 'What caused the series to exist at all?' or, yet more abstractly, 'Why should there *be* any events?': not just, why should there be *this* event or *that*, but why is there *anything*? In the nature of the case, scientific investigation, which takes us from what is given to what explains it, presupposes the existence of things. Hence it cannot solve this more abstract and more puzzling question. It is a question that seems to reach beyond empirical enquiry and yet at the same time to arise naturally out of it. Science itself will not provide the answer, and yet it does not seem nonsensical to suggest that there might *be* an answer.

At every point we find that science generates questions which pass beyond its own ability to solve them. Such questions have been called metaphysical: they form a distinctive and inescapable part of the subject matter of philosophy. Now, in considering the particular metaphysical problem that I have mentioned, people might have recourse to an authoritative system of theology. They might find their answer in the invocation of God, as the first cause and final aim of everything. But if this invocation is founded merely on faith, then it claims no rational authority beyond that which can be attributed to revelation. Anyone who lets the matter rest in faith, and enquires no further into its validity, has, in a sense, a philosophy. He has staked his claim in a metaphysical doctrine, but has affirmed that doctrine *dogmatically*: it is, for him, neither the conclusion of reasoned argument, nor the result of metaphysical speculation. It is simply a received idea, which has the intellectual merit of generating answers to metaphysical puzzles, but with the singular disadvantage of adding no authority to those answers that is not contained in the original dogmatic assumption.

Any attempt to give a rational grounding for theology will, for the very reason that theology provides answers to metaphysical questions, itself constitute a form of philosophical thought. It is not surprising, therefore, that, while theology alone is not philosophy, the question of the *possibility* of theology has been, and to some extent still is, the principal philosophical question.

In addition to metaphysical questions of the kind I have referred to, there are other questions that have some *prima facie* right to be considered philosophical. In particular there are questions of method, typified by the two studies of epistemology (the theory of knowledge) and logic. Just as scientific investigation may be pushed back to the point where it becomes metaphysics, so may its own method be thrown in question by repeatedly asking for the grounds for each particular assertion. In this way science inevitably gives rise to the studies of logic and epistemology, and if there is a temptation to say that the conclusions of these studies are empty or meaningless, or that their questions are unanswerable, that in itself is a philosophical opinion, as much in need of argument as the less sceptical alternatives.

To the studies of metaphysics, logic and epistemology one must add those of ethics, aesthetics and political philosophy, since here too, as soon as we are led to enquire into the basis of our thought, we find ourselves pushed to levels of abstraction where no empirical enquiry can provide a satisfactory answer. For example, while everybody will realise that a commitment to a moral principle forbidding theft involves an abstention from theft on any particular occasion, everybody also recognises that a starving man's theft of bread from one who has no need of it is an act which must be considered differently from a rich man's theft of another's most precious possession. But why do we regard these acts differently, how do we reconcile this attitude, if at all, with adherence to the original principle, and how do we justify the principle itself? All these questions lead us towards distinctively philosophical regions; the purviews of morality, of law, of politics themselves will be left behind, and we find ourselves reaching out for abstractions, often with little conviction that they might suffice to uphold a system of beliefs, and often with a renewed desire to take refuge in the dogmas of theology.

What, then, distinguishes philosophical thought? The questions that philosophers ask have two distinguishing features from which we might begin to characterise them: abstraction, and concern for truth. By abstraction I mean roughly this: that philosophical questions arise at the end of all other enquiries, when questions about particular things, events and practical difficulties have been solved according to the methods available, and when either those methods themselves, or some metaphysical doctrine which they seem to presuppose, are put in question. Hence the problems of philosophy and the systems designed to solve them are formulated in terms which tend to refer, not to the realm of actuality, but to the realms of possibility and necessity: to what might be and what must be, rather than to what is.

The second feature – the concern with truth – is one that might seem too obvious to be worth mentioning. But in fact it is easily forgotten, and when it is forgotten philosophy is in danger of degenerating into rhetoric. The questions that philosophy asks may be peculiar in that they have no answer – some philosophers have been driven to think so. But they are nevertheless questions, so that any answer is to be evaluated by giving reasons for thinking it to be true or false. If there are no answers, then all putative answers are false. But if someone proposes an answer, he must give reasons for believing it.

During the course of this work we shall come across several writers and schools of thought which have been founded in what one might call 'meta-philosophy' – that is, in some theory as to the nature of philosophical thought, designed to explain how there can be an intellectual discipline that is both wholly abstract and yet dedicated to the pursuit of truth. Such meta-philosophies tend to belong to one of two kinds, according as they uphold speculation or analysis as the aim of philosophical thinking.

Some say – following in the tradition of Pythagoras and Plato – that philosophy gains its abstract quality because it consists in the speculative study of abstract things, in particular of certain objects, or certain worlds, which are inaccessible to experience. Such philosophies are likely to denigrate empirical investigation, saying that it yields only half-truths, since it studies appearance alone, whereas speculative philosophy has the superior virtue of attaining to the realm of necessity, where the true contents of the world (or the contents of the true world) are revealed. Others regard philosophy as reaching to abstraction not because it speculates about some other more elevated world, but because it occupies itself with the more mundane task of intellectual criticism, studying the methods and aims of our specific forms of thought, in order to reach conclusions concerning their limits and validity. According to this second approach, abstraction is merely abstraction *from* the particular; it is not abstraction *towards* something else, in particular not towards some other realm of being. As for the pursuit of truth, that is explained immediately as an offshoot of the desire to settle what can be known, what can be proved – philosophical truth is simply truth about the limits of human understanding.

This analytical or critical philosophy, manifested at its most magisterial in the writings of Kant, has also dominated Anglo-American philosophy during this century, in the special form of 'conceptual' or 'linguistic' analysis. But the history of the subject suggests that, in questions of philosophy, analysis, in whatever high respect it may be held, always creates a desire for synthesis and speculation. However narrow a particular philosophy may look at first sight, however much it may seem to be mere verbal play or logic-chopping, it will in all probability lead by persuasive steps to conclusions, the metaphysical implications of which are as far-reaching as those of any of the grand speculative systems.

I have said that it is an essential feature of philosophical thought that it should have truth as its aim. But, faced with the bewildering variety of the conclusions, the contradictions of the methods, and the darkness of the premises of philosophers, the lay reader might well feel that this aim is either unfulfillable, or at best a pious hope rather than a serious intention. Surely, the reader will say, if there is such a thing as philosophical enquiry, which aims at and generates truth, then there ought to be philosophical progress, received premises, established conclusions; in short there ought to be the kind of steady obsolescence of successive systems that we observe in natural science, as new results are established and old ones overthrown. And yet we find no such thing; the works of Plato and Aristotle are studied as seriously now as they ever were, and it is as much the business of a modern philosopher, as it was the business of their philosophical contemporaries, to be familiar with their arguments. A scientist, by contrast, while he may have an interest in the history of his subject, can often ignore it with impunity, and usually does so. A modern physicist who had never heard of Archimedes may yet have a complete knowledge of the accepted conclusions of his subject.

It would be an answer to this scepticism to argue that there *is* progress in philosophy, but that the subject is peculiarly difficult. It lies at the limit of human understanding; therefore its progress is slow. It would also be an answer to argue that the nature of the subject is such that each attempt is a new beginning, which can take nothing for granted, and only rarely reach conclusions that have not been already stated in some other form, clothed in the language of some other system. It is useful here to contrast philosophy with science on the one hand, and literature on the other. As I have suggested, a scientist may with impunity ignore all but the recent history of his subject and be none the less expert for that. Conversely, someone with only a very inadequate grasp of physics (of the system of physics which is currently accepted as true) may nevertheless prove to be a competent historian of the subject, able to explore and expound the intellectual presuppositions and historical significance of many a dead hypothesis, and many an outmoded form of thought. (Thus we find that science and the history of science are beginning to be separable academic disciplines, with little or no overlap in questions or results.)

When we turn to literature, however, we find a completely different state of affairs. First, it is implausible to suggest that there is an innate tendency of literature to progress – since there is nothing *towards* which it is progressing. Science, which moves towards truth, builds always on what has been established, and has an inalienable right to overthrow and demolish the most ingenious, satisfying and beautiful of its established systems, as Copernicus and Galileo overthrew the Ptolemaic and Aristotelian cosmology. It follows that someone who had never heard of Ptolemy or even of Aristotle might still be the greatest living cosmologist. Literature, by contrast, has its high points and its low points, but no semblance of a necessary progression from one to the other. The perspective across this landscape will change with time: what had appeared towering will in time be diminished, and (more rarely) what now appears insignificant will from a distance appear great. But there is no *progress* beyond Homer or Shakespeare, no necessary expectation that a person, however talented, who has stuffed his brain with all the literature produced before him must therefore be in a position to do as well or better, or even in a position to understand what he has read. Associated with this evident lack of a determinate direction are two important features of literary scholarship: first, it is impossible to engage in literary history without a full understanding of literature, and secondly, we cannot assume that a full understanding of literature will come from the study of contemporary works alone. History and criticism here penetrate and depend on each other; in science they are independent.

Philosophy seems to occupy some intermediate place between science and literature. On the one hand, it is possible to approach it in a completely unhistorical spirit, as Wittgenstein did, ignoring the achievements of previous philosophers and presenting philosophical problems in terms that bear no self-confessed relation to the tradition of the subject. Much contemporary philosophy is in this way unhistorical, and often none the worse for it. Philosophers have succeeded in isolating a series of questions to which they address themselves in a manner that increasingly concerns itself with what has been most recently thought, and with the intention of improving on that recent thought. The image is generated of 'established results', and of a movement which, because it is progressive, can afford to be unhistorical. But with the help of a little ingenuity, it is usually possible to discover, concealed in the writings of some historical philosopher, not only the most recent received opinion, but also some astonishing replica of the arguments used to support it. The discovery that the latest results have been anticipated by Aristotle, for example, has occurred many times during the history of philosophy, and always in such a way as to lead to the recognition of new arguments, new difficulties, and new objections surrounding the position adopted, whether that position be the scholastic theology of Aquinas, the romantic metaphysics of Hegel, or the dry analysis of the contemporary linguistic school.

Moreover, it is an undoubted fact that to approach the works of historical philosophers without the acquisition of some independent philosophical competence leads to misunderstanding. A purely 'historical' approach as much misrepresents the philosophy of Descartes or Leibniz as it misrepresents the plays of Shakespeare or the poetry of Dante. To understand the thought of these philosophers is to wrestle with the problems to which they addressed themselves, problems which are usually still as much the subject of philosophical enquiry as they ever were. It seems to be almost a precondition of entering the thought of traditional philosophers that one does not regard the issues which they discussed as 'closed', or their results as superseded. To the extent that one does so regard them, to that extent has one removed them from any central place in the history of the subject. (Just as a poet drops from the corpus of our literature to the extent that his concerns seem merely personal to him.)

Pursuing this thought, one comes very soon to the conclusion that two philosophers may arrive at similar results, but present those results so differently as to deserve equal place in philosophical history. This is the case with William of Ockham and Hume, with Hegel and Sartre. We will come across this phenomenon repeatedly in what follows.

We are now in a position to make a preliminary distinction of the greatest importance, the distinction between the history of philosophy and the 'history of ideas'. An idea may have a complex and interesting history, even when it is obvious to every philosopher that it has no persuasive power. (Consider the idea that there is more than one God.) Likewise an idea may have serious philosophical content, but owe its influence not to its truth but to the desire to believe it. (Consider the idea of redemption.) To be part of the history of philosophy an idea must be of intrinsic philosophical significance, capable of awakening the spirit of enquiry in a contemporary person, and representing itself as something that might be arguable and even true. To be part of the history of ideas an idea need only have an historical influence in human affairs. The history of philosophy must consider an idea in relation to the arguments that support it, and is distracted by too great an attention to its more vulgar manifestations, or to its origins in conceptions that have no philosophical worth. It is surely right for the historian of philosophy to study Kant's ethics, and to ignore Luther's *Bondage of the Will*, even though, from the historical point of view, the former would have been impossible had the latter not been written. In conceding such points, we concede also that the best method in philosophical history may be at variance with the practice of the historian of ideas. It may be necessary for the philosopher to lift an idea from the context in which it was conceived, to rephrase it in direct and accessible language, simply in order to estimate its truth. The history of philosophy then becomes a philosophical, and not an historical, discipline.

If the historian of philosophy studies influences, therefore, they will be the influences that derive not from the emotional or practical appeal but from the cogency of ideas. Hence the influence of Hume and Kant will be of the greatest philosophical significance, while the influence of Voltaire and Diderot will be relatively slight. To the historian of ideas, these four thinkers each belong to the single great movement called the 'Enlightenment', and in human affairs, where what matters is not cogency but motivating force, their influence is tangled inextricably.

It may happen that an historian of ideas and an historian of philosophy study the same system of thoughts; but it will be with conflicting interests, demanding different intellectual expertise. The historical influence of Rousseau's *Social Contract* was enormous. To study that influence one requires no better philosophical understanding of the document than belonged to those through whom the influence was most deeply felt – men and women of letters, enlightened sovereigns, popular agitators. The question of its philosophical interest, however, is an independent one, and, in order to approach the document from the philosophical view one must understand and set forth its conclusions with the best intention of determining their truth. To be able to do this one will need capacities of a different kind from those of the people most strongly influenced by the doctrine. One may indeed come to the conclusion (not in this case but certainly in the case of Tom Paine's *Rights of Man*) that a philosophical work of immense historical importance has no significant place in the history of philosophy.

In what follows the reader must bear in mind this distinction between the history of philosophy and the history of ideas, and recognise that the history that I am outlining is as much created by as it has created the current state of philosophical understanding. My method, however, will be, not to expound the arguments of philosophers in full, but to outline the main conclusions, their philosophical significance, and the kinds of consideration that led their authors to espouse them.

2

THE RISE OF MODERN PHILOSOPHY

The tradition which has marked out Descartes as the founder of 'modern' philosophy should not lead us to erect an impassable barrier between the thought of the seventeenth century and all that had preceded it and made it possible. The method of philosophy changed radically as a result of Descartes' arguments. But much of its content remained the same. It should not therefore be regarded as surprising if some modern philosophical idea can be shown to have been anticipated by the thinkers of the Middle Ages, in their manifold attempts either to reconcile religion and philosophy or else to divide them.

The spirit of Plato, and that of his pupil and critic Aristotle, have haunted philosophy throughout its history, and it is to them that almost all medieval controversies in the subject can ultimately be traced. They each bequeathed to the world arguments and conceptions of superlative intellectual and dramatic power, and it is not surprising that, wherever they were read, their influence was felt. Each of the important Mediterranean religions – Judaism, Christianity and Islam – attempted either to assimilate their doctrines or to present some alternative that would be equally persuasive and equally compatible with our intuitive sense of the nature of the world and of our place within it.

From Plato and the neo-Platonic tradition the medievals inherited a cosmology which both justified the belief in a supersensible reality, and at the same time presented an elevated picture of our ability to gain access to it. Plato had argued that the truth of the world is not revealed to ordinary sense-perception, but to reason alone; that truths of reason are necessary, eternal and (as we would now say) *a priori*; that through the cultivation of reason man can come to understand himself, God and the world as these things are in themselves, freed from the shadowy overcast of experience. The neo-Platonists developed the cosmology of Plato's *Timaeus* into a theory of creation, according to which the entire world emanates from the intellectual light of God's self-contemplation. Reason, being the part of man which participates in the intellectual light, knows things not as they seem but as they are. This theory – initially metaphysical – seemed to imply a corresponding 'natural philosophy' (a natural philosophy which had both Platonic and Aristotelian variants). According to this natural philosophy the earth and earthly things reside at the centre of the turning spheres, each representing successive orders of intellection, and each subordinate to the ultimate sphere of immutability, where God resides in the company of the blessed. Reason is the aspiration towards that ultimate sphere, and man's mortality is the occasion of his ascent towards it. This ascent is conditional upon his turning away from preoccupation with the ephemeral and the sensory towards the contemplation of eternal truth. This 'natural philosophy', persuasively expounded by Boethius (c. 480–524 AD) in his *Consolation of Philosophy* (one of the most popular works of philosophy ever to have been written), influenced his predecessor St Augustine (354–430 AD) – who nevertheless retained a sceptical stance towards much of Plato's metaphysics – and reappears in one or another variant, described, upheld and celebrated in countless works of medieval and early Renaissance literature, from popular lyrics to such masterpieces of high art as Chaucer's *Knight's Tale*, Dante's *Divine Comedy* and Spenser's *Faerie Queene*.

The consoling vision of neo-Platonic physics was accompanied, however, by no prescription against metaphysical uncertainty. At every point in the neo-Platonic system problems of seemingly insuperable difficulty were presented to the enquiring mind. What, for example, is this 'reason' upon which our knowledge of ultimate truth depends, and what are the laws of its operation? In what sense does it generate eternal, as opposed to transient, insights, and how do we learn to distinguish between the two? What is the nature of God, and how do we know of his existence?

What are the laws which govern the movement and generation of sublunary things, and how is the Platonic hypothesis – that man's residence among them is temporary, and that the end of his being lies elsewhere – compatible with his subjection to those laws? At every point the neo-Platonic cosmology raises problems of a philosophical kind. These problems seem not to be amenable to scientific resolution. On the contrary, they are posed precisely by the suggestion that sensory perception, which is the principal vehicle of scientific thought, leads us not to truth but to systematic (if sometimes persuasive) illusion.

As the theories of Aristotle began to become known among European thinkers – filtered through the writings of Arab philosophers and theologians who had gained them, as it were, by right of conquest – they were avidly studied as the source of new answers to these metaphysical queries. Some of the Aristotelian arguments were familiar to the early Christians. In particular, these arguments had been used in giving philosophical formulation to the doctrine of the Trinity. It was thanks to the philosophers of Alexandria, in particular to Clement (c. 150–215) and Origen (c. 185–254), both of whom had seen the inadequacies inherent in the neo-Platonism of their day, that all the resources of Greek philosophy were used together in the attempt to achieve a coherent statement of Christian dogma. And with the victory over Arianism, and the consequent acceptance of the doctrine of the Trinity, one of the most important of all Aristotelian concepts, the concept of substance, took a central place in the formulation of the credo of the Christian Church. Thus already, by the time that the Council of Nicaea (325) declared the Son to be consubstantial with the Father, a dependence of theology upon Aristotelian metaphysics had arisen. Boethius, in his writing on the Trinity and his surviving translations of Aristotle, did much to reinforce this dependence. But it was only later, at the end of the 'dark ages', that the full content of Aristotelian metaphysics began to enter into the philosophical speculations upon which the Christian world-view sought to found itself; and by then the Aristotelian theories had been systematised and adapted by such thinkers as Al-Farabi (875–950), Avicenna (890–1037) and Averroës (c. 1125 to c. 1198), all of them Moslems, and Moses Maimonides (1135–1204), a Jew well versed in the philosophical speculations by which the doctrines of the Koran were currently supported. Aristotelian doctrine therefore entered the arena of theology already bearing the stamp of a monotheism which had found it congenial.

The final conversion of Christian theologians to Aristotelian ways of thinking occurred during the eleventh and twelfth centuries, and led, with the founding of universities at such important centres as Paris and Padua, to the rise of that philosophical movement now known as 'scholasticism'. The greatest luminary of this movement was St Thomas Aquinas (1225–1274), whose *Summa Theologica* purported to give a complete description of the relation between man and God, relying only on philosophical reasoning, and without recourse to mystical assertion or unsupported faith. His master at every point was Aristotle, and the subsequent synthesis of Christian doctrine and Aristotelian metaphysics – known after its creator as Thomism – has remained to this day the most persuasive of the foundations offered for Christian theology.

In order to understand subsequent developments in the history of philosophy it is necessary to grasp some of the conceptions, disputes and theories that emerged from the attempt to set neo-Platonic and Aristotelian doctrine into a framework of monotheistic religion, and in the course of doing so to reconcile classical science and morality with the dogmas of faith. Contrary to the opinion of their successors, the medieval philosophers were not merely slaves of authority, nor were they easily deterred from speculations which led them into conflict with Church or State. As the scholastics themselves were given to saying, 'authority has a nose of wax', meaning that if you can get hold of it you can bend it as you will. Nevertheless it is undeniable that, looked at as a whole, their philosophy has a conciliatory aspect, upholding through reason doctrines that either coincide with or leave room for the articles of faith. Consequently, if we are to see what is distinctive in the speculations of this period, we must look behind the doctrines to the logical and metaphysical arguments that were used to support them.

The concept of substance

The Aristotelian logic, expounded in the works known as the *Organon*, was preserved in part by Boethius, and later delivered up in full by the scholars of Islam. Fundamental to this logic is the distinction between subject and predicate. Every proposition, it was thought, must consist at least of these two parts, and, corresponding to these parts, reality itself must divide into substance and attribute, the latter being 'predicated of' or 'inherent in' the former. The distinction has its origins in logic, and in the

Aristotelian attempt to classify all the valid 'syllogisms' within a single scheme. But it has clear metaphysical implications. Since substances can change in respect of their attributes, they must endure through change. Moreover, if we can refer to substances it must be possible to separate them, at least in thought, from the attributes with which they might at some particular moment be encumbered. Hence we should distinguish the 'essence' of a substance – that without which it could not be the particular thing that it is – from its 'accidents', the properties in respect of which it might change without ceasing to exist altogether. Finally, it is substances, in the Aristotelian view, which are the ultimate constituents of reality, and our knowledge of the world consists in our various attempts to classify them into genera and species.

One of the problems that the medievals bequeathed to their seventeenth-century successors was that of whether, and how far, it makes sense to say of a substance that it can cease to exist, or be created. We find that there is an innate tendency in the Aristotelian metaphysic to regard all change as a change in the attributes of a substance. Hence the coming to be or passing away of a substance demands a very special – indeed metaphysical – explanation. For many philosophers influenced by Aristotle, these 'existence changes' *have* no explanation. Later philosophers such as Leibniz went further, arguing that a substance must contain within itself the explanation of all its predicates. In which case it becomes hard to envisage how one substance might create or destroy another, except by a miracle which, in the nature of things, it lies beyond the capacity of human intellect to understand. A further problem arose from the inability of the traditional logic fully to distinguish individual and species terms from quantitative (or 'mass') terms. For example, 'man' which can denote both an individual and the class which subsumes him – refers to individual substances. It also expresses a predicate which generally describes them. But what about 'snow' or 'water'? There are not individual 'snows' or 'waters', except in an attenuated sense which would seem to obliterate a distinction fundamental to scientific thought. This is the distinction between 'stuff' and 'thing', between what can be measured and what can be counted. The difficulty of forcing the idea of 'stuff' into the conceptual frame of 'substance' is responsible for much of the rejection of Aristotelian science during the seventeenth century, and for this reason, if for no other, the concept of substance became the focus of philosophical enquiry.

The nature of universals

Any philosophy which asks itself serious questions as to the nature of substances, must also examine the nature of the 'attributes' or 'properties' that inhere in them. The neo-Platonic cosmology had transformed the original Platonic realm of Ideas – the realm where the 'forms' reside, unchanged, unchanging and known to reason alone – into the blessed sphere of immutability. But the old metaphysical dispute between Aristotle and Plato as to the nature of universals remained central to medieval thought. This was because the dispute bore on what is perhaps the single most important issue in the theory of knowledge, the issue of how far the world is knowable to reason. Using as their basic text a passage from Porphyry's *Isagoge*, transmitted and commented upon by Boethius, philosophers enquired whether genera and species exist only in the mind or in reality; and, if the latter, whether they exist in individual substances or in separation from them. In answer to this question some philosophers reaffirmed the original Platonic position, upholding the independent existence of universals, in the realm of 'Ideas'; others went to the opposite extreme, the extreme of nominalism, holding that universals are mere names, and that only individuals exist. There is no independent reality to the idea of 'blue': the only fact of the matter here is that we classify things under that label.

One of the most important thinkers to defend a version of the nominalist theory – William of Ockham (*floret* 1300–1349) – also combined it with a doctrine which seems to be its natural associate. This is the doctrine of empiricism, according to which reason, far from being the sole authority in determining how things are, is subordinate to and dependent upon the senses (upon empirical enquiry). Such empiricism was by no means unusual in medieval thought; it is foreshadowed in Aristotle, and to some extent approved by Aquinas, who lent support to the scholastic tag '*nihil in intellectus quod nisi prius in sensu*' ('there is nothing in the understanding that is not first in the senses'), a saying which, under one interpretation at least, implies a thoroughgoing scepticism as to the powers of reason. Ockham was prepared to develop that scepticism to the full, and to combine it, as later empiricists combined it, with a theory of the nature and function of language which would remove the basis from much of the traditional claims made on reason's behalf. In the course of developing this theory, Ockham was to anticipate many of the major conceptions of later philosophers, including Hume's theory of causality, Leibniz's theory of relations, and the attack on absolute space and time. Followed in his scepticism by the vigorous Nicolas d'Autrecourt (c. 1300–after 1350), he provided a powerful challenge to many of the dogmas of the Church, arguing that these must be founded not in reason, which could never stretch so far as to comprehend them, but in faith. In this way, the ancient dispute about the nature of universals served as a focus for the growing disagreement between empiricism and rationalism (as they came to be known). Moreover, it became increasingly apparent, during the course of these disputes, that much in philosophy, perhaps the very possibility of philosophy, depends upon the truth about language. It was consequently in the scholastic age that philosophy began to incorporate the theory of meaning and the study of usage as a central focus of its arguments. Out of this study there emerged important specific theories – such as that of abstract ideas (adopted by Peter Abelard (1079–1142) and bequeathed to Locke and British empiricism) and the doctrine that entities should not be multiplied beyond necessity. This last doctrine, known as Ockham's razor (though not in fact found in Ockham's writings), provided the inspiration to much later scientific thought. There also emerged at this time a sense of the centrality of logic to philosophy, and of the need for fine distinctions in the discussion of all philosophical problems.

The ontological argument

Not surprisingly, the rationalist, Platonic tradition of speculative thought lent itself more readily to the support of theological dogma than the empiricist scepticism which took so much inspiration from Aristotle's attack on Plato's theory of Ideas. Nevertheless it was an argument that was Aristotelian both in content and in form which was to have the decisive influence upon medieval theology. This argument is known as the ontological proof (adopting a term of Kant's) for the existence of God. The discovery of this proof is normally credited to St Anselm, Archbishop of Canterbury (1033–1109), but it is not too great a distortion to find glimpses of it in certain passages of Aristotle's *Metaphysics* and in the commentaries of Al-Farabi and Avicenna. It was rejected by Aquinas in his systematic exposition of the basis of Christian doctrine, but nevertheless belongs to a class of arguments others of which he was inclined to accept, and all of which derive their proof for the existence of God by way of the concept of a necessary being – a being whose essence involves existence.

Put very simply, St Anselm's argument is as follows. By 'God' I mean an entity than which no greater can be thought. Suppose that God, so defined, does not exist; I can nevertheless *think* that he exists. But an entity is greater if it does exist than if it does not. Hence it is possible to think of something greater than God – namely an entity which is not only greater than any that can be thought, but which also exists. But this is contrary to the definition. Hence the hypothesis – that God does not exist – must be false.

If valid, the argument establishes not merely that God exists, but that he exists by necessity, since it follows from his nature (his essence) that he exists. Later versions (such as that endorsed by Descartes) rely on the idea that existence is a perfection and therefore a property of whatever possesses it. It is not clear that St Anselm's argument relies on this assumption; indeed, to this day it is not clear that the argument makes any questionable assumptions at all. Some philosophers think that it is valid, although only when stated in a refined and novel way; others think it was decisively refuted by Kant, with his attempted proof that 'existence is not a true predicate'. In any case, despite its sophistical appearance, the argument had a peculiar philosophical tenacity, being accepted in one or another version by all three of the major rationalist thinkers of the seventeenth century.

There is a special reason for the argument's popularity with medieval theologians, which is that it gives credibility to the idea of God as a 'necessary being'. Many writers had tried to show that there must be something which exists of necessity (or which is *causa sui*, cause of itself) if anything is to exist contingently. The ontological argument provides a description of this necessarily existing being, and therefore an answer to the fundamental question of metaphysics, the question why (for what reason) *is* there anything? Or (to put it more tendentiously) why should Being be? We see here too the origin of that dark dispute, which still appears to live in the obscure pages of existentialist philosophers, as to the relation of existence and essence. If there is no being for whom existence and essence coincide, then what of the remainder? Do contingent objects (among which we must place ourselves) partake of an essence that precedes their existence, or is it the case that, for them, existence must take priority over essence? When we come to discuss this, as yet scarcely intelligible, question, it will be important to bear in mind its relation to those medieval discussions of the nature of God and of universals, which many modern thinkers might unreflectingly suppose to be of merely academic interest.

Free will and human nature

The acceptance of the ontological argument and the resultant conception of a 'necessary being', endowed with omnipotence and omniscience, leads almost inevitably to a rigid determinism. If all that is contingent depends ultimately upon the divine nature, and if that nature is governed by necessity, then the world too must follow its course in accordance with the laws which express God's nature. How then is human freedom possible? This problem arises in slightly different form for those philosophers who adopt the more Platonic conception of the divine nature. Hence it had already been discussed by the Fathers of the Church, and in particular by St Augustine. With the acceptance of the Aristotelian metaphysics it acquired a new dimension, and some of the greatest achievements of modern philosophy result from the continued attempt to describe human freedom, following arguments that had already been surveyed and as often as not abandoned by the scholastics, in their endeavour to fit a plausible account of human nature and human morality into the theological absolutism which reason seemed to demand.

The greatest of these attempts to describe the relation between God and man and to fit the full complexity of human nature into a coherent theology, is undoubtedly the *Summa Theologica* of St Thomas Aquinas. This work contains what is perhaps the most subtle and complete philosophical account of the nature of human emotion that has ever been produced. As well as incorporating into his work what he considered to be the totality of what was true and well argued in the classical sources available to him, Aquinas attempted to bring to completion the picture of human nature and human virtue presented by Aristotle in his *Nicomachean Ethics*, and to show its compatibility with the doctrines of revealed religion. While many of Aquinas's assumptions were soon to be subjected to the scepticism of Ockham and his followers, there is no doubt that he succeeded in convincing his contemporaries that philosophy could not only generate the truth about human nature but also sustain the doctrines of the Christian faith, in such a way as to leave little room for doubt about the major questions of morality and religion which all of us must at some stage in our thinking lives encounter.

Aquinas's philosophy leaned heavily upon the Aristotelian doctrine of substance and upon the achievements of medieval logic. But, despite its frequent digressions towards empiricism, it was assiduous in the support that it offered to the doctrine of the power and autonomy of human reason. In particular Aquinas did much to revive interest (an interest already exhibited by Abelard) in the Aristotelian theory of 'practical reason', as definitive of the active nature of man. The theory of practical reason was held to provide an account of human freedom, together with a description of the 'good life for man' that would recommend itself on the basis of reason alone. Aquinas thus handed on to later philosophers a concept without which the study of ethics is either empty or non-existent.

The rejection of scholasticism

The triumph of Thomism was, however, short-lived. Its first serious enemy was the humanism of the early Renaissance. This was accompanied by revolutions in the practice of education which tended to take intellectual authority from ecclesiastics and vest it in the hands of courtiers and literary men; and also by the gradual ascendancy of a spirit of scientific enquiry hostile to the ready reception of theological dogma. During the fourteenth and fifteenth centuries there was therefore increasing criticism of the influence of the schools, and increasing awareness of the lacunae in the systems which they propagated. The intellectual history of this period is complex, and the transition from medieval to modern approaches in education and intellectual life was far less abrupt than our modern taste for clear transitions represents it to be. As late as 1685 William of Ockham's textbook on logic was standardly used in the University of Oxford, while as early as the *Metalogicon* of John of Salisbury, Bishop of Chartres (1120–1180), the seeds of Renaissance humanism had been sown, and the medieval theories of education thrown in doubt. Nevertheless, it is clear that between these two periods a change took place in the intellectual climate of Europe that could not but have the profoundest repercussions on the history of philosophy. And two philosophers in particular stand out both as embodying the new spirit of criticism and as laying down the intellectual presuppositions of that style of philosophy which we choose to call modern: Francis Bacon and René Descartes. These two are united by their rejection of traditional authority and their radical search for method. But in the case of Bacon neither motive led him in the direction of those philosophical enquiries which we, with hindsight, see as proper to the modern age, so that, for all his brilliance and learning, it is difficult to see him as the founder of the modern, rather than a destroyer of the medieval, modes of thought. Nevertheless it is fitting to conclude this brief summary with a few remarks about Bacon's distinctive contribution to modern philosophy.

Sir Francis Bacon (subsequently Viscount St Albans and Lord Chancellor of England) was born in about 1561 and died, dismissed from courtly offices, in 1626. He was a polymath and scholar of the highest order, and even had he never engaged in philosophical or scientific speculation, he would be known through his *Essays* as one of the great stylists of the English language. But his distinguished place in intellectual history lies in his exploration of the fundamental principles of scientific thought, summarised in the *Novum Organum* (1620). In this work Bacon sets out to show the inadequacies of Aristotelian science and of the barren *a priorism* which he associated with the traditional Aristotelian logic of the *Organon*. He argued that the Aristotelian logic, being purely deductive in character, provides no method for the discovery of new facts, but only a means of arriving at the logical consequences of what is already known. The resulting science must therefore have a purely classificatory character, contenting itself with a division of the known contents of the world into 'species' and 'genera', without understanding the true causality which leads objects to manifest the similarities whereby we could so classify them in the first place. Instead of Aristotelian science he proposed his method of 'induction' – the postulation of universal laws on the basis of observed instances – and thereby hoped to promote the 'true and lawful marriage between the empirical and the rational faculty'. While Bacon's development of this method was of necessity speculative and incomplete, he did in the course of it make various striking criticisms of the Aristotelian tradition, and at the same time introduce conceptions which were later to prove fundamental to scientific thought. He criticised the theory of 'final causes' (the theory that the cause of an event might be found in its purpose), and with it many of the rationalist preconceptions about causation that we shall encounter in later chapters. In place of these ideas he put forward the notion of causality as the generation of one thing from another, in accordance with underlying 'laws of nature'. He argued that science must always aim at greater and greater universality and abstraction, so ascending 'the ladder of the intellect'. This could be achieved by a theory whose fundamental laws were expressed not in qualitative but in quantitative terms, since 'of all natural forms . . . Quantity is the most abstracted and separable from matter'. It was this conception of science, as the formulation of quantitative laws, that was shortly to gain intellectual ascendancy in the wake of the discoveries of Galileo and Harvey. Bacon also attacked what he saw as the arbitrary and conventional element in the Aristotelian science, and in the course of doing so introduced his doctrine of 'Forms', which foreshadowed another, entertained by Locke, that science should treat of the real and not of the nominal essences of things (see p. 90).

But before Bacon's influence could be widely felt, philosophy had undergone a radical convulsion. This was induced by Descartes' declaration that all of philosophy's results were without foundation until its premises could be agreed, together with a method whereby to advance from them. Only in the wake of Cartesianism was the nature of Bacon's thought fully to be appreciated, and by then the disputes of scholasticism seemed irrevocably distant.

Part One

Rationalism

3

DESCARTES

René Descartes (1596–1650), the principal founding father of modern philosophy, and well known as a mathematician, deserves the eminent place accorded to him on two accounts. First, because of his single-minded search for method in all branches of human enquiry; secondly, because he introduced into philosophy, largely on account of that search, many of the concepts and arguments which have since served as its foundation.

A contemporary of Bacon and Galileo, and immediate predecessor of Newton (many of whose thoughts he anticipated), Descartes was a perfect representative of the new scientific spirit. While he feared and respected the censure of the Church (as is shown by his withholding from pub-lication the *Treatise on the Universe*, 1633, upon hearing of Galileo's condemnation), he deferred to no intellectual authority other than the 'natural light' of reason. This set him apart both from the scholastic traditions to which we have referred and also from the worldly preoccupa-tions of the Renaissance humanists. For Descartes the results of all previous speculation had to be set aside or suspended, until clear and indubitable principles could be established against which to measure them. Without the aid of such principles, no system, scientific or meta-physical, could warrant assent. Descartes could not find these basic principles in the works that he had read. He therefore embarked on a programme of radical intellectual reform, which resulted in a change of philosophical perspective so great that scholasticism fell into lasting disrepute. Even now medieval philosophy is rarely studied in our universities and yet more rarely understood.

Descartes' first important work was the *Discourse on Method* (1637), written in French in a style of remarkable elegance and distinction. In this book Descartes sets forth his life's aim of directing his reason to the systematic discovery of truth and the elimination of error. The *Discourse* was followed by Descartes' masterpiece, the *Meditations of First Philosophy*, published in Latin in 1641, which was soon followed by sets of objections from various writers together with Descartes' replies to them. His other major philosophical works were *The Principles of Philosophy* (1644) and *The Passions of the Soul* (1649), the first being an ambitious attempt to systematise his philosophical method and derive from it foundations for an account of the physical world. The second was an exploration in the philosophy of mind which, while of considerable interest in itself, cannot be treated in what follows.

It is true to say that, despite the enormous influence of experimental science, the distinction between science and philosophy was not clear to the philosophers of Descartes' day. Descartes himself – despite great expertise in physics and genuine mathematical genius – was slow to appreciate the difference. However, he came to believe that, as he put it, human knowledge is a tree, the trunk of which is physics, and the root of which is metaphysics. It is only through the exploration of metaphysics that the basis of human knowledge can be discerned. And 'for right philosophising . . . the greatest care must be taken not to admit anything as true which we cannot prove to be true.' We must therefore adopt a 'method of doubt', in order to arrive at propositions which could not be reasonably doubted.

Two arguments persuaded Descartes that he could doubt virtually all his normal beliefs. The first is the argument from dreaming. I believe that I am sitting by the fire with a piece of paper in my hand. Why? Because my senses tell me so. But could I not be dreaming? In dreams my senses present me with information of the same kind as I receive waking. So how do I know that I am not dreaming now?

There are beliefs which are not shaken by the argument from dreaming – beliefs about what is most general, such as we encounter in mathematics. 'Whether I am awake or asleep,' Descartes writes in the first Meditation, 'two and three added together are five, and a square has no more than four sides.' He therefore asks us to imagine a spirit of such power and such malignity, as to cause in me all the experiences that I have, and all the beliefs that are associated with them, with the express intention of deceiving me about both. What assurance have I that this 'evil genius' is not the real cause of my present beliefs and experience? It is useless to reply that the hypothesis is highly improbable. In the abstract, with no certainties to rely upon, I can have no grounds for knowing what is probable and what is not. My own experience, since it is equally well explained by common-sense beliefs about an external world and by the hypothesis of an evil genius, gives no grounds for choosing between them. Descartes even admits (see, for example, *Principles*, 1, 5, 6) that the evil genius might be deceiving me 'in those matters which seem to us supremely evident', such as mathematics – an admission that threatens his own solution to these sceptical problems.

Descartes drew the conclusion that he could begin from no premise except those which he could not doubt. Metaphysics must begin from truths that are not just evident, but in some sense self-verifying: otherwise it will never be more than a shot in the dark. He went on to identify such a truth, arguing that 'from the mere fact that I thought of doubting the truth of other things, it followed quite evidently and certainly that I existed' (*Discourse on Method*, 32) – in other words, 'I think, therefore I am' ('*Cogito ergo sum*'). This original statement of Descartes' master-premise has given rise to the mistaken impression that the *cogito* is some kind of inference. In the *Meditations*, however, he corrects that impression: 'the proposition *I am, I exist* is necessarily true whenever it is put forward by me or conceived in my mind.' In other words, the proposition that I exist is self-verifying. I cannot assert it or think it without its being true. Likewise the proposition that I do not exist is self-defeating: to assert it is to give conclusive grounds for its disproof.

A similar argument can be mounted for the proposition that I think, which verifies itself in the very act of being doubted. Neither 'I think' nor 'I exist' expresses a necessary truth: each might have been false. Nevertheless, whenever they are true, I know for certain that they are true. My philosophy can begin from two indubitable premises which also express contingent and substantial truths about the world.

We should say that the truth that I exist is self-evident. Descartes wrote rather that it is manifest to the 'natural light' of reason. In other words, it is known by a process that can be perceived to be valid by anyone who reasons at all. The existence of this 'natural light' is not so much an arbitrary assumption as a precondition of all philosophical argument. There must be some point at which reason simply *finds manifest* the validity of an argument or the truth of an idea. Otherwise the process of reasoning itself will be thrown in doubt, and absolute scepticism will ensue. Without some reliance on reason, neither scepticism nor its opposite can be proven. Absolute intellectual darkness is the result. It is clear that Descartes in no way intended his method of radical doubt to bring about absolute scepticism; indeed he would have rightly regarded such scepticism as incoherent.

But what is the point at which the truth of an idea or the validity of an argument are revealed to reason? This question is one of the basic questions of philosophy. It is the question of the nature and limits of what has come to be known as *a priori* knowledge. The prime example of such knowledge for Descartes (who did not use the term '*a priori*') is knowledge of the validity of a step in an argument. For example, I can see that from the proposition '*p* and *q*' it follows that *p*. By way of explaining this as a basic operation of the natural light, Descartes would say that the relation between '*p* and *q*' and '*p*' is something that I perceive clearly and distinctly. Anything that I perceive clearly and distinctly is something the truth of which I can discern without recourse to anything other than the natural light of reason. Clearness and distinctness are not the same: I perceive an idea clearly when I comprehend it intellectually without any assistance from the senses or from agencies outside my own innate reasoning powers. But such an idea may be mixed with less clear, more confused intellectual notions, in which case it is not distinct. It is only when I consider it in its distinct form that I am in a position to judge of its truth or falsehood.

Having established his own existence and introduced the concept of a 'natural light' of reason whereby to advance from this premise to whatever conclusions may spring from it, Descartes went on to reflect on his own nature. It is clear, he argued, that I am a thing which thinks. Moreover, since I cannot conceive myself except as thinking, it is of my essence to think. ('Think' – *cogitare* – was a word of wide application for Descartes, and covered all conscious manifestations of the mental life.) Now, however hard I try, I can find no other property besides thought which belongs to my essence. For example, although it seems to me that I have a body which I can move at will, I can readily conceive of myself as existing without this body. Hence it is not an essential property of me that I have a body. I could conceivably (although it is a matter of faith that I will in fact) exist after the body's demise. And in so existing I shall continue to exist as a thinking thing.

That argument, which contains Descartes' grounds for asserting at least the possibility of immortality, can be criticised on many grounds. (In particular there is a confusion in the idea that since I cannot conceive myself as not thinking it is therefore of my essence to think.) However, it formed the basis of a Cartesian thesis of great importance, a thesis which dominated philosophy for centuries, and which Descartes expressed by saying that there is a 'real distinction' between body and soul. Associated with this thesis is a view to which we shall shortly return and which I shall label, in deference to recent discussions, the 'Cartesian theory of mind'.

Having established his own existence and nature, Descartes now seeks to overcome the corrosive doubt which had earlier beset him, so as to be able to set up a sure foundation for his knowledge of the external world. So far, it will be noted, Descartes' conclusions have concerned only himself and the contents of his own consciousness. And his very method of doubt has forced him into the confines of what I shall call 'the first-person case', beyond which he has so far found no argument that will open the passage. However, it is clearly important that he should find that argument, for his enterprise requires it. He wishes to arrive at a view of the world which is, in a quite specific sense, objective. That is to say, he wishes to show that a world exists independently of his thoughts and perceptions, a world that might at any moment be other than it appears to him to be, a world of which he is but one finite, fallible part, and the true nature of which he may discover only by laborious enquiry. The peculiarity of the first person is, roughly speaking, that from the first-person point of view the distinction between being and seeming does not arise. My conscious mental states are as they seem to me, and seem to me as they are: what else, after all, is meant by 'consciousness'? Knowledge of the first person signally fails to reach out beyond subjectivity to the concept of an objective independent order. For the concept of such an order is the concept of a potential divergence between being and seeming. This divergence will not be made available to Descartes simply by reflecting on his own present state of mind.

Descartes therefore needed to establish the existence of at least one being independent of himself and in relation to which he could situate himself as part of an objective world. It is characteristic of Descartes' time, and of the element in his philosophical method that was later to be designated as 'rationalism', that he should choose at this point to establish the existence of God. The methodological importance of this choice was, as we shall see, enormous.

Descartes had two arguments for the existence of God, versions of the 'cosmological' and the 'ontological' arguments respectively. Both of them illustrate the extent to which his thought, for all its radical departures from scholastic tradition, remained true to the medieval conceptions which his philosophical education had bequeathed to him. The two arguments are as follows. First: I am an imperfect being (as is proved by the fact that I can doubt and therefore do not have perfect knowledge). But I have the idea of a most perfect being (of God), and whence came this idea? It could not be of my own devising, since it is manifest to the natural light of reason that there must be 'as much reality (perfection) in the cause as in the effect'. Applying this principle to ideas, it manifest that there must be as much 'formal reality' in the cause of an idea as there is 'objective reality' in the idea itself. 'Formal' means actual, and 'objective' represented. The more reality represented by an idea, the greater the reality that produced it. My idea of God represents the highest degree of reality; its cause therefore must be real in the highest degree; in short, it must be God himself.

The argument depends upon the premise, said to be manifest to the natural light, but in fact hardly intelligible, that there is at least as much reality in the total cause as in the effect. Included in this premise is precisely the set of suppositions required by the second argument – namely, that reality admits of degrees and is therefore a predicate or property of things, and that reality (or existence) is a positive property or 'perfection'. If we allow these suppositions, then Descartes' version of the ontological argument follows at once. I have an idea of a most perfect being; I clearly and distinctly perceive that such a being must contain all perfections, and therefore reality in every degree. Hence this idea contains existence, which means that God's essence contains his existence. (Of no other thing, Descartes adds, can this be said.)

The first argument is 'cosmological' in that it starts from a premise about the actual world (the premise that I have an idea of God) and asks what caused that premise to be true. The more usual form of such an argument simply asks again and again what caused the world to be as it now is, until the question seems to demand the answer that there was a *first* cause, which has the property of being '*causa sui*', or explanation of itself. Hence the cosmological argument, as Kant points out in his famous critique of rational theology, will always require an ontological argument to support it, the ontological argument being simply the attempt to explain how it is that God can be *causa sui* (*Critique of Pure Reason*, A.608). In Descartes the interdependence of the two arguments is shown succinctly in the scholastic principle, which he claims to derive from the natural light, that there must be at least as much reality in the cause as in the effect. This principle is vital for Descartes' cosmological proof and also dependent upon the fundamental preconceptions of the ontological argument for its intelligibility.

Having, as he thinks, established the existence of God, Descartes goes on to draw his desired conclusions. First, that there is an objective world of which he, Descartes, is but a small, dependent and finite part. Secondly that, since God is all-perfect, he is no deceiver. From which it follows that those faculties that Descartes has innately will, when used in accordance with their true and God-given nature, lead him, not into error, but towards genuine discovery. In other words, the hypothesis of the evil genius can be dismissed, as can every other form of radical doubt. The existence of God guarantees those claims to knowledge which, by using his faculties to their greatest ability, Descartes will be naturally inclined to make.

Two difficulties arise at this point, and were already pointed out to Descartes in the series of objections collected by Mersenne (see p. 40). The first is, how does Descartes account for the possibility of error? If God is no deceiver, why does he permit error in any form? The second is this: if the existence of God is needed to guarantee the judgements about the world which we would, using our faculties to their best measure, instinctively arrive at, then do we not need to be assured of God's existence before we can guarantee that the 'clear and distinct' perceptions whereby that existence is proven do really have the authority which they appear to have? In which case does not the validity of the argument for God's existence covertly rely on the truth of its conclusion? In other words, is it not viciously circular? In answer to the first of these difficulties Descartes developed a complex theory of 'assent' to truth, a theory which assigns 'assent' to the will rather than the intellect. Ideas in themselves contain no error: but error is in us when we choose to assent to an idea that we do not clearly and distinctly perceive. Human error is therefore the necessary consequence of human freedom, and this seeming evil is part of a real and greater good.

In answer to the second difficulty – the so-called 'Cartesian circle' – Descartes was apt to be impatient, and commentators do not agree as to the real nature of his reply. One theory is that Descartes held clear and distinct perception to be a guarantee of truth, so that the only error that could occur when working through an argument each step of which is clearly and distinctly perceived would be an error of memory. This error would be eliminated merely by rehearsing the proof at such length that it can be grasped in a single act of intellectual 'intuition'. Even if this *was* Descartes' reply, however, it has not satisfied many of his critics. Indeed, the Cartesian circle remains a major difficulty for the whole method of doubt. For if the evil genius really *can* deceive me in what I perceive most clearly and distinctly, then there is no hope of proving anything that is not self-verifying in the manner of 'I exist' and 'I think'. I must then remain locked within my own subjective viewpoint, and deprived of all knowledge of an objective world. The difficulty is not one for Descartes only. All philosophical reasoning relies on principles that can be proved only by arguments that presuppose them. There is no point of view outside human reason from which reason can be judged. The nature of this difficulty, and the way in which it might be overcome, became clear only with Kant's *Critique of Pure Reason*.

It is now necessary to return to the parts of Descartes' philosophy for which he is chiefly remembered – his views concerning mind and matter on the one hand, and intellect and the senses on the other. It is on account of these views that we can now see Descartes as a founding force behind both the prevailing philosophies of the seventeenth and eighteenth centuries: rationalism and empiricism. Descartes' view of matter is in fact closely bound up with his epistemology. In a famous passage of the *Meditations* he reflects roughly as follows: consider a lump of wax; it has a certain shape, size, colour, perfume. In short, it has certain qualities which I can perceive through the senses. It is tempting to say, therefore, that my senses reveal the nature of this lump of wax and tell me what it really is. But when I approach it to the fire I find that its colour, shape, hardness, perfume – in short, all those qualities in terms of which I might have sought to describe it and distinguish it from other things – undergo a change and may even disappear entirely. And yet it is the same piece of wax. It follows, Descartes thought, that it possesses its sensible qualities only accidentally – they are not 'of its nature' or 'essential'.

Reflecting on this point Descartes came to the conclusion that not only are the senses intrinsically unreliable in discerning the reality of the physical world, but also that the real nature of physical objects must consist in something other than sensible qualities. These qualities simply constitute the passing mode in which the true physical essence clothes itself, and if we are to know that essence then we must consult, not the senses, but the intellect, which is alone capable of grasping the essences of things. What, then, is the essence of physical objects – what, as Descartes put it, is corporeal substance or body? The only properties that the wax seems to have essentially are extension in space, together with flexibility and changeability. In other words, material substance consists in extension (space) together with the various modes in and through which extension may change. This conclusion gives us the first principle of physical science, and Descartes was further confirmed in it by his reflections on geometry. These reflections had shown him that we really do have 'clear and distinct' perceptions of all the ideas of extension, and can reach knowledge of its properties through reason alone, by a deductive science that makes no reference to the sensible properties of things.

The argument, which I have very much abridged, was of considerable historical importance, being a direct precursor of Locke's distinction between primary and secondary qualities (see chapter 7), and also the clearest statement in Descartes of the position that was later to be known as rationalism. Rationalism finds the key to knowledge, even of 'sensible' things, in rational reflection rather than in empirical observation. The argument about the wax shows that the distrust of the senses and the rationalist doctrine that there are knowable essences are intimately linked, and that together they go with a search for *a priori* principles of enquiry. Such principles will issue (like the axioms of geometry) in necessary, universal truths. As we shall see when we consider the philosophy of Leibniz, the difficulty for the rationalist is to explain the nature and possibility of contingent truths – of propositions which, while true, might have been false.

But while Descartes was, in this way, the founder of rationalism, there was another aspect to his philosophy which approached him more to later empiricists than to his immediate rationalist successors. This was the subordination of metaphysics to epistemology. Two consequences immediately stemmed from that. First, the conception of the first-person case as prior; secondly, the so-called Cartesian theory of the mind.

The priority of the first-person case follows from the Cartesian method. Descartes begins from the question 'How can *I* know, be certain of, the things that I claim to know?' Immediately his thought is turned inwards, to the contents of his own mind, and the specific certainties which attach to them. Although the peculiarity of the 'cogito' lies in its self-verifying nature, there lurks behind it a host of other certainties. These certainties we might call the certainties of 'first-person privilege'. I am able to know what I think, feel, experience with an authority that is quite different from any authority that attaches to my knowledge of another person or thing. In the case of my own mentality, what is, seems, and what seems, is. The first-person case appears therefore to provide a paradigm of certainty, and from this certainty one may perhaps advance by degrees to a systematic vision of the world. While Descartes did not himself develop such a view of the 'foundations' of knowledge – relying as he did on a rationalistic argument for the existence of God, the premise of which was not first-person privilege as such but only the peculiar logical status of the 'cogito' – he provided it with significant impetus. It is to later empiricism, however, that we must turn in order to find the view developed to its full.

The phenomenon of first-person privilege – variously described and explained – led directly to the Cartesian view of the mind. My immediate certainty of my own mental states is contrasted with my uncertainty about all corporeal things, in such a way as to lend support to the contention that what I am is an immaterial, substantial being, accidentally and temporarily connected with the body through which I act. I am a substance, but not a corporeal substance, and my privileged awareness of the contents of my own consciousness is supposed somehow to be explained by that. Descartes recognised that a difficulty must arise as to the mode of connection of mind and body: he proposed various half-formed and ultimately absurd hypotheses as to how this mental thing might interact with bodily substance, and his eminent failure to produce an explanation prompted Spinoza to provide a revolutionary account of how soul and body are related.

The Cartesian theory of mind has seemed obvious and compelling to philosophers throughout the centuries. Caricatured by Ryle* as the view of mind as 'the ghost in the machine' (and despite Descartes' claim that he is

---

* Gilbert Ryle, *The Concept of Mind*, London, 1949.

not lodged in his body like a pilot in a ship, he said little or nothing to prevent this caricature from remaining persuasive), it represents a deep illusion, generated by almost all epistemological thought. Epistemology usually assumes that it is from my own case that my knowledge derives, and that the certainty of self-awareness is to be explained only by the peculiar nature of the mind as an object of its own knowledge. One of the most impressive features of recent philosophy has been the demolition of this body of assumptions, and the consequent destruction of the dualistic vision of the world.

4

THE CARTESIAN REVOLUTION

In the last chapter I gave some philosophical reasons in support of what is now the commonplace opinion that modern philosophy begins with Descartes. But there are further reasons for isolating him as the founder of philosophy in its modern form, reasons which are apt to seem more pertinent to the historian of ideas than to the philosopher.

First, Descartes was not only a philosopher; he was also a great mathematician and a founder of modern physics. While it may now be usual practice to distinguish these subjects, this was not the common practice of Descartes' time, nor would such practice have encouraged the development of any of them. Descartes belonged to that post-Reformation world in which, as the authority of Church and scripture receded, so did speculation and experiment advance. While almost all the philosophers and scientists of the time sincerely believed in the tenets of religion, they worked independently of its intellectual constraints, confident that by diligence alone they would establish the truth about matters which for centuries had remained in darkness.

It has been said of the scientific revolution of which Descartes was a part that

> since [it] overturned the authority of the science not only of the Middle
> Ages but of the ancient world – since it ended not only in the eclipse of
> scholastic philosophy but in the destruction of Aristotelian physics – it
> outshines everything since the rise of Christianity and reduces the

Renaissance and Reformation to the rank of mere episodes, mere internal displacements, within the system of mediaeval Christendom.*

And it is impossible to doubt now that the predilection of cultural historians to find the great divide between medieval and modern at the Renaissance has obscured and to some extent misrepresented the true development, not only of Western philosophy, but of Western thought as a whole. From ancient times until the mid-eighteenth century science and philosophy went hand in hand. For the historian of ideas, it is impossible to separate the development of philosophy from that of scientific thought, and, when taken together, it becomes apparent that the most significant point in the development of each occurred, not at the Renaissance, but in the early seventeenth century, in the intellectual turmoil that to some extent caused, and to a large extent was caused by, the thought of Descartes.

Already in the sixteenth century the problems of scientific method had been vigorously discussed – notably at the University of Padua, where it was recognised that experiments are of the first importance in scientific investigation, and also that experimental results can be fully understood only by a science of quantity and not by one of quality. Bacon had attempted to describe the form of such a science and the logic which would govern it, and such men as Harvey and Galileo had exemplified it in their writings and researches. But Descartes, partly because of his deep epistemological preoccupations, introduced with a novel explicitness the suggestion that there must be fundamental physical laws, of a kind so general as to provide the explanation of everything, and yet so abstract as to be the outcome not of experiment but of *a priori* reflection. He enunciated such laws in his *Principles of Philosophy* (1644), showing both their deductive dependence on metaphysics and their power to generate comprehensive explanations. Much of the content of the *Principles* was influenced by what Descartes had understood of the work of Galileo (whose comprehensive attack on the Aristotelian physics, the *Dialogues of the Two Principal World Systems*, was published in 1625– 1629). But Descartes was perhaps the first to give clear prominence to the law of inertia. This law says that a body continues at rest or in motion in a straight line until something intervenes to halt, slacken or deflect its movement. The law makes movement into a basic fact of the physical universe, which may sometimes neither require nor permit further

* Sir Herbert Butterfield, *Rise of Modern Science*, p. vii.

explanation. It reverses the traditional physics, which had postulated a 'mover' for every movement, believing motion as such to stand in need of an explanation. By accepting the law of inertia, and also embedding it at the heart of what he considered to be a rigorous, axiomatic system, Descartes changed the aspect of physical science and prepared the way for Newton.

However important Descartes' contribution to science, he gave only a subordinate role to experiment, and a far more elevated role than would now be considered acceptable to metaphysical speculation. He wished to deduce the nature of the whole universe from the nature of God, with each step bound to its predecessor in an unbreakable chain of 'geometrical' reasoning. Everything was to be accounted for mathematically, either by configuration or by number, since mathematics gives us the most complete tabulation of 'clear and distinct perceptions' that we could ever hope to arrive at. No rival explanation therefore could compete with it. Any science that started from the mere evidence of the senses must be inferior in its conclusions to a science that began from principles so abstract that their persuasive power would be apparent to reason alone. It was not until Newton's *Principia* (1687) that it was definitely established that the geometrical method could not prove the propositions of physics, and that it was only through a new, and previously unthought of, alliance of geometrical reasoning and experimental method that significant progress could be made. It is fair to say, however, that without Descartes Newtonian physics would have been impossible, and that since Descartes' physics was the child of his philosophy there is a further historical reason for thinking that the Cartesian philosophy marks the birth of much that we would recognise as peculiarly 'modern' in the spirit of scientific investigation.

In philosophy itself the immediate impact of Descartes was enormous. The lucidity of his style, his contempt for scholastic technicalities, the clarity, honesty and unassuming objectivity of his approach, made it impossible to resist the appeal of his writings. Many of the greatest thinkers of the time felt called upon to respond to Descartes' *Meditations*, offering their objections either directly to the author, or else indirectly, to the tireless impresario Father Marin Mersenne (1588–1648), who, with a humility remarkable in a man of less than total genius, acted as go-between among the scientists and philosophers of his age, achieving for the France of his day what the Royal Society was later to achieve for

England. The objectors included Thomas Hobbes, Pierre Gassendi and the young priest Antoine Arnauld (1612–1694), who put forward the objection referred to in the previous chapter, arguing that Descartes' proof for the existence of God must be circular. The interest of this objection lies in the suggestion that a search for method as absolute as Descartes' must in the end rely not only upon 'self-verifying' truths such as the 'cogito', but also, and more generally, upon some characteristic of our mental processes whereby we recognise the intrinsic validity of ideas. The 'clear and distinct perception' of Descartes must itself be immune from Cartesian doubt. If this is so, then the faculty which governs clear and distinct perception, the 'natural light' of reason, is our ultimate guarantee of knowledge. It is in the recognition of this commitment that Cartesian rationalism is born, out of a sceptical epistemology that seemed at first to make rational enquiry as dubious as our other claims to knowledge.

Arnauld is significant not only as a critic of Descartes but also as expressing the spirit which arose, partly in opposition to Cartesian enlightenment and partly as its natural corollary, in the philosophy of Jansenism. Cornelius Jansen (1585–1638) was bishop of Ypres and an enthusiastic exponent of doctrines which, while seemingly compatible with the new findings of science, exalted the act of faith above the conclusions of reason as our guide to theological and metaphysical truth. He joined with the Abbé de Saint-Cyran in founding what is known as the Port-Royal movement, after the abbey where its activities were located. Arnauld was a member of this movement, and was associated with two decisive thinkers of the time: the moralist Pierre Nicole (1625–1695) and the famous mathematician and philosopher, Blaise Pascal. Together with Nicole, Arnauld wrote a textbook of logic for the Port-Royal School, under the title *La Logique ou l'art de penser* (1662), usually known as the Port-Royal logic. This work exemplifies the profundity of the Cartesian revolution in philosophy, and also anticipates the difficulties which the Cartesian 'geometrical method' was soon to encounter.

Judged from the historical point of view, the Port-Royal logic is merely one among a multitude of manuals designed to abbreviate and restate a discipline that had become too deeply overlaid by the pernickety squabbles of the scholastics to recommend itself to the new man of science. In 1556, Petrus Ramus had published his *Animadversiones*

Aristotelicae, in which he claimed to discredit the whole science of logic as Aristotle had invented and the scholastics embellished it. By the mid-seventeenth century faith in Aristotelianism was so much shaken that it seemed vital to achieve some rival logic with which to record and validate the 'method' of the new philosophy. In fact no systematic alternative to the Aristotelian logic was to emerge until the nineteenth century, and, despite many attempts (culminating in some notable ones from Leibniz), the seventeenth-century logic was less new than it claimed to be. It served partly to mask the old Aristotelian theories in Cartesian jargon. Without Aristotelian logic the rationalist conception of substance is, after all, scarcely intelligible; and yet it is this concept which lies at the heart of the philosophy of Descartes, Spinoza and Leibniz, surviving, in modified form, even in the works of Kant.

There are, however, important philosophical reasons for noticing the Port-Royal logic at this juncture. First, it represents an attempt to examine the nature of human reasoning in the light of the Cartesian theory of ideas. Traditional logic had spoken of the relations between judgements or propositions. It was unclear to Arnauld and Nicole how this logic bore on those more important relations without which there could be no such thing as the Cartesian 'method': the relations among ideas. The Cartesian 'idea', seeming to be both concept and proposition at once, has no claim to be the true subject matter of logic. As philosophers came to perceive this, so logic began again to make the progress which for centuries had been denied to it.

There are two further respects in which the Port-Royal logic deserves recognition. First, because of its quasi-mathematical development of part of the medieval logic. This development must have seemed natural to any follower of Descartes, but it contained the first premonition of modern formal logic. Secondly, because of its distinction, again novel at the time but now considered fundamental to logic, between the 'comprehension' and 'extension' of a general term. The word 'comprehension' denotes that which is understood in understanding a term – in other words, the idea that the term expresses. The extension of a term, on the other hand, is the set of things to which it is applied. (Thus the comprehension of the term 'man' is the idea of manhood, its extension is the class of men.) Following the nineteenth-century Scottish philosopher Sir William Hamilton, the distinction is now often expressed as that between the intension and the extension of a term. It was important to Arnauld and

Nicole, since they wished to isolate the former (the realm of 'ideas') as giving the true subject matter of logic; it is important in modern thought for the opposite reason, because logicians have come increasingly to realise that logic is the science not of the intension, but of the extension of terms (see chapter 17).

The Port-Royal school projected a manual on mathematics, and, as a preface to this, Blaise Pascal (1623–1662) wrote his *De l'esprit géometrique*, an investigation into the philosophy of mathematics designed to display not just the nature of the 'geometrical' method, but also its limits. Pascal, like Descartes, was a great mathematician and a deeply religious man. But his faith, which he acquired by conversion, took the passionate form characteristic of Jansenism, according to which the claims of reason could never suffice as foundations for so great a thing as religious doctrine. Pascal argued that the indefinability of terms and the need for axioms in the 'geometrical method' showed not the absolute validity of the 'clear and distinct idea', but rather the imperfection of finite minds, which must always rest content with indefinables. Our reason may give us some guarantee of the methods of the geometer, but it could never provide the same guarantee for his axioms.

In the famous *Pensées* (published posthumously) Pascal takes further his strictures on the use of reason, arguing that, since God is hidden from mortal view, it is futile to attempt to discover his essence through rational enquiry. 'We know truth not only by reason but more by the heart.' And it is from the heart that we sense the meaning of life and its divine eschatology. Pascal stopped short of total scepticism, believing it to be self-defeating, and qualified his strictures against rational theology with a curious argument for the existence of God: 'Pascal's wager'. The argument goes roughly as follows: 'If God exists He will reward belief in Him: while if He does not exist, such belief leads to no harm. Hence the best bet is to believe in Him.' The argument reflects Pascal's concern with the concept of probability; it is interesting because it offers practical reasons (rather than theoretical reasons) for an article of faith, so connecting the logic of religious belief not with that of science but with that of practice. This singularly modern idea – which resurges periodically in later philosophy, for example in Kant's conception of the 'ideas' of reason, in Kierkegaard's notion of the 'leap' of faith, in the neo-Marxist theory of *praxis* and in the existentialist concept of commitment – possesses less philosophical merit than rhetorical impact. For while it is indeed a striking suggestion that religious belief may be constituted by a form of voluntary activity, and so be inaccessible to metaphysical doubt, it seems hard to reconcile with the obvious fact that the question of the existence of God is a question about what is true, and not a question that could be resolved by mesmerising ourselves into a state of unfounded belief in Him.

Perhaps the greatest of the many philosophers who could reasonably be called Cartesian was Nicolas Malebranche (1638–1715), a priest of the Oratory who engaged in a vivid and at times bitter controversy with Arnauld over matters of theology and metaphysics. Like Pascal, Malebranche was distinguished by his literary gifts and produced – in his *Dialogues on Metaphysics* (*Entretiens sur la métaphysique et sur la réligion*, 1688) – some of the finest philosophical prose since Plato. But he did not share Pascal's distrust of metaphysics and conceded to mysticism only a narrow region of carefully circumscribed darkness. Malebranche had thoroughly absorbed the principles and proofs of the Cartesian philosophy, but, like many who were convinced that Descartes' method was both valid and comprehensive, he remained unsatisfied with the Cartesian picture of the relation between body and soul.

Descartes' views of causation are such that there is a *prima facie* contradiction between the thesis that body and soul are (or exemplify) separate substances, and the thesis that there is also interaction between them. Malebranche did not seek to question the Cartesian idea of substance, although his writings are remarkable for containing an extended metaphysics from which that idea could be eliminated without detriment to the system's integrity. Instead, he questioned the theory of causation implicit in Descartes: the theory that the states of a substance must be explained in terms of its essential nature. It seemed to Malebranche that such a theory could explain neither our ability to perceive the material world, nor our ability to act on it. Furthermore (and in this he showed how much he had let the Cartesian conception of material substance fall into the background of his philosophy, replacing it with the more modern idea of the material object), he even regarded it as incompatible with the view that there is causal action between separate bodies, since it seemed to imply that each body, being complete in itself, had nothing to gain from or to impart to its surroundings. Rejecting the view that bodies have an intrinsic 'power' to affect us and each other as a mere superstition, Malebranche adopted the theory, already proposed by the Cartesians du Cordemoy (c. 1605–1684) and Arnold Geulincx (1624–1669), of 'occasionalism', which he defended with great vigour. This theory – perhaps the first developed account of the concept of causation in modern philosophy – argues that, since the laws of the universe have their origin in God, it is God who produces the events that conform to them. No event produces another of its own nature. Rather, when one thing occurs, then this is the occasion for God's production of that thing which we know as its 'effect'. In this view, there is no special difficulty posed by the relation between mind and body, since to speak of interaction between them can only be a manner of speaking: just as it is only a manner of speaking to refer to interaction between anything.

There is much more to Malebranche's metaphysics than this theory (often wrongly thought to be, not a general philosophy of causation, but rather an *ad hoc* apologetic whereby to reconcile the Cartesian theory of mind with the obvious). In particular Malebranche upheld and developed the Cartesian theory of continuous creation; he supported the view that science must be rooted in *a priori* metaphysical principles; and he reaffirmed the distinction between the rationally conceivable essence and the empirically perceivable properties of things. But his influence in these matters was less great than it might have been. The Cartesian philosophy was already being eclipsed by the more systematic work of Spinoza and Leibniz, and by the powerful attack on rationalism initiated by Hobbes and given magisterial form in Locke's *Essay on the Human Understanding.*

It is impossible to leave the subject of the Cartesian revolution without taking a brief forward glance into that intellectual movement known to the historian of ideas as the 'Enlightenment', and known to philosophers either as the eighteenth century, or as nothing at all. By the end of the seventeenth century, scientific knowledge, and the Cartesian clarity of expression, had become universal properties of the educated class; and a new literature began to arise, encyclopaedic in its aims, anti-authoritarian in its preconceptions and outspoken in its style (see especially Pierre Bayle (1647–1706): *Dictionnaire historique et critique,* 1696). Culminating in the writings of Voltaire, Diderot and d'Alembert, this movement has gained international status in the eyes of the intellectual historian. But it remains decidedly French in its tone and manners. Clear, elegant, haughty and ironical, the '*philosophes*', as they came to be known, stand at the end of a century in which intellectual, political and moral revolutions had upset the authority of Church and State, and humbled in their eyes all mortals whose pretensions to eminence could be backed neither by reason nor by experiment. Most of the *philosophes* had their intellectual roots in Cartesian scepticism; but by now this scepticism, separated from the intellectual accomplishment of the metaphysics which stemmed from it, had become a literary device, a means to sustain a detached attitude of rational unbelief, while treating of matters that could allow neither systematic development nor the easy extraction of a moral.

The *philosophes* and the figures of the literary Enlightenment, authors of literary masterpieces as diverse as Voltaire's *Le Siècle de Louis XIV* and Diderot's *Le Neveu de Rameau*, would not have existed but for the decades of Cartesian metaphysics which cleared the intellectual air for them. Nevertheless, they play an insignificant part in the history of philosophy, neither adding to nor subtracting from the metaphysical ideas which their urbane scepticism made it more agreeable to them to ridicule than to understand. No doubt it is a further tribute to Descartes that his method should transmute itself into so many literary forms. But the history of philosophy proceeded independently, returning to the legacy of Descartes with a spirit which he would have recognised, but which was not his own.

5

SPINOZA

Benedict de (Baruch) Spinoza (1632–1677), like Descartes and Leibniz, was a philosopher immersed in mathematical and scientific investigation. The greatest single influence on his thought was Descartes; he corresponded with men of science, such as Oldenburg (secretary to the newly formed Royal Society) and Boyle, and became an acknowledged expert in the science of optics, making his living (according to some accounts) as a lens-grinder. He was educated at the Jewish College in Amsterdam, to which city his Jewish parents had come from Portugal to escape persecution. Ex-communicated from the synagogue for his sceptical beliefs, he settled among a group of enlightened Christians, who had formed a philosophical circle of which he soon became the leader. Then, leaving Amsterdam, he lived a secluded unworldly existence, refused offers of money and academic distinctions, and even withheld his great *Ethics* from the press, as much from love of truth and intellectual independence as from any fear of the censor. He died of consumption, leaving his major work unpublished.

Spinoza's philosophy rests on two principles. First, a rationalist theory of knowledge, according to which what is 'adequately' conceived is for that reason true; secondly, a notion of substance, inherited through Descartes from the Aristotelian tradition of which Descartes himself was the unwilling heir. From the standpoint of metaphysics it is perhaps Spinoza's greatest distinction that he examined this notion of substance, and refused to let it go until he had extracted from it every particle of philosophical meaning.

Like Descartes, Spinoza sought for what is certain, and regarded the pursuit of certainty as providing the only guarantee of human knowledge. However, unlike Descartes, he did not seek to found his system in the single indubitable premise of the 'cogito'. The proposition 'I think' has two features which rendered it useless to Spinoza. First, it expresses a merely contingent truth, whereas for Spinoza all certainty must ultimately be founded in necessities. Secondly, it contains an ineliminable reference to the first person, while for Spinoza access to philosophical truth comes only when we rise above preoccupation with our own limited experience and mentality, and learn to see things from the impartial point of view of the rational observer to whom things appear 'under the aspect of eternity' (*sub specie aeternitatis*).

The geometrical method

Spinoza took as his model of objective rational enquiry the geometry of Euclid. This, he believed, began from axioms, the truth of which could be seen to be necessary, and from definitions which clarified the concepts used to formulate them. Furthermore it advanced by indubitable logical steps to theorems which, by virtue of the deductive method, must be as certain and free from error as the axioms from which they were derived. In setting up the geometrical method as his philosophical ideal, Spinoza expressly laid aside ordinary conceptions and everyday language. He argued that his definitions were not arbitrary plays on words, but the instruments whereby certain antecedent ideas may be formulated in a language more precise than that made available by the vernacular.

One of the few works published in his lifetime was *The Principles of Cartesian Philosophy* (1663), in which he tried to lay down all the fundamental axioms to which Descartes' metaphysics could be reduced, and then to deduce from those axioms the actual content of Descartes' philosophy. The work is a brilliant summary, and of great interest in being written from outside the artificial standpoint of Descartes' *Meditations*, in which metaphysical doubt is cured only by the invocation of a highly specific contingent premise. But the principal exemplification of Spinoza's geometric method is in the *Ethics*, where Spinoza's own philosophy is set out in axiomatic form. Beginning from what he took to be correct definitions of notions indispensable to the description of reality, Spinoza attempted to prove not only propositions of a metaphysical system as ambitious as any since Plato, but also the precepts of rational conduct and the description of our moral and emotional nature. His system moves with equal geometrical rigour towards the proposition that 'a substance is prior in nature to its modifications' and towards the proposition that 'there cannot be too much merriment, but it is always good; but on the other hand melancholy is always bad.' (The proof of this second proposition involves, when traced back to original axioms, something like a hundred separate steps; it looks less inaccessible to rational thought when placed beside Spinoza's view that merriment can be 'more easily conceived than observed'.)

Substance

The Cartesian notion of substance, appealing though it was on logical, scientific and metaphysical grounds, gave rise to problems that steadily increased in significance as their depth was perceived. What is the relation between substance construed as individual and substance construed as matter or stuff? How many substances are there? How, if at all, can we explain their interaction? If they can sustain themselves in existence, why do we need an explanation of their origin? Descartes and the Cartesians gave various answers to those questions, none of them felt to be satisfactory. Spinoza was quick to observe that the concept of substance is, nevertheless, the cornerstone of Cartesian metaphysics. Hence each of those questions must be answered unequivocally and consistently if the metaphysical structure is to stand up to philosophical examination. If metaphysics collapses, then, Spinoza believed (and in this he was at one with all rationalist thinkers), so does the possibility of science.

In the *Principles* Descartes had touched on the problems posed by the concept of substance and made a distinction between the 'principal attribute' of a substance (the attribute which constitutes its nature, as extension is the nature of physical things and thought the nature of mind) and its 'modifications' or 'modes' – the properties in respect of which it can change without ceasing to be what it is. He also noted an ambiguity in the term 'substance', which might be used in a wide sense, to denote any individual object, or in a restricted sense, to refer to that which depends upon nothing outside itself for its existence. In this restricted sense, he argued, only God is a substance.

It is this restricted idea of substance that provides the cornerstone of

Spinoza's metaphysics. A substance, he writes, is 'in itself and conceived through itself', or is 'that the conception of which does not depend upon the conception of another thing from which it must be formed'. A substance must be intelligible apart from all relations with other things. Hence a substance cannot enter into relations and, in particular, can be neither the cause nor the effect of anything outside itself. To the extent that a thing is caused, it must be explained in terms of, and therefore 'conceived through', other things. A substance therefore cannot be produced by anything else: it is its own cause (*causa sui*) – which means, according to Spinoza's definition, that its essence involves existence.

Spinoza, evidently influenced by Descartes, distinguishes the attributes of a substance from its modes. An attribute is that which 'the intellect perceives as constituting the essence of a substance', whereas a mode is that which is 'in something else' through which it must be conceived. The word 'in' here creates difficulties, but here is an analogy: a group of people join to form a club which then does things, owns things, organises things. When I say that the club bought a house, I really mean that the members of the club did various things, with a specific legal result. But none of the members bought a house. Hence it looks as though the club is an independent entity, existing over and above the people who compose it. In fact, however, it is entirely dependent for its existence and nature on the activities of its members. The club is 'in' the members, in Spinoza's sense. And when x is 'in' y, x can be understood fully only *through y*. Another way to put the point is: y is 'prior to' x, since we cannot understand x without a prior conception of y. In this sense, 'a substance is prior in nature to its modes'.

The first part of the *Ethics* is devoted to God, defined as 'a substance consisting of infinite attributes, each one of which expresses an eternal and infinite essence'. Spinoza follows Descartes in giving a version of the ontological argument. However, the proof has an interesting twist to it. Spinoza believes that all substances exist necessarily, since 'it belongs to the nature of substance to exist'. But he also argues that 'there cannot be two or more substances with the same nature or attribute'; in other words, substances cannot share attributes. Since God possesses all attributes, therefore, there can be no other substance besides God. Everything that exists is 'in' God.

God has 'infinite attributes'. Extension is an attribute, since we perceive it as constituting the essence of the corporeal world: there is nothing more basic than extension to which the explanation of corporeal things could be referred. We have full (or, as Spinoza puts it, 'adequate') knowledge of the nature of extension through the science of geometry, and the existence of this systematic science of necessary truths is further proof that the idea of extension delivers God's essential nature to our intellect.

Monism

Extension is an attribute of God, and like all the attributes of God it is infinite in quantity (which means, to put it crudely, that space has no boundaries, a proposition for which Spinoza provides an independent proof). It remains to examine what other attributes God might have. The other candidate bequeathed by Cartesian philosophy was thought, which Descartes put forward as the essential characteristic of mind. Spinoza argued that this too must be an attribute of the single divine substance, since it can be conceived in itself and there is nothing beyond itself by reference to which we must conceive or explain it. It has modifications – specific thoughts, images and agglomerations of the same – just as extension has its modifications. But in the rational explanation of these it is to thought alone that we need refer; having referred to thought, we do not need to go beyond it to some more basic attribute through which thought itself must be conceived. This explains why the properties of thought are pellucid to us (although it is clear on reflection that thought and extension are pellucid in a different way and for different reasons). Thought, therefore, is another attribute of the divine substance.

While there are of necessity infinitely many such attributes, to finite beings only finite knowledge is available. Thus we can conceive God through the attribute of extension and through that of thought, while other manners of conception lie outside our intellectual capacity. In so far as the world is knowable to us, therefore, it consists of one thing, seen under two aspects, which correspond to its two knowable attributes. It can be seen either under the aspect of thought, in which case we call it God, or under that of extension, in which case we call it Nature. God or Nature (*Deus sive Natura*) is the single existing thing which exists of necessity and, being cause of itself, persists through all eternity. Thought and extension are not mere properties of God: they each constitute God's essence, and each therefore present to the intellect a full and adequate idea of what God is.

It is of course extremely puzzling to imagine in this way *one* thing with more than one essence: the concept of an 'attribute' only seems intelligible when construed epistemologically, as a reference to the two possible ways of knowing God; the alternative, ontological, conception, which attributes two separate essences to God, is extremely difficult to understand. But Spinoza definitely meant us to construe his theory ontologically, believing that only then will the full intellectual consequences contained in the concept of substance be understood. Only then could it be seen that the very same ontological argument that shows the existence of a substance, explains also the existence of thought and of extended matter. There ceases to be a distinction between creation and the creator, and the greatest theological problem therefore dissolves. Likewise there ceases to be a real distinction between mind and matter: so the greatest metaphysical problem also dissolves. Mind, matter, creation, creator – all these are simply names of the same eternal self-sustaining thing.

Mind and its place in nature

The theory of the attributes was partly intended by Spinoza to solve an outstanding question raised by Descartes' philosophy of mind. If the mind is, or belongs to, a separate substance from that of the body, then how do mind and body interact? What mechanism can join two substances, so that changes in the one are explained by changes in the other? On Spinoza's reading of 'substance' the suggestion is a nonsense, and his reading, he thought, is the only consistent one.

Spinoza's solution to the problem of mind and body is ingenious, although hard to understand in its entirety. 'The mind and the body are one and the same thing, which is conceived now under the attribute of thought, now under the attribute of extension.' The theory of the attributes implies not only that the one substance can be known in two ways, but that the same two ways of knowing apply also to the modes of that substance. The mind is a finite mode of the infinite substance conceived as thought; the body is a finite mode of the infinite substance conceived as extension – and these two finite modes are in fact one and the same. Spinoza summarises the theory by saying that the mind is the idea of the body.

However, when we describe a mode of thinking (an idea), we situate it in the total system of ideas (which is God, conceived under the attribute of thought). No explanation of an idea can be formulated, except in terms of other ideas. Similarly, when we describe a mode of extension, we situate it in the system of physical things, and explain it accordingly, through the attribute of extension. Mind and body are one *thing*; but they are conceptualised under rival and incommensurable systems. Hence, while we can assert in the abstract that they are identical, we can never *explain* a physical process in terms of a mental one, or a mental process in terms of a physical. This combination of doctrines has proved immensely puzzling to Spinoza's commentators. On the one hand, he is a monist, believing that there is only one ultimate reality, of which everything is a mode; on the other hand, he admits a kind of dualism into his system, reaffirming the separateness of mind and body in the very act of denying it.

Perhaps the best way to grasp what Spinoza is saying is through a somewhat distant analogy. When I look at a picture I see physical objects: patches of pigment smeared on a canvas. And I can describe these objects so thoroughly as to account for the entire picture. In doing so, I do not mention the other thing that I see: a stag hunt passing before a country house. This too I could describe so thoroughly as to give a complete account of the picture. But the two accounts are incommensurable: I cannot cross from one to the other in midstream, so to speak. I cannot describe the lead hound as frantically pursuing a patch of ochre, or the area of chrome yellow fused with oxydised linseed oil as resting on the huntsman's knee. In some such way, Spinoza is saying, the complete description of the body describes the very same thing as the complete description of the mind; but to explain mental states in terms of physical causes is to cross in midstream to another and incommensurate language.

Persons and things

What, then, *are* we? To say that we are modes of the divine substance is not to say enough, for, as Spinoza realised, this does not yet grant to us our individuality. In particular, it does not settle the important question of how we can come to consider ourselves as things, even though, in the nature of the case, we cannot be substances. Thus Spinoza, having argued that there can be only one substance, attempted to reconcile this doctrine with the view that there is a potentially indefinite number of things. He did this by reversing Descartes' argument about the wax.

The wax, it will be remembered, seemed not to possess any essential unity or identity beyond that of the stuff out of which it was composed. It could be broken up, melted, transformed in respect of every one of its properties except those which pertained to matter as such. Its individuality counted for nothing in comparison with its constitution. By contrast, Spinoza observes, there are certain modifications of fundamental substance which have a kind of innate resistance to changes of the kind undergone by Descartes' lump of wax. Things resist damage, fracture and so on, or perhaps, if injured, they restore themselves out of their own inherent principle of existence. They endeavour, as Spinoza puts it, to persist in their own being. This endeavour (*conatus*) constitutes their essence, in so far as it makes sense to attribute essence to something that has neither the completeness nor the self-sufficiency of a genuine substance.

The obvious examples of these partial substances or individual things are organisms; and in describing their identity in terms of a *conatus* Spinoza was in effect reviving a concept from Aristotelian biology. Organisms seem to have more *conatus* than inanimate things: they avoid injury, resist it, restore themselves when it is inflicted. This is why we are ready to attribute to them an individuality that we are not always willing to attribute to inanimate objects. We speak of a tree, a bird, a man; but only of a *lump* of wax, a *heap* of snow, a *pool* of water; thus identifying the first as individuals, the second only as quantities of some independently describable *stuff*.

In the case of persons we are also able to know this '*conatus*' not only under the aspect of physical cohesion such as characterises all organic life, but also under the aspect of thought. Under this aspect *conatus* appears as desire, or rather (since human beings have adequate knowledge of mentality) as desire accompanied by its own idea: what we might call self-conscious desire. It is this which (judged from the mental standpoint) constitutes our striving, and the satisfaction of which therefore constitutes our good.

Knowledge

Spinoza's theory of knowledge is an extension and refinement of the Cartesian theory of clear and distinct perception. For every idea there is an *ideatum* – an object conceived under the attribute of extension which exactly corresponds to the idea in the system of the world. Every idea is 'of' its *ideatum*, and therefore every idea possesses what Spinoza calls the 'extrinsic' mark of truth, namely an exact and necessary correspondence to its *ideatum*. Error is possible, however, since many ideas fail to possess the 'intrinsic' mark of truth, which is present only in 'adequate' ideas. Although the term 'adequate' comes from Descartes, it effectively replaces the notion of a 'clear and distinct perception', as Descartes had discussed this.

Every adequate idea is self-evident to the one who grasps it, and 'falsity consists in privation of knowledge, resulting from inadequate or mutilated and confused ideas'. A prime example of this inadequacy is sensory perception. My image of the sun, for example, is of a small red disc resting on the horizon: and if I trusted sense-perception alone, I should be led into false conceptions, believing that the sun itself is the *ideatum* of this image, when in fact its *ideatum* is a process in me – something going on in my eye or brain.

Knowledge gained through sense-perception is assigned, in the *Ethics*, to the lowest of three levels of cognition: the level that Spinoza calls imagination or opinion. Such cognition can never reach adequacy, since the ideas of imagination do not come to us in their intrinsic logical order, but in the order of our bodily processes. By the accumulation of confused ideas we can arrive at a grasp of what is common to them – a 'universal notion', such as we have of man, tree or dog. But these are not in themselves adequate ideas, even if they constitute the meaning of our everyday general terms.

The second level of cognition, exemplified by science and mathematics, comes from the attempt to gain a full (adequate) conception of essences. This involves adequate ideas and 'common notions', since 'those things which are common to all and which are equally in a part and in the whole can only be conceived adequately'. To return to our example: not being part of my body, the sun cannot be adequately known through modifications of my body, but only through the science – astronomy – that aims to provide an adequate idea of the heavenly bodies. This science will begin from geometry, which is the science of extension; but it will also employ such common notions as those of 'motion and rest'.

The third level of cognition is intuition, or *scientia intuitiva*. 'This kind of cognition proceeds from an adequate idea of the formal essence of certain attributes of God to the adequate knowledge of the essence of things.' Spinoza seems to mean by intuition the comprehensive understanding of the truth of a proposition that is granted to the person who grasps it, together with a valid proof of it from self-evident premises, in a single mental act.

'Cognition of the first kind is the only cause of falsity . . . while cognition of the second and third kinds is necessarily true.' From our point of view, therefore, the truth of an idea consists in, and is understood through, its logical connection to the system of adequate ideas. The advance of knowledge consists in the replacement of confused and inadequate ideas by adequate conceptions, until, at the limit, all that we think follows inexorably from a self-evident conception of the nature of God.

Every idea is a mental glimpse of a physical process, and conversely every physical process is no more than an extended embodiment of an idea. It follows that 'the order and connection of ideas is the same as the order and connection of things'. This proposition encapsulates a thoroughgoing rationalism. The relation between ideas, when considered purely from the aspect of thought, is a relation of logic: one idea follows from or provides a logical ground for another. And the only way in which an idea can give a satisfactory explanation of another idea is through such logical relations. We can explain the conclusion of a proof only by showing its logical relation to the premises. And that relation is one of necessity.

Likewise the order of things is an order which allows for explanation. In Spinoza's view everything that happens, since it stems from the same ineluctable nature of the single divine substance, happens not by chance but by necessity. So the order of things must exhibit that necessity. We show why one event happens in nature by showing it to be a necessary consequence of all that preceded it. And the necessity here, which compels the sequence of nature, is exactly the same as the necessity explored in a mathematical proof. Indeed, if we saw all nature adequately, so that we conceived it not only under the aspect of extension but also under the aspect of thought, then it would appear to us exactly like a mathematical proof. Physical events, seen as their corresponding ideas, would be seen to follow from each other as ideas in a mathematical sequence.

Adequate knowledge of physical things comes about because we can have ideas of what is common to all physical processes. These common notions will reflect the universal properties of extension; hence, whatever they indicate by way of logical implications will correspond accurately to reality, since nothing in the physical world will originate in those universal properties except in accordance with the logical sequences of ideas which our common notions generate. It is the mark of such adequate ideas that, as soon as presented, they are grasped and adopted with certainty, like the clear and distinct ideas of Descartes. The certainty here is nothing but the reflection of the fact that we are so constituted that we cannot think otherwise. To be differently constituted is to be possessed of a nature that does not correspond to the common notions. But, *ex hypothesi*, these common notions are common because they reflect what is universal and necessary in nature. It is by abstract reasoning concerning these notions that an accurate understanding of the essence of things is obtained.

Freedom

The theory just sketched has a powerful, and to many unacceptable, consequence. It turns out that there is as little freedom in the world of physical things as in the world of ideas: an effect follows from its cause with all the necessity of a mathematical theorem. Moreover, every human action arises out of the same unbroken chain of causal necessity as do the movements of the planets, the falling of trees, and the steady flow of rivers. Spinoza's determinism is in fact totally rigid, and can be seen as a consequence not of some one or other dispensable metaphysical doctrine, but of the very conception of philosophy from which he began. Once we grant the conception of God as *causa sui*, together with the rationalist premise that there must be an explanation of everything, we are compelled to accept the view that the explanation of every event must refer back to God. For to find an explanation is to find a cause, and the cause of anything must lie either in it or outside it. If the cause lies in it, then the thing is *causa sui*, and therefore is itself God and identical with the whole of things. If the cause lies outside it, then it must lie in something else which in its turn must have a cause. Suppose that some given event might have been other than it is. It could have been otherwise only if it had been preceded by a chain of causes different from those which in fact occurred; and this would have been possible only if the first cause had itself been different. But that first cause, God, is *causa sui*, and therefore has all its properties by necessity. Therefore it could not be other than it is. Hence the supposition that anything might have been otherwise is absurd.

Spinoza writes

> the order of concatenation of things is a single order, whether Nature is conceived under one or the other attribute; it follows therefore that the order of the action and passions of our body is simultaneous in nature with the order of the actions and passions of the mind . . . Now all these things clearly show that the decision of the mind, together with the appetite and determination of the body, are simultaneous in nature, or rather that they are one and the same thing, which, when it is considered under the attribute of thought and explained in terms of it, we call decision, and when considered under the attribute of extension, and deduced from the laws of motion and rest, we call causation.

Thus Spinoza's solution of the problem concerning the relation between mind and body (namely that they are simply one and the same thing), while it overcomes all the difficulties concerning interaction which had bothered the Cartesians, has the inescapable consequence that there is no human freedom. Human beings are part of Nature, and the causal order of Nature is as rigid and unbreakable as the logical order of ideas. The unfolding of events in Nature proceeds with the ineluctability of a mathematical proof pursued by an omniscient mind. What then does human freedom amount to, when the origins of every human act are contained incipiently in the primeval idea of God or Nature just as are the origins of every occurrence?

It is in addressing himself to this question that Spinoza developed the part of his philosophy for which he has ever since been most admired, the theory of human freedom, and the associated analysis of the passions.

Emotion

As its title implies, the *Ethics* was not designed merely as a treatise on metaphysics with various moral asides. On the contrary it was designed to treat of the moral life in terms which, while they gained their validity from a sound metaphysical base and implied no confusion concerning Nature or God, were sufficiently definite to entail an account of the place of man in the natural world. This account would in its turn be adequate to found a true system of moral behaviour. Given his premises, Spinoza was more or less successful in this enterprise. The fact is the more surprising in that his moral views were by no means the received platitudes of the day, nor in any way predictable from the literature of the Christian and Jewish moralists who had been the overseers of his life and education. Not only did Spinoza argue that pity is 'bad and useless', and that 'self-complacency is the greatest good that we can expect'; he also poured scorn on the resentment of the poor and ungifted, and recommended humility and repentance only to those unable to live according to the dictates of reason. The necessary bridge from the uncompromising determinism of the metaphysics towards this almost Nietzschean moral vision lies in the philosophy of the emotions.

Although Descartes had written a treatise on the 'passions', it is fair to say that Spinoza was the first great philosopher since Aquinas to attempt to explore human passions systematically, in full consciousness that man's place in nature could not otherwise be described. It is from his theory of the passions that Spinoza derived his idea of freedom. God is free in that he is self-determining. But human beings cannot be free in that sense (a sense which can, logically, apply only to substance). What, then, does the distinction between freedom and unfreedom amount to? Spinoza recognised that the distinction between the free and the unfree must be expressed in other terms than that of the distinction (imaginary for Spinoza) between the caused and the uncaused. In this he has been followed by many more recent philosophers. The first step in reconstructing the distinction between the free and the unfree lay in his theory of the passions.

In some respects Spinoza's theory of the emotions shows similarities to the far sketchier and less imaginative theory propounded by his empiricist predecessor Hobbes. In particular, he took after Hobbes in supposing the various human emotions to be definable in terms of a relatively simple number of mental states, together with a specification of the content of the thoughts and desires peculiar to each individual passion. Thus Hobbes had defined fear as 'aversion, with opinion of hurt from its object' (*Leviathan*, I, vi). Hobbes thought he could specify the range of the emotions in terms of the specific beliefs and desires characteristic of each of them, although he was very unclear as to how those beliefs and desires are united.

In similar fashion Spinoza attempted to define emotions in terms of desire, pleasure and pain (for which he in turn offered definitions), and certain characteristic causes. These causes were so explained by Spinoza as to involve the concept of mentality. They involved particular conceptions of the world, and these define not just the causes but also the objects of the emotions. (The distinction here, between object and cause, is made clear by an example: I am afraid of what will happen at my meeting with the Chairman; what has caused my fear is thoughts about the Chairman's past behaviour. The object here (my meeting with the Chairman) lies in the future and so cannot be the cause. This distinction between object and cause, vital to the theory of the emotions, was made with finesse by Aquinas, but not by Spinoza whose theory of the mind nevertheless brought it about that the oversight was cancelled out in the general account of the emotional life which followed from his premises.) It may seem odd that phenomena seemingly as arbitrary and fluctuating as the human passions could be treated by the geometrical method, so that conclusions concerning the nature of grief, remorse and jealousy could be seen to follow from the definitions and axioms of an incontrovertible metaphysics. But Spinoza, who in this, as in many respects, was close to medieval thought, was dissatisfied with conventional assumptions concerning the disorderliness of this material, and believed that many assertions about the emotional life which might appear to be the fruits of prolonged and fallible observation, were in fact demonstrably necessary. In thus reopening the field of the emotions to philosophical thought he became a principal guide to those later philosophers who have sought to understand them. There are many philosophers who would agree with Spinoza, for example, that we cannot hate a thing which we pity, or that no one envies the virtue of anyone save his equal; and who would agree with him, too, in seeing these propositions as necessary truths, to be established not by empirical investigation but by philosophical argument. In his definitions of the individual emotions and his drawing of such conclusions from them, Spinoza's most lasting contribution to philosophy was made.

Activity and passivity

The essence of all emotion, for Spinoza, is passion. To the extent that he reacts to the world in an emotional way, a person is held to be passive towards it. Emotion is something suffered. The next step in Spinoza's theory of freedom was to try to show an identity between suffering passion and being the victim of an external cause. A person is passive to the extent that his actions have their origin outside him. He is active to the extent that they have their origin within him. Now of course it

follows from the metaphysics that, literally speaking, every action origi-
nates outside the agent, in God. But there is a matter of degree here. Just
as the doctrine of *conatus* allows us to postulate indefinitely many quasi-
individuals in a world which, literally speaking, contains only one
individual, so does it enable us to speak of the greater or lesser degree to
which the causes of an action are contained within the body of the agent
and therefore within his mind. Passivity is therefore a matter of degree.

The next step is to argue, from the premise that to every physical
event in the body there is a mental event that constitutes its idea, to the
conclusion that the more active a person is, the more his mind contains
adequate ideas of the causes of his action. A person is more active in
respect of his behaviour the more his consciousness contains an adequate
idea of the behaviour and its cause. To have a completely adequate idea of
the cause is to see it in relation to its own cause and so on, to the point of
grasping the full necessity of the system of which the causes form a part.
Spinoza further argues that this ever-increasing understanding of the
causes of our action is the only legitimate concept of human freedom
that we can postulate. Freedom is not freedom from necessity, but the
consciousness of necessity.

Now an emotion, since it already involves an obscure perception of
reality, can be refined, as it were, from the passive to the active, as that
perception is improved. To the extent that this refinement occurs – to the
extent, as we might put it, that the object of a feeling is more clearly
and completely understood – to that extent does the emotion pass from
passion to action, from something suffered to something done. The free
man is the man who thus gains mastery over his emotions, transforming
them into accurate conceptions of the world which he thereby dominates.
The change from passivity to activity is precisely what we mean by
pleasure, and the reverse what we mean by pain.

It is a small step from there to the conclusion that only the free man
is truly happy, and that his freedom and his reason are one and the same.
From these noble ideas Spinoza then unfolds his moral system, one
aspect of which here deserves mention.

The intellectual love of God

Spinoza's final moral vision has an Aristotelian and a Platonic aspect. Like
the philosophers of the Platonic tradition, Spinoza wishes to locate the

final wisdom and happiness of humans in the intellectual love of God (the love which informs the blessed souls of Dante's Paradise). And he thinks he can make clear what this love consists in. To the extent that we understand something we obtain pleasure from it, and to the extent that such pleasure is pure – unmingled with confused ideas – to that extent does it constitute love. Now, understanding the universe in its totality cannot produce confused ideas, since the idea of the universe in its totality is the idea of God, which, to the extent that we grasp it, is adequate in us. The attempt to understand reality through that idea necessarily leads us to the love of reality; in other words to the love of God. But this love is active and intellectual, not passive and emotional; in acquiring it we come to participate in the divine nature. We see the world in its fullness, under the idea of God, and not in partial, confused or passive form. Seeing things thus, we see them, as Spinoza puts it, 'under the aspect of eternity'. Eternity means, not endless time, but timelessness. We see the world as an entity which endures because it has no duration, which is infinite because it has no parts, and in which we participate because in it we are dissolved. Seeing the world thus is to see God. Other ways of representing God – as the personal, anthropomorphic, passionate creature of established religion – might be useful in encouraging moral sentiments among the ignorant, bringing as they do the ideas of divine retribution and reward; but they are insignificant to the philosophical mind. Moreover the moral life of the enlightened has no need of anthropomorphic religion. Seeing things *sub specie aeternitatis*, they recognise that happiness, freedom and virtue are one and the same, and therefore that virtue is strictly its own reward.

Conclusion

Spinoza's vision, as it emerges in the *Ethics*, is thus one of sublime impersonality. We are happy to the extent that we share in the objective vision which is God's (the vision of the world *sub specie aeternitatis*). The first-person viewpoint of Descartes has been lost entirely. The 'cogito' appears only dimly reflected (in one of the incidental propositions of Part I); it plays no role in the validation of the system, and inevitably gives way to the third-personal vision towards which the *Ethics* tends. This loss of epistemological doubt, and consequent abandonment of first-personal privilege as the basis of philosophy, is characteristic of post-Cartesian metaphysics, and the origin of the more powerful of the critiques which were to destroy it. In Spinoza, we see the most adventurous development possible of the ideas of God and substance as the medievals had expounded them. With rare intellectual honesty, he worked out what he considered to be the inevitable logical consequences of those concepts, at the same time arguing for their indispensability. The result was a complete description of humanity, of nature, of the world and of God. The weak point of the philosophy lay not in its conclusions, but in its premises, and in particular in that fatal idea of substance which Spinoza had thought he both needed and could make intelligible.

6

LEIBNIZ

Gottfried Wilhelm von Leibniz (1646–1716) shared with Newton the discovery of the calculus, and contributed the concept of kinetic energy to mechanics. He was accomplished in history, law, chemistry, geology and mechanics, made many incidental scientific discoveries of importance, was a tireless politician and courtier, founded the Academy of Berlin, wrote fluently in French, German and Latin, corresponded with every man of genius from whom he could learn, and produced a philosophical system of astonishing power and originality, which provided the basis of German academic philosophy throughout the century following his death. Embedded in this system are the foundations of a new logic, and, with the discoveries of modern logic, interest in the thought of Leibniz has been reawakened. But so fertile was his mind, and so prodigious his output, that even now many of his writings are unpublished, and few scholars can claim familiarity with every aspect of his thought.

Leibniz published little during his lifetime, and his philosophical masterpiece – the *Monadology* – is such a triumph of succinct expression that, fully to interpret it, one must look to many other works and to his correspondence, in order to know the detailed arguments which underlie its conclusions. Among the most important of these works are the *Discourse on Metaphysics*, *The New Essays on the Human Understanding* (written partly in answer to certain theories of the empiricist Locke), *The Theodicy** and the correspondence with Arnauld, Clarke, de Volder and Des Bosses.

---

* Published in 1710. The other works mentioned are posthumous. See bibliography.

Interpretation of Leibniz is made doubly difficult by the fact that he changed his mind about certain of his most influential ideas during the course of his lifetime, while remaining obstinately attached to them and unable overtly to reject them. Thus the picture to be obtained from reading the earlier works – such as the *Discourse on Metaphysics* – is different from that obtained from the mature *Monadology*, or the posthumous *New Essays*. In this brief summary, I shall tend more in the direction of the later Leibniz, while drawing on the earlier writings wherever these seem to be illuminating.

Substances and individuals

Spinoza's thesis that all apparent individuals are merely 'modes' of the one substance is inherently paradoxical. For the distinction between substance and mode derives in part from the ancient attempt to distinguish individuals from their properties. Spinoza seems to have abolished individuals from his world-view, reducing them to properties of something that is neither individual nor universal but a strange metaphysical hybrid: a universal with a single instance. Leibniz's philosophy arose from the attempt to provide a concept of the individual substance, and to use it to describe a plural universe – indeed, a universe in which there is not one substance but infinitely many.

Spinoza argues for human immortality; but he concludes that we survive only in part, dispersed in the infinite mind of God. Leibniz also believed in immortality; but immortality would be worthless, he thought, if it did not involve the survival of the soul. And the soul is an individual, something which is numerically the same at one time as it was or will be at other times. But what exactly *is* an individual? What is the distinction between the individual and its properties, and what do we mean by saying that this individual is identical with the one I saw last week? These are the deep and difficult questions that Leibniz placed on the agenda of modern philosophy.

Monads

Every entity is either composite or simple, and simple entities do not contain parts. It is the simple entities that are the true substances, from which all other things are composed. These simple entities cannot be extended in space, since everything extended is also divisible. They are not to be confused, therefore, with the atoms of physical theory, and can best be understood in terms of their one accessible instance – the human soul, which is neither extended nor divisible, and which seems to be self-contained, simple and durable in exactly the way that a substance must be. Such basic individuals Leibniz called 'monads'; and although the soul is our clearest example, there are and must be other kinds of monads, which do not share our distinguishing attributes of rationality and self-consciousness.

Leibniz's theory of monads (the 'monadology') contains three parts, being the theories of the monad, of the aggregates of monads and of the appearances of monads. These tend in three separate directions, and much ingenuity was needed in order to attempt a reconciliation. The theory of the monad can be briefly summarised in the following six propositions:

1 Monads are not extended in space.
2 Monads are distinguished from one another by their properties (their 'predicates').
3 No monad can come into being or pass away in the natural course of things; a monad is created or annihilated only by a 'miracle'.
4 The predicates of a monad are 'perceptions' – i.e. mental states – and the objects of these mental states are ideas. Inanimate entities are in fact the appearances of animated things: aggregates of monads, each endowed with perceptions.
5 Not all perceptions are conscious. The conscious perceptions, or apperceptions, are characteristic of rational souls, but not of lesser beings. And even rational souls have perceptions of which they are not conscious.
6 'Monads have no windows' – that is, nothing is passed to them from outside; each of their states is generated from their own inner nature. This does not mean that monads do not interact; but it does mean that certain theories as to *how* individual substances interact are untenable.

Those propositions follow, Leibniz thinks, from the very idea of an individual substance, once the idea is taken seriously. But they can also be derived independently, from certain metaphysical principles which it would be absurd to question.

Principles

Leibniz's rationalism is displayed most vividly by his guiding principles, which he held to be at one and the same time laws of rational thinking and deep descriptions of reality. We need only follow these principles in order to arrive at a description of how things are – indeed, of how things *must* be. Naturally, this description of the world must be compatible with natural science. But science can be incorporated into metaphysics, Leibniz believed, once it is seen that scientific discoveries concern the 'phenomena' and not the underlying reality. Natural science is the representation of the world as it systematically appears, while the world as it really is can be known only from the self-evident principles of rational thinking.

There are two supreme principles, which Leibniz treated as axiomatic to the end of his philosophical career:

1 The Principle of Contradiction, 'in virtue of which we judge that which involves a contradiction to be false, and that which is opposed or contradictory to the false to be true';

2 The Principle of Sufficient Reason, 'by virtue of which we consider that we can find no true or existent fact, no true assertion, without there being a sufficient reason why it is thus and not otherwise, although most of the time these reasons cannot be known to us'.

Corresponding to those two principles there are two kinds of truth: truths of reason, which depend upon the first principle, and truths of fact, which depend upon the second. Truths of reason are necessary, and their opposite impossible; truths of fact are contingent, and their opposite possible. Leibniz's rationalism is reflected in his belief that for every truth of fact there is a sufficient reason, so that there is no *bare* contingency in the world, and the structure of reality conforms to the principles of rational argument.

A third principle is given equal prominence in Leibniz's earlier writings:

3 The Predicate-in-Subject Principle. This is stated in various ways, for instance: 'when a proposition is not an identity, that is, when the predicate is not explicitly contained in the subject, it must be contained in it virtually ... Thus the subject term must always contain the predicate term, so that one who understands perfectly the notion of the subject would also know that the predicate belongs to it' (*Discourse on Metaphysics*). More succinctly: 'in every true proposition, necessary or contingent, universal or particular, the concept of the predicate is in a sense included in that of the subject, *praedicatum inest subjecto*, or I know not what truth is' (Letter to Arnauld).

This third principle has posed many difficulties to commentators, and Leibniz was himself aware of objections to it: in particular, it seems unable to deal with negative propositions, such as 'No good person is unhappy'. He had intended the principle as a general theory of truth: the truth of a proposition is supposed to consist in the fact that it attributes to the subject a predicate which is already contained in its concept. Whether or not Leibniz still believed in the principle when he wrote the *Monadology* is a moot point. But it should be understood in terms of the following.

The complete notion

To every individual substance there corresponds a 'complete notion', which is given by the complete list of its predications. This notion identifies the substance as the individual that it is, and is the conception given in God's mind when he chooses to create it. Since there is no truth about a substance that is not a predication of it, substances must be distinguished by their predications. To enumerate those predications is to give the *whole* truth about the individual to which they apply. Moreover, anything less than the whole truth will not identify the individual as the thing that it is; a monad can share any of its predications, short of the total list, with another monad. If God is to have a reason to create a given monad, therefore, it is only because he has a complete notion of it. The Principle of Sufficient Reason – which implies that there is a sufficient reason for the existence of each contingent thing – also implies that there is a complete notion for every substance.

If that is so, however, then the Predicate-in-Subject Principle is true, even if we ourselves could not make use of it. For God, at least, the truth of every subject–predicate proposition consists in the fact that the concept of the predicate is contained in the complete notion of the subject. One consequence of this is another famous Leibnizian principle:

4 The Identity of Indiscernibles. If *a* has all its properties in common with *b*, then *a* and *b* are one and the same. Hence, if *a* and *b* are not identical, then there must be some difference between them.

The converse of this principle says that if *a* and *b* are identical, then they have all their properties in common. It is sometimes known as Leibniz's law, and is rarely disputed by modern philosophers. The Identity of

Indiscernibles, however, is highly controversial, since it is used by Leibniz to prove the relativity of space and time, and to establish a metaphysical distinction between the world of substances and the world of their appearances.

God

Like the other rationalists, Leibniz accepted a version of the ontological argument for God's existence. However, the proof works, he argued, only on the assumption that the concept of God contains no contradiction. We are entitled to this assumption, he supposed, since the concept of a being with all perfections (including existence) contains nothing negative which would contradict any of the positive predications.

Leibniz also arrives at the existence of God in a more interesting way, through the Principle of Sufficient Reason. The sufficient reason for the existence of contingent things cannot be found in other contingent things, which always demand an explanation for their existence. This explanation can be found only on the assumption that a necessary being also exists – a being which 'carries the reason for its existence within itself'. And 'this ultimate reason for the existence of things is called God'.

God is supremely good, and therefore must have created the best of all possible worlds. This conclusion is sometimes proposed in the form of another principle:

5 Principle of the Best. The actual world is the best of all possible worlds. 'Best' means 'simplest in hypotheses, richest in phenomena'. The best world is an optimal solution to two simultaneous require-ments: it contains as much reality (perfection) as possible, while being maximally simple and therefore intelligible.

The concept of a 'possible world' entered philosophy for the first time with Leibniz. It enabled him to formulate some of the intuitions about necessity and contingency which had proved fundamental to the argu-ments of Descartes and Spinoza, but which neither of them had made fully clear.

Contingency

The truth of the proposition that Caesar crossed the Rubicon consists in the fact that the predicate 'crosses the Rubicon' is contained in the complete notion of Caesar. But in that case, someone might object, it is true by definition, and therefore necessary, that Caesar crossed the Rubicon. What remains, then, of the distinction between necessary and contingent truth?

There is indeed a sense in which it is necessarily true of Caesar that he crossed the Rubicon: anyone who did not do so would not be Caesar. Still, Leibniz argues, Caesar might not have crossed the Rubicon, for there might have been no such individual. Caesar's existence is a contingent fact, dependent on the will of God. Another way of saying this is that there are possible worlds in which there is no such person, and in which therefore the event of Caesar's crossing the Rubicon does not occur. Hence the proposition that Caesar crossed the Rubicon might have been false.

A necessary truth, by contrast, is one that is true in all possible worlds; and the marks of a necessary truth are that it is universal and knowable *a priori* by finite minds. Only God can know a *contingent* truth *a priori*, since only God possesses the complete notion of contingent things. We must know such truths *a posteriori*, by investigation and experiment, if we are to know them at all.

This account of necessity and *a priori* knowledge indicates a radical division between God's view of the world and our view. God knows everything *a priori*, and it is this *a priori* aspect of things that is captured by the controversial Predicate-in-Subject Principle. In creating contingent things, God is also creating the possible world that contains them, and therefore so ordering them as to form a consistent and harmonious totality. Indeed, Leibniz argues, each individual monad is like a mirror of the universe that contains it, and the universe itself is contained implicitly in all its parts.

Freedom and necessity

What place is there, in Leibniz's system, for human freedom? In the *Discourse on Metaphysics* he writes as follows:

> We must distinguish between what is certain and what is necessary. Everyone grants that future contingents are certain, since God foresees them, but we do not concede that they are necessary on that account. But (someone will say) if a conclusion can be deduced infallibly from a definition or notion, it is necessary. And it is true that we are maintaining

that everything that must happen to a person is already contained virtually in his nature or notion, just as the properties of a circle are contained in its definition.

Yet, he argues, human freedom is a reality, since although it is necessary in *this* sense that Caesar should cross the Rubicon, it is still not impossible that the event should not happen. God chose the best possible world, and in that world Caesar crosses the Rubicon; but there is no contradiction in supposing that God had chosen otherwise.

But surely God, being supremely good, *must* choose the best of all possible worlds – any other choice is incompatible with the nature of God. And in what sense am I, created according to God's complete notion of me, free to do other than I do, when what I do is contained in my notion from the start? Leibniz seems to say that there are two kinds of reason. In a mathematical proof reasoning necessitates the conclusion. In reasoning about what is best to do, however, our reasons 'incline without necessitating'. Such are God's reasons for creating the actual world; and such are our own reasons for behaving as we do. It is in this sense that both we and God are free.

Most commentators have found Leibniz's treatment of free will obscure at best; part of the problem is that Leibniz has two contrasting ways of envisaging the individuality of monads.

Activity and *vis viva*

Monads are individuated in God's mind by their complete notions. But the complete notion merely lists the predicates of a monad and says nothing about the link between them. Looked at in another way, each monad can be seen as a centre of activity, whose perceptions are generated successively by a living force, or *vis viva*. Like Spinoza, Leibniz was impressed by the substantial unity of organic beings, and believed that we observe in them, from another perspective, the individuality that is revealed in a timeless way to God. He sometimes writes of the *conatus* of individual substances and defended a theory of dynamics which gave pride of place to the living force in things, as opposed to the 'dead force' or momentum that features in Cartesian physics. In defending this idea, Leibniz introduced the concept of kinetic energy into mechanics, and thereby set physics on a new path.

The active principle enables us to individuate monads, even though we do not possess their complete notions. I can identify the individual substance that is Caesar in terms of the living force that propels him, without already predicating of him that he will cross the Rubicon. The active principle binds Caesar's predicates together, and inclines him from the outset towards the decision that he will one day make, to cross the Rubicon – inclines, but does not necessitate.

Leibniz also refers to the activity of monads in another sense, familiar from Spinoza: a monad is active to the extent that its ideas are 'distinct', passive to the extent that they are 'confused'. To understand this aspect of Leibniz we must turn to the theory of aggregates.

Aggregates of monads

In speaking of organic things we are not, as a rule, talking of individual monads. Every living organism is an aggregate of many monads. What binds them together, and what enables us to speak of *one* organism, when we have a plurality of simple individuals? It seems that the original problem that motivated Leibniz – the problem of accounting for the actual individuals in our world – remains with him.

Leibniz has recourse to the theory of ideas, which he inherited from Descartes. Each monad has perceptions or knowledge, which may be more or less clear and distinct, and more or less adequate.

> When I can recognise a thing from among others without being able to say what its differences or properties consist in, the knowledge is *confused*. It is in this way that we sometimes know something *clearly*, without being in any doubt whether a poem or a picture is done well or badly, simply because it has a certain something, I know not what, that satisfies or offends us. But when I can explain the marks which I have, the knowledge is called *distinct*. And such is the knowledge of the assayer, who discerns the true from the false by means of certain tests or marks which make up the definition of gold.

Distinctness, so defined, admits of degrees, since the notions that enter into the definition of something themselves stand in need of definition. Only when everything that enters into the definition of a thing is known distinctly, can the knowledge of the thing be called *adequate*.

What then is the relation between an idea and its object? For example, what happens when I perceive something? Nothing is passed to me from the thing perceived; yet there is a sense in which all my perceptions represent the world around me. They do this because the predicates of other monads unfold in harmony with mine: each of my perceptions corresponds to perceptions in surrounding monads and enables me to infer, with a greater or less amount of confusion, what is going on in them. This is guaranteed by another Leibnizian principle:

6 The Principle of Pre-established Harmony. Each monad has a 'point of view' on the world, defined by the totality of its perceptions; and because our perceptions evolve in harmony with each other, my perceptions can be treated as representations of the objective order.

Another way of putting this is to say that each monad 'mirrors' the universe from its own point of view. As Leibniz writes in the *Monadology*: 'the interconnection or accommodation of all created things to each other, and each to all the others, brings it about that each simple substance has relations that express all the others, and consequently, that each simple substance is a perpetual living mirror of the universe.'

How then are monads related? Such influence as there is between monads is only 'ideal', an effect of God's ceaseless intervention. Nevertheless, monads can have a more or less clear idea of each other and of their situation – as I have a clear idea of my body, even though I do not know how it is composed, and therefore even though my idea of my body is not distinct. The varying clarity and distinctness of our perceptions can be understood as defining the 'distance' between us and surrounding things. And we can speak of being 'affected' by those things, to the extent that our perceptions give us a clear idea of them.

In each organism there is a 'dominant monad', distinguished by the clarity of its perceptions of all the others; and this dominant monad is the source of the organism's unity. Leibniz, following Aristotle, describes this dominant monad as the form or 'entelechy' of the body; it is the animating principle or soul. In some way that Leibniz does not succeed in explaining, it binds the aggregate of monads into a quasi-substantial unity: it provides a *vinculum substantiale* – a 'substantial chain' – making a new quasi-individual from the simple individuals of the human body.

The appearance of monads

That is confusing enough. But matters are made worse by Leibniz's growing conviction that the appearance of the world is organised and understood in ways that do not represent the underlying reality. The familiar world around us appears ordered in space and time; it contains extended and durable things, which interact and obey causal laws. Yet monads are not extended – perhaps they are not 'in time' in the way that physical objects are. Moreover, they do not interact in the way that physical objects appear to interact, according to causal laws which are established *a posteriori*, by observation of the physical world. Such laws do not describe the activities of monads, but only the regular connections in the world of appearance, which are the by-product of transformations most of which we do not observe.

Thus, if I see a car passing my window my perception constitutes a state of this monad; this state mirrors the states of the monads which collectively constitute the car, as they are then disposed, in such a way that, to my confused perception, a car is represented in a state of motion. The perceptions of individual monads harmonise, and the phenomenal world which they 'perceive' obtains coherence because of the pre-established harmony, according to which the histories of individual monads proceed according to successive 'mirrorings' of the whole of things. God established this harmony at the creation, monads then proceeding according to their own individual inner momentum, yet in such a way as to share the collective illusion of a common physical world, in which they participate and of which they have experiential knowledge. Once established, the harmony proceeds forever: it no more needs the intervention of God to see that the laws of the universe appear to be obeyed from any particular point of view, than it needs the intervention of the watchmaker to ensure that two perfectly made watches, once wound up, will go on keeping time.

Leibniz also argued against Newton (through Newton's representative Samuel Clarke), in favour of a relative as opposed to an absolute view of space. If space is absolute, and possessed of reality over and above the spatial relations between individuals, then the whole universe might be moved through space without discernible change. But then consider the position of the universe as a whole. Why should it be situated in one area rather than another? This question can have no answer. By the postulated nature of space, there will be no discernible difference between the two arrangements. Hence there is no explanation of the actuality of either; which violates the Principle of Sufficient Reason. Hence space must consist in the totality of spatial relations between objects. And if one asks for a definition of a point in space, Leibniz says, he can provide it by showing what it is for two objects to occupy the same point. Two objects occupy the same point in space if they stand in the same spatial relation to all other things.

But now what of spatial relations? What we perceive as a relation between *A* and *B* consists in fact of particular modifications of *A* and of *B*. To take an example: John's being taller than Henry consists in two facts; first that John measures six feet, secondly that Henry measures five. Thus what we perceive as spatial relations are really certain modifications of monads. These could be called their 'space-generating' properties; Leibniz referred to them as their individual 'points of view'. The familiar world that surrounds us appears spatial, even though monads have no extension and indeed, strictly speaking, no spatial properties at all. Space, as a system of relations, can only be an *appearance*; however, is not just any kind of appearance. Although when we perceive things as spatially organised, we do not perceive them as they really are, space is still to be distinguished from a mere hallucination. This is what Leibniz meant by describing space as a 'well-founded phenomenon'.

With this phrase Leibniz introduced one of the crucial concepts underlying the philosophy of Kant. The physical world was described as 'systematic appearance'. On the Leibnizian system, the whole physical world turns out to be a well-founded phenomenon. Which is to say that the dynamic and static properties of matter, its spatial and even its temporal organisation, and finally the causal laws which govern its behaviour, are assigned by Leibniz to the world of appearance.

The interesting result of this is that, having tried to reconcile the rationalist concept of substance with the common-sense concept of an individual, Leibniz ends by saying that the apparent individuals in our world are for the most part not individuals at all. Moreover, he is unable to give a coherent account of the fact that they nevertheless appear to be individuals. No example of a monad presents itself, save the individual soul. And yet the soul is as much outside the natural order (the order of well-founded phenomena) as every other substantial thing.

Part Two

Empiricism

7

LOCKE AND BERKELEY

It cannot be said that philosophical empiricism is either peculiar to Britain or predominant there. Nevertheless, it is a fact worth remarking that, since the Middle Ages, there has been a succession of gifted British writers who have defended a version of the empiricist outlook, so that 'British empiricism' is now the name of a recognised strand of philosophical history.

Empiricism sees human understanding as confined within the limits of human experience, straying outside those limits only to fall victim to scepticism or to lose itself in nonsense. In the Middle Ages William of Ockham had already put forward empiricist theories about causality, about the mind and about the nature and limits of science; these were later to find wide acceptance. In the late Renaissance too, Francis Bacon had expressed, in a manner more fulsome than systematic, a theory of knowledge in which the habit of empirical investigation was given precedence over metaphysics.

Hobbes and the philosophy of language

Empiricism only began to come of age as a philosophy, however, when it was able to align itself with a comprehensive theory of language. It was then, when it felt able to determine what can and what cannot be *said*, that empiricism was able to challenge rationalism in what proved to be its weakest spot. Rationalism must assume that humans possess ideas the significance of which outstrips the limit of any experience which might provide their content. Among such ideas were those of 'God', 'substance', 'cause', and 'self', upon which the rationalist world-view had raised its foundations. It is this assumption that the new philosophy of language was to deny.

The empiricist theory of language finds expression in the works of Thomas Hobbes (1588–1679) who, while he is now best known for his political writings, gave considerable thought to questions of metaphysics and epistemology. Hobbes wrote extensively, with the ambition of expounding a complete philosophy of man. He had encountered the influence of Descartes, and had been among those invited by Mersenne to submit their objections to *The Meditations*. His objections, crude though they sometimes were, show already the workings of a powerful and enquiring mind, and a dissatisfaction with the rationalism that Hobbes discerned in Descartes. Hobbes sought for a theory which would tell him how words acquire meaning, in order to demonstrate that certain metaphysical theories are, quite literally, meaningless. Like later empiricists, he was tempted to reject not just this or that metaphysical notion, but the *whole* of metaphysics, as a science forced to use words in a manner that transcends the limitations which determine their sense: 'if a man should talk to me of a *round quadrangle* . . . or *immaterial substances* . . . or of a *free subject* . . . I should not say he were in error, but that his words were without meaning' (*Leviathan*, 1651).

In common with many other empiricists, Hobbes gave a genetic account of the origins of meaning: words acquire meaning through representing 'thoughts', and the origin of all thought is sense-experience, ' for there is no conception in a man's mind, which hath not first, totally or by parts, been begotten upon the organs of sense.' In order to discover the meaning of any utterance, we must trace it back to the observations which gave rise to it. Moreover, because sensory experience gives us knowledge of particulars, then the words (names) which express our thoughts must ultimately have reference to particulars. Thus a general term could not denote a 'universal'; rather it denotes indeterminately the particular members of a class. In this way Hobbes expressed a thought already familiar in the works of Ockham. He perceived a connection between empiricism and nominalism (see chapter 2, p. 17). One of the principal preoccupations of succeeding empiricist philosophy was to determine just what this obligatory nominalism amounts to, and how far it is tenable without the simultaneous denial of scientific thinking.

Hobbes foreshadowed Locke and Berkeley in many other ways. In a confused but determined manner, he tried to reject the rationalist concept of causation, although he was unclear as to what to put in its place. His unclarity was shared by every other thinker with whom he might be compared, being overcome only when Berkeley made the first steps towards the radical theory of causality that is found in Hume. Hobbes inherited from Descartes and Pierre Gassendi (1592–1655) the distinction between 'primary' and 'secondary' qualities, as Robert Boyle was to call them. In his theory of these, he presaged a fundamental advance normally attributed to Locke. He also attempted to give a general theory of the passions and of human nature based on empiricist assumptions alone. He combined this theory with an account of good and evil which represents moral judgements as entirely subjective.

Locke and the theory of ideas

However, in order to understand the philosophical significance of empiricism, and the true nature of its opposition to the philosophies of Descartes, Spinoza and Leibniz, we must consider its mature expression in the arguments of Locke. There had been a reaction to the empiricism of Hobbes. In Cambridge an anti-empiricist school had been founded (known as the Cambridge Platonists, and including such men as Ralph Cudworth (1617–1688) and Henry More (1614–1687)). This school upheld many of the traditional claims made on behalf of metaphysics; however, it took its authority from the speculative metaphysics of Plato, rather than from the methodological rationalism of Descartes. It was of little lasting significance, and the publication of Locke's *Essay*, which followed closely on that of Newton's *Principia*, gave such complete expression to the new empiricist spirit, that it could not but eclipse the opposing efforts of these lesser writers.

John Locke (1632–1704) was a student of Christ Church, Oxford, a lawyer and a medical practitioner. Becoming embroiled, through a position as tutor in the household of the first Earl of Shaftesbury, in the political controversies of his day, he spent part of his life exiled in Holland. There he awaited that 'glorious revolution' which was to place William of Orange on the throne of England and vindicate the ideal of legitimacy defended in Locke's own political writings. These political writings I shall discuss in chapter 14; what is of immediate concern is the change wrought in philosophy by Locke's highly ambitious and influential theory of knowledge, contained in the *Essay Concerning Human Understanding* published in 1689.

The *Essay* is the fruit of a lifetime's interest in philosophy and the foundations of natural science. It is a vast, disorganised and repetitious work, written in a sinuous style, full of hidden subtleties and difficult to grasp in its totality. The arguments are directly opposed to many of the most important tenets of Cartesian rationalism. Yet the language of the book is through and through influenced by Descartes and can be read, from one point of view, as an extended critical reflection on the crucial term 'idea', which Locke took from Descartes with the intention of freeing it from its rationalist connotations. Ideas are the immediate objects of the understanding:

> every man being conscious to himself that he thinks; and that which his mind is applied about whilst thinking being the ideas that are there, it is past doubt that men have in their minds several ideas, – such as those expressed by the words whiteness, hardness, sweetness, thinking, motion, man, elephant, army, drunkenness, and others.

And the first thing to note about ideas, according to Locke, is that they all, without exception, come to us from experience.

Innate ideas

Hence there are no innate ideas or principles. In making this claim, Locke is explicitly going against Descartes, who had argued that the principles of rational argument, and ideas like those of God, thought and extension which we perceive clearly and distinctly and which provide the rational foundations of our knowledge, are innate, implanted in us by God without the help of any sensory experience. On the contrary, Locke argued, the mind of the infant is a blank slate – a *tabula rasa* – until experience imprints it with the ideas that are necessary for thinking. We have no awareness of either ideas or rational principles, until we have begun to exercise the mind in the attempt to understand experience. Nothing is innate to the mind, apart from the faculties whereby we acquire knowledge.

One of Leibniz's intentions, in his *New Essays on the Human Understanding*, was to mount a defence of innate ideas against Locke's attack on them. Spinoza admitted – what can scarcely be denied – that the laws of logic and mathematics, and the concept of metaphysics, are not part of an infant's new-born consciousness. But the issue, he believed, cannot be settled by such an observation. We possess innate ideas and innate knowledge in a *virtual* manner. The mind should be compared, Spinoza suggested, to a block of marble, veined in such a way that a figure of Hercules emerges, just as soon as it is struck with a hammer. In like manner, the impact of experience creates the ideas to which our minds are by nature predisposed, since they are the preconditions of thinking.

The controversy between the defenders and attackers of innate ideas was long-drawn-out and bewildering. It might seem to be of parochial interest now, but in fact this is not so, for two reasons. First, because it has been revived in recent times on account of Chomsky's work in linguistics; secondly, because beneath the bluster of this quarrel lies concealed a more serious dispute over the status of *a priori* truths. The first of those reasons concerns us little. Those linguists who argue that there must be innate concepts if language acquisition is to be possible, do no more than repeat an old fallacy adequately exposed by Locke himself. They confuse the possession of a concept with the power to acquire it. As Locke points out, it is trivial to assert the existence of innate ideas if we mean only that the child is born with the *power* to acquire those ideas which are later displayed in him. For how could it be otherwise?

But this brings us to the second and more important reason for taking an interest in the controversy. At first sight it seems rather odd that philosophers, from Descartes to Hume, should have spent so much of their labours disputing over a point of little consequence. For what does it matter, philosophically speaking, whether we choose to believe with Locke that the mind of the infant is a *tabula rasa* awaiting the inscription of experience, or with Leibniz, that this board comes to us, as it were, already lined and ruled, with markings the significance of which has yet to be discerned? In what way is our view of human knowledge, or of reality, changed by these theories? To see the dispute in its modern significance we must, as always with early empiricist philosophers, rephrase a theory that is expressed genetically (in terms of the 'history' of the acquisition of a concept) as a theory concerning the nature of a concept, however that concept is in fact acquired. We will then see that Locke and Leibniz were arguing over whether there are concepts which are *a priori*, in a sense later to be made precise by Kant. Locke wishes to show that everything that we understand (every idea) we understand *in virtue of* its connection with experience. The content of every idea is revealed by tracing it back to experience. (Whether or not it has its *origin* in experience is another question, and one that is irrelevant to epistemology.) Leibniz had many philosophical interests to urge against that assertion, as well as against its mistaken formulation in genetic terms. In particular he wished to defend the premise of rationalism, that there are ideas whose content can be revealed by no experience, but by reason alone. Moreover we can generate from that content a system of truths whereby we know the universe as it really is, and not as it appears to our fallible organs of sensation. Into that knowledge we may then fit our experience, as best we can. But it is not experience which tells us what we mean.

This controversy was not to become clear until Kant formulated his theory of synthetic *a priori* truth. However, to understand Locke's intention we need only recognise that he was not putting forward a psychological hypothesis. He was proposing, rather, an empiricist theory of understanding. According to this theory all communication depends upon the common significance of words. This significance can be identified only by referring to the experiences which lead us to apply or revoke the words whose significance we seek to explain. That way of putting it is not Locke's, and indeed it conflicts with Locke's own formulation, according to which 'ideas' are private mental particulars, and accessible only through the words that denote them. Nevertheless it is the most plausible thesis contained in Locke's discussion of innate ideas. It is also a thesis that caused him to deny the possibility of rationalist metaphysics by denying all significance to the words that such a metaphysics would be compelled to employ.

This is not to say that Locke was wholly clear about the extent to which he rejected rationalism. He took over in modified form the Cartesian notion of 'intuition', arguing that I do have intuitive knowledge of certain truths (including the truth that I exist), and contrasting this intuitive knowledge with the 'demonstrative' knowledge of mathematics. He also argued that we have 'demonstrative' knowledge of God. It might therefore be thought that Locke was disposed, like the rationalists, to accept at least in part the idea that the ultimate truth about the world can be derived from the exercise of reason alone. It turns out, however, that this is not so. His demonstration of the existence of God has a purely contingent (if intuitive) premise, namely, that I exist. It concedes to rationalism only the principle which it employs to advance from that premise. This principle (for which Locke offers no argument and which stands out as peculiarly isolated from the rest of his thought) is the following: 'everything which has a beginning has a cause.' In other words, Locke's demonstration of the existence of God is a form of the 'cosmological' argument. And this does not lead him to reject the fundamental principles of empiricism. Moreover he held that 'demonstration', including all mathematics, provides no new knowledge of the world. It speaks only of the relations among ideas. That theory of mathematical truth finds further elaboration in the philosophy of Hume, and is the ancestor of the modern empiricist doctrine that necessary truths are 'tautologous' or 'verbal' (see chapter 19).

The theory of ideas

There are two forms of experience through which ideas are acquired – sensation and reflection. Ideas of sensation come to us through the senses – through seeing, hearing, touching, tasting and smelling things. Ideas of reflection come to us through the activity of the mind as it observes its inner processes. Since the soul does not think until the senses have furnished it with ideas, sensation has a primary importance in delivering our theory of the real world.

Locke follows Descartes in distinguishing the understanding from the will – the first being the passive power of the mind to receive ideas, the second the active power of the mind to affirm or act on them. But he seems to treat sensations (including visual and other forms of sensory perception) as a distinct kind of mental event – one from which we may *receive* ideas, but which is not itself a kind of idea. Locke's ideas are really *concepts*; and although he sometimes writes of them as though they were images, he clearly distinguishes them from complete thoughts or propositions. Ideas are of the following kinds.

Simple and complex. A simple idea is one like the idea of redness, which cannot be analysed into its components. It is 'not in the power of thought to make or erase' these simple ideas, which come to us through sensation or reflection. All ideas that are not simple are complex; and if you can define a in terms of b, c, d, etc., then the idea of a is composed of the ideas of b, c, d. He writes of ideas as a kind of mental object, which can be pushed around in the mind and combined and separated just as physical objects might be. This picture of the mind survives in other British empiricists, and is one cause of the antiquated feel to their arguments.

Ideas of one sense, of more than one sense, of reflection, and of both sense and reflection. The idea of greenness is derived from one sense, the visual. The idea of solidity corresponds to both visual and tactile experiences. The idea of imagination comes from inner awareness of the operations of the mind. The idea of action derives from all those sources working together.

Ideas of modes, substances and relations. A mode is a property, a substance the bearer of properties. Locke means two things by 'substance': the individual, for example John Smith; and the basic *kind*, such as gold or water. Both individuals and kinds are bearers of properties, and both endure through time. Modes are simple or complex, and a complex mode may also be 'mixed', when its idea is put together from ideas derived from different sources. 'Table' signifies a mixed mode, whose idea is unified by 'an act of the mind'.

Finally there are *abstract* ideas, which deserve a section to themselves.

Abstract ideas

Locke, in common with other empiricists, felt called upon to explain our ability to form general notions. This ability is exercised in every application of a predicate and therefore in almost every thought. He was well aware that, if all ideas derive from experience, they ought, in the first instance, to reflect the particular features of the experiences from which they stem. How then can any of our thoughts become general in its nature, when experience itself is irremediably particular?

We form complex ideas either by bringing together separate ideas into a composite whole (and among such composite wholes are all our ideas of relation), or else by separating ideas in such a way as to generate what is common to all of them. This second process Locke called abstraction, regarding it as of considerable importance in the genesis of human knowledge. Locke thought that abstraction enabled him to explain, without departing from the theory of ideas, our ability to use general terms. 'Words', he wrote, 'become general by being made the sign of general ideas', and these general ideas are derived from particular ideas (or ideas of particular things) by a process of abstraction. The theory is roughly as follows: I have many ideas of particular men, some tall, some short; some fat, some thin; some intelligent, some stupid; some white, some black. All the respects in which these ideas might differ, while yet remaining ideas of men, cancel each other out in the composite idea formed by their agglomeration. What remains is an 'abstract' idea which contains only those features which are in common to all the instances. These features are the defining properties of manhood, the idea of which is abstract, because, being incomplete, it can identify no particular thing.

Ideas and words

Like Hobbes, Locke attached his empiricist account of the origin of ideas to a theory of meaning. He was motivated by a belief that scholastic and Cartesian philosophy achieve their interesting results largely by assuming that certain key terms have a meaning and that the meaning is understood. On examination, however, these terms are often found to have a meaning other than the one intended, or sometimes no meaning at all.

Words have meaning, according to Locke, because they are the 'signs' of, or 'stand for', ideas. (Not much of a theory, of course, since 'sign' and 'stand for' are precisely the terms that need to be explained by a theory of meaning.) Communication is the process whereby words, which are attached to ideas in my mind, issue from my mouth and impinge on your ear, so causing the same ideas to arise in your mind.

The theory is open to serious criticism. In particular, it confuses the relation of meaning, which is governed by rules and conventions, with the natural relation between a word and the ideas that are aroused by it. The word 'cow' conventionally signifies a certain kind of animal; but it arouses in many people the ideas of milk, farmyards and pasture. Laurence Sterne put the criticism in a nice piece of satire:

– My young master in London is dead! said Obadiah –

– A green satin nightgown of my mother's, which had been twice scoured, was the first idea which Obadiah's exclamation brought into Suzannah's head. – Well might Locke write a chapter on the imperfection of words. – Then, quoth Suzannah, we must all go into mourning. – But, note a second time: the word *mourning*, notwithstanding Suzannah made use of it herself, failed also of doing its office; it excited not one single

idea, tinged either with grey or black, – all was green. – The green satin
nightgown hung there still. (*Tristram Shandy*, Book 5, chapter 7).

One of the achievements of modern philosophy, an achievement
which is owed largely to Wittgenstein, is that it has taken the point
of such satire seriously. It has given proper foundation to the view of
language as a practical skill, governed by conventions which need make
no reference to such accidental occurrences as Locke's mental 'ideas'.
It could be further objected to Locke that, on his own account of what
an idea is, I could never know that you mean the same by a word as I
do. In particular, the idea that I associate with the word 'pain' might be
associated by you with the word 'pleasure'; this difference between us
lying as it were undisclosed beneath the mask of our common usage.
Such a theory, which removes from meaning its essential 'publicity',
would for this reason now be almost universally rejected.

The physical world

It remains now to state briefly the view of the world and of scientific
enquiry that Locke derived from his theory of knowledge. In many
respects this view reflected an improved theory of the nature of science;
some aspects of it have indeed been restored to favour in recent years as
scientists have come to understand their utility. Locke derived from his
friend Robert Boyle and ultimately from Pierre Gassendi (1592–1655)
an interest in the distinction between primary and secondary qualities.
He also enquired – in a wholly novel and illuminating way – into the
concepts of essence and substance, endeavouring both to reinstate them
as fundamental scientific notions, and at the same time to free them from
the metaphysical confusion introduced by rationalist ways of describing
them. In this he made a philosophical step the significance of which was
unappreciated for over two centuries.

Among complex ideas Locke distinguished those of modes, substances
and relations. These correspond to the grammatical categories of predicate, subject and relation. As he sometimes seemed to recognise, however,
it is not right to say that we have an idea of the individual substance. Part
of the obscurity in the theory of abstract ideas comes about because all
ideas seem to be inherently general: that is, they represent properties, of
which it would make sense to say that more than one object possesses

them (just as more than one person may exactly correspond to the image in a painting). How then do we arrive at a conception of the individual thing which is the subject of predication? Locke was anxious to avoid the paradoxes of Spinozism, and to preserve a notion of substance that allowed for the existence of many – possibly infinitely many – substantial things. So he could not take refuge in the Cartesian idea of substance.

It is first necessary, Locke thought, to distinguish ideas from qualities; qualities being the *powers* of objects to produce ideas in us. Primary qualities are supposedly both inseparable from the objects in which they inhere, and also generative of simple ideas. They are the qualities of extension, motion, mass and so on, and are the true subjects of scientific investigation. Secondary qualities are nothing but certain powers to produce sensations (the power of sugar to produce a sweet taste, of red things to produce certain characteristic visual impressions, and so on).

It is difficult to be precise about this distinction (which could be drawn differently for different purposes). But one assertion that Locke makes about it is certainly of crucial significance, both historically and philosophically. Whereas primary qualities resemble the ideas that are produced by them, secondary qualities do not. And this enables us to say that there is a sense in which primary qualities are really *in* the objects which possess them, whereas secondary qualities are not. Berkeley objected to this, saying that it is absurd to suppose that any quality of a material substance can resemble an idea, since ideas are mental entities, belonging to a wholly different realm, and it is *prima facie* absurd to suppose that ideas can resemble things which are not ideas.

In order to reply to this objection, we must attempt once more to free Locke's insight from the dead theories which enclose it. We must recognise that, in speaking of a resemblance between ideas and qualities, he was misdirecting his thoughts in a way encouraged by his theory of meaning. In some sense, as Locke saw, certain scientifically determinable and measurable qualities are basic to the reality of a thing in a way that other qualities are not. The secondary qualities seem to stand in need of a perceiver, the primary qualities only in need of an object. One way of putting the point is this: if you know all the primary qualities of an object, and the nature of the man who perceives it, then this alone will enable you to explain how that object appears to him. There is no need to refer to the secondary qualities of the object in order to explain how it is perceived. The primary qualities can be said to resemble our perceptions of them in the sense that they themselves must be invoked in explaining that perception. To say this is to deny not the reality of secondary qualities, but only their centrality in any scientific view of the nature of the object that possesses them.

Real and nominal essence

Seen in this way, the distinction between primary and secondary qualities relates to another of Locke's distinctions, that between real and nominal essence. Locke makes this new distinction in the course of exploring the nature of material things, and in subjecting the scholastic ideas of 'substance' and 'essence' to critical examination. If we construe 'substances' to be individual things, the bearers of qualities, then we can have no positive conception of them. They are the ineffable substrata which 'support' those qualities through which any object is known. Any positive conception of the individual is the idea of a quality and therefore not of the substratum itself.

Let us leave aside the (for Locke) extremely difficult question how we might then come to have such an idea as that of substance. Locke, in common with many philosophers, influenced directly or indirectly by Aristotle, recognised that such a negative conception leaves us with the task of defining the nature of an individual. An individual cannot be identified as a particular substance (even if it is identical with such a substance) since of substances, considered in isolation from their qualities, nothing can be said. As the scholastics put it, '*individuum est ineffabile*' ('the individual is ineffable'), a doctrine which Locke in the end is driven to support. It is therefore necessary to separate among the properties of a thing those which define its essence from those in respect of which it might change without changing its nature. This is the closest we can get to the idea of an individual.

But what is this essence? In fact, Locke now speaks not of individuals but of kinds. The scholastic idea of an individual essence seemed to him to be incoherent. He regarded all problems of individuality as exhausted by enquiries on the one hand into the fundamental kind to which an individual belongs, and on the other hand into the conditions of its identity. Except for the general idea of a 'substratum' there was nothing to be said by way of characterising the nature of a thing. And it is possible to doubt that Locke's empiricist theory of meaning could give him grounds for the assumption even of this 'general' idea of substratum. It seems absurd to suggest that we arrive at this general idea by abstraction, since abstraction would have to go so far in such a case as to leave us, so to speak, with no remainder.

As I implied, Locke's purpose in exploring the concept of essence is partly polemical. He wished to attack the Aristotelian science which had erected itself upon a system of rigid classifications. These classifications seemed to be conceived *a priori* and without reference to the actual constitution of the objects which fall under them. For Locke, the only significant idea of essence must be one of constitution. The constitution of an object cannot be determined by fiat, but only by exploring the reality of the thing itself. Hence it cannot be determined *a priori*. Locke therefore introduced the idea of a real essence, to be distinguished from the nominal essence bestowed on an object by the arbitrary classification under which we subsume it.

Consider the classification 'bachelor'. This defines a nominal essence, which is to say, a set of properties which we consider to be the qualifying attributes of the class of bachelors. The classification is arbitrary; we could have defined the word differently. But in so far as it exists it enables us to speak of a certain 'essence'. We can say, for example, that it is an essential feature of a bachelor that he is unmarried, meaning that, *qua* bachelor, he is of necessity unmarried. But it is not an essential feature of John, who is a bachelor, that he is unmarried: on the contrary, he might choose to marry tomorrow, in which case, in ceasing to be unmarried, he ceases also to be a bachelor. Nominal essences are therefore accidents of classification; they reflect constraints embedded in our language, but these constraints do not operate on the things themselves. They hold, as the medieval logician would have put it, not *de re* but *de dicto*. Locke thought that it is only nominal essences that could be known *a priori*, and this is only because such knowledge would be the empty reflection of our own linguistic habits, not knowledge of the things themselves.

Now consider the classification 'gold'. This is associated, according to Locke, with a nominal essence – gold is a yellow, metallic substance, etc. But gold has a real essence as well, in respect of which it could not change without ceasing to be the kind of stuff that it is. This real essence is not (unless by some extraordinary accident) given by the nominal essence. It has to be discovered by scientific investigation. The nominal essence guides us in that investigation only to be overthrown by it. As a matter of fact, Locke was inclined to think that real essences are unknowable. This was partly because he thought that the underlying reality of material substances must remain hidden from observation. Since his day we have found reason to reject that belief. We might come to the conclusion that what really matters to something's being gold is, for example, its atomic weight, and not those properties in which we first based our classification. Hence empirical enquiry can decide the real essence of gold: the matter, however, could never be settled by convention.

In the case of modes, and of simple ideas (in other words in the case of the ideas corresponding to qualities), real and nominal essence cannot be distinguished. It is only in the case of substances that the distinction can be made. But as the example indicates, there are definite 'kind' terms – such as 'gold' – which admit of the distinction. Do they therefore denote substances? Surely not – at least, not in the sense Locke intended. Gold is not an individual thing, but a stuff. In other words, it is a substance in the more familiar, common sense of the term. And now we begin to see, what neither Locke nor the rationalists were equipped to see, that real essences belong not only to individuals but also to kinds.

Personal identity

Locke's explorations of the concept of essence did not provide a satisfactory account of the nature of individual substances. He came to realise that the concept of identity must play an important part in distinguishing individuals from kinds. He made suggestions as to the deep intrinsic connection between the individuation of a thing and its location in space and time; but his most important contribution in this area was to raise the problem of personal identity in its modern form. Locke argued that to be a human being is one thing, to be a person is another. Human beings can endure where a person ceases, and perhaps vice versa. A human being is an organism, whose identity is determined by the continuity of that organism in accordance with the real essence which it possesses. But the organism is not identical with the person; men can suffer radical changes of personality; or we can imagine a personality that, after enduring in one organism, suddenly disappears to reappear simultaneously and intact in some other, erstwhile sleeping body. Many thought-experiments can be performed which will point to the conclusion that identity of man and identity of person are separate ideas. In which case, in what does the identity of a person consist?

Locke proposed a criterion of identity, sometimes described as 'the continuity of consciousness'. So far as my memories link me to the past and my desires and intentions project me into the future, so far am I the same person over time. Thomas Reid famously objected that such a criterion could deliver two conflicting answers to the question of identity. The old general may remember the young officer, who remembers the boy who stole the apples, even though the boy has been forgotten by the general. So the general both is and is not identical with the boy. But the objection is not lethal and suggests merely that we should amend Locke's approach. We should define personal identity in terms of a *chain* of interlocking memories, linking the general to all his previous activities: the old man remembers the middle-aged man who remembers the youth who remembers the child. If the chain is unbroken, then perhaps identity is secure.

More serious is the objection made by Bishop Butler. Suppose I have the thought of standing in this room once before. What makes this thought into a *memory*? Surely, the fact that I identify *myself* as standing in this room. But how do I know that this identification is correct? I must have grounds for judging that it was once *I* who stood in this room. False memory claims are no grounds for identity; true memory claims ('genuine' memories) are grounds for identity, but only because their truth depends upon the truth of a claim about identity. The criterion, in short, is circular.

Butler's objection is still much discussed. Locke's criterion may have an appearance of circularity: but perhaps the circle is not *vicious*. It is vicious only if it presupposes what it sets out to prove; and it is by no means obvious that this is so.

The concept of cause

Throughout Locke's lifetime the scientific revolution had proceeded unabated. The Royal Society had been founded, and Boyle (1627–1691) had written widely and sceptically of the traditional science, in a way that engaged directly with contemporary philosophical issues. Boyle followed Bacon in rejecting all research into final causes as irrelevant to science; but he was reluctant, in his search for the particular causes of observable phenomena, to take too much guidance from Descartes' *a priori* method, which assumed that fundamental principles could be derived from metaphysics alone. In particular, Boyle rejected the very metaphysical-seeming law that Descartes had put at the heart of his physics: the law of the conservation of motion. This law was to be revived in a new form by Newton, and, when the *Principia* was finally published almost simultaneously with Locke's *Essay*, philosophers were confronted with an extraordinary synthesis of *a priori* speculation and empirical method, in which seemingly irrebuttable laws were held forth as governing and explaining the whole chaotic world of transient phenomena. It was not until Kant that the philosophical significance of Newton's theories was finally encompassed. Meanwhile Leibniz vigorously combated Newton's absolute view of space, while the empiricists occupied themselves with understanding the deep and difficult concept of causality upon which Newtonian physics had been erected.

Locke had already recognised that, in accordance with his principles, it must be possible to give an account of the *experience* from which the idea of causality derives its content. He had no difficulty in resolving this problem to his satisfaction. The exercise of will presents us, he thought, with an experience of causality which is immediate, indubitable and irreducible to anything more basic. In a sense Berkeley followed Locke in this doctrine: that is to say, he thought that in so far as we have an idea of true causality, it can only be one of will, the exercise of which is experienced by us both as an activity and as something suffered. When we observe nature, however, we are confronted by the regular succession of events, but not by any experience of volition. To say that there is a will to attract that draws masses together is to speak in a way that is misleading and unwarranted, since all we can observe is the confluence of masses. If we refer to a law of nature here, then that law is nothing more than the expression of the regular and seemingly immutable fashion in which this motion occurs. (Berkeley thus attacked Newton for speaking of 'attraction' or 'force' in his theory of gravity, since these terms imply the presence of something more than is strictly observable.)

Berkeley, like Locke, was an empiricist. He believed that everything that we say derives its sense from experience. Since our experience of the relation among things in the 'external world' presents us only with regular succession, and not with any spirit or will that animates it, we can mean nothing more when we invoke causal laws, than to refer to this regularity. This theory of Berkeley's presaged Hume's radical attack on the traditional concept of causality. It also echoed Leibniz's theory that causal laws express 'well-founded phenomena'. It showed the extent to which the concept of causality was becoming uppermost in the minds of philosophers, beginning to take its place as one of the central concepts, indicative of a central problem, in metaphysics.

Berkeley's criticism

George Berkeley (1685–1753), Bishop of Cloyne, was perhaps the greatest of the philosophers to derive his main inspiration from the metaphysics of Locke. He is best known for his idealism, expounded in the *Treatise Concerning the Principles of Human Knowledge* (1710), according to which the world contains nothing but spirits and their 'ideas'. Berkeley thought that this theory was an ineluctable consequence of the empiricist method that Locke had put forward. Since he accepted that method – and moreover thought that it was the only one that accorded with human common sense – he accepted the consequence. However, his idealism was consequent upon a clearer, though far narrower, presentation of the concept of an 'idea' than can be derived from Locke. For Berkeley 'ideas' are mental particulars, the immediate objects of the 'perception' whereby the contents of our mind are revealed to us, and they comprise all actual mental contents. Images, sense-experiences, thoughts, concepts – all are 'ideas' in Berkeley's sense, since all are immediate objects of mental perception. (Kant was not the only one to complain about this assimilation of items so diverse into a single category. But it was perhaps Kant who made the most telling criticism, in arguing that the empiricists find their conclusions persuasive only because they confuse sensibility and understanding, and so 'sensualise' the concepts of the understanding, and misrepresent their nature and function in the derivation of human knowledge.)

Having made this assumption, however, Berkeley went on to draw conclusions which seemed compelling both to him and to many of his contemporaries. First, he attacked Locke's theory of abstraction, arguing that since everything that exists is a particular, there can be no such thing as an abstract idea. For consider the abstract idea of a triangle: it is supposed to be neither scalene nor isosceles, to have all triangular shapes and no specific triangular shape at once. And is it not an absurdity to think of a triangle that is indeterminate in all its properties? There is an obvious reply: Locke was referring, not to a triangle, but to the *idea* of a triangle; it is ridiculous to suppose that an idea of a triangle is itself a triangle and therefore determinate in its shape. But this reply was forbidden by Berkeley's assimilation of ideas and images under a single mental category. An image of a triangle in some sense shares the properties of the triangle it represents. Berkeley is right in assuming therefore that there can no more be an abstract image of a triangle than there can be an abstract triangle. And since images are his model for all the 'ideas' of the mind, his conclusion must therefore appear correspondingly more plausible.

But why should that assimilation of ideas to images have appeared persuasive? The answer is to be found in Berkeley's attempt to fill in the gap, left open by Locke's empiricist theory of meaning, between experience and idea. Berkeley makes experiences and ideas *one and the same*: a perception of a red book, an image of a red book, an idea of a red book – these are all examples of one kind of thing, different in name, but not in nature. Hence there is no difficulty in showing how words are given sense by their application in experience: everything denoted by a word is, in effect, an experience (or idea), and there need never be any doubt in our mind as to what we mean by the words we utter. We need only refer back to the experience which the word denotes. (It is a characteristic of rationalist philosophy to bring all mental processes under one label. But it is also characteristic of rationalism to distinguish very carefully between those 'clear and distinct' perceptions which belong to reason and those more confused mental items that display the workings of sense and imagination. For Berkeley such a distinction is empty.)

Idealism

Berkeley feels that he can now provide an answer to the fundamental question of philosophy as he saw it. This is the question of existence. What *is* existence? Berkeley's first answer is that to be is to be perceived: *esse est percipi*. If everything which confronts us is an idea, then the principle of existence must be found in the nature of ideas. It is absurd, however, to think of ideas as existing outside the mind. And to exist *in* a mind is to be perceived by that mind. Hence, nothing can exist which is not perceived; any metaphysical assertion that commits itself to the existence of an imperceivable thing is absurd. In particular, Berkeley thought, the belief in what he called 'material substance' is absurd: this term corresponds to no idea, and therefore has no sense. We do not even know what we mean to assert when we commit ourselves to the existence of that which it purports to name.

This radical conclusion (which Dr Johnson thought he could refute by kicking against a heavy stone) was not, according to Berkeley, repugnant to common sense. On the contrary, it is only metaphysical confusion that could lead the ordinary person to doubt it, since he applies words according to their proper meanings, and therefore affirms existence only of those things of which he has an idea; in other words those things which he experiences. What then are the 'material objects' to which we so repeatedly refer? Berkeley refrains from saying that they are *ideas*: for to every table there exists not one but many, perhaps infinitely many, perceptions. Hence the term 'table' denotes, not a single idea, but 'a collection of ideas'. This theory is obscure, as is shown by Berkeley's answer to the question 'What does it mean to say that the table exists while I am not perceiving it?' His answer (in the first instance) is that such an assertion means no more than that, if were to return to the place where the table stands, then I would have a certain perception. In other words, it makes reference not to an actual but to a possible idea. This introduces a complication into Berkeley's philosophy which he brushes aside somewhat peremptorily, but which has been recognised in recent years as the major source of difficulty for theories such as Berkeley's: how can there be such entities as possible ideas?

Berkeley's arguments for his view, in so far as they are not merely reaffirmations of the immediate consequences of his theory of 'ideas', consist in spirited, but as it now seems, often misguided, attacks against Locke. Berkeley rejects the distinction between primary and secondary qualities. He thinks that whatever arguments are given for the unreality of the second must equally establish the unreality of the first. He also dismisses Locke's view of substance, arguing that we can have no idea of the pure 'substratum' divested of its qualities, and therefore cannot know what we mean in referring to such a thing. He argues from the subjectivity of ideas directly to the subjectivity of the qualities represented through them, in a manner that betrays his too easy assimilation of thoughts to sensations, and which therefore establishes the inadequacy of the former by reference to the well-known Cartesian arguments for the inadequacy of the latter.

It is now perhaps more apparent than it was to Berkeley's contemporaries that these negative arguments trade on inapposite conflations and hasty analogies. Berkeley confuses (though the fault is not entirely his) the Lockean 'substance' with the material stuff of the physical world; he ignores the distinction between real and nominal essence and uses the word 'idea' to name, indiscriminately, qualities, sensations and the concepts which result from them. In short, he fails to present in a cogent manner the issue which really concerns him, which is that of the relation between appearance and reality. His slogan that 'to be is to be perceived' might be better expressed as 'being is seeming'. And the true epistemological weight of his argument can then be seen to amount to this: it is a necessary truth that all my evidence for how things are is derived from my immediate and incorrigible knowledge of how things seem. But I cannot mean, in referring to the world, to refer to a world other than the one that I know (for otherwise I would not know what I mean). So what I speak of, in speaking of objects, is not some underlying reality that lies beyond all my powers of observation, but rather the totality of appearance. In other words, in speaking of objects, I am speaking of the sum of what I can, from my own point of view, observe. My *world* is *my* world. It is not just unverifiable but meaningless to speak of some other world which transcends the world as it appears to me. Since 'appearance' or 'how it seems' are terms which refer, of necessity, to the mental state of an observer, it seems that the observer has neither reason nor capacity to affirm the existence of things that are not mental.

God and the soul

The real problem that arises for Berkeley, and one which he recognised, was this: how can one accept such a view and escape from the conclusion that all I think and know is contained within the sphere of my own consciousness, so that I have no grounds for asserting the existence of spirits besides myself? This difficulty Berkeley confronted in a manner reminiscent of Descartes. He argues for the existence of an omniscient and omnipotent God who sustains not just the illusion but the reality of a many-souled universe. As Berkeley clearly saw, however, he could not confront the question immediately, without first showing that terms like 'soul', 'mind' or 'spirit' are indeed meaningful according to his own precepts. He admitted some difficulty over this, arguing that the mind is not itself an idea since it is not identical with any of its contents. So do we have an idea *of* the mind? If you take away all the contents of a mind, you do not take away the mind itself, since it is not identical with any of its contents nor with all of its contents taken together. Indeed, the mind seems to be a substance precisely in the Lockean sense: it is an unknowable substratum. Being forced to admit as much, Berkeley found it necessary to say (as though it made things clearer) that we have not an idea, but a 'notion' of this substratum. The suggestion is to some extent redeemed by the following observations. First, we do have a unique experience which is associated with the mind: the experience of volition, through which we derive our idea of a *true* causality. Secondly, we can make sense of 'mental substance' by extending the maxim that was applied to ideas, that to be is to be perceived, to apply to notions of substance. In this case the maxim becomes: to be is to perceive. It is therefore through the relation of perception that we understand the nature of mind. Perception requires two terms; the reality of one term (the idea) and the reality of the relation (perception) necessitate between them the reality of the other term (the mind). It is as though perception is the hidden 'bond' between substance and attribute. Certainly Berkeley's confusion of ideas with qualities, and his view that substance must contain some active principle and therefore can only be mental, seem to imply some such conclusion.

Having resolved the problem of the nature of mind to his satisfaction, Berkeley felt able to lean on the Cartesian part of his argument. This proceeds, via the proof of the existence of God, to the not surprising conclusion that the world *is* in fact more than it merely seems to be: it *is* as it appears to God. While our knowledge of this divine appearance is imperfect we can be fairly sure that we are not deceived in those beliefs that arise cogently and naturally from the perceptions which God vouchsafes to us.

The most interesting part of Berkeley's theology lies in a novel argument for the existence of God. This argument both clarifies and depends upon Berkeley's notion of spiritual substance as the only source of activity. He rightly observes that, among ideas, we can distinguish those in respect of which we are active from those in respect of which we are passive. I can voluntarily call an image or thought to mind, and recognise it as the product of my mental activity. But other ideas – in particular those which go under the denomination of sensation and belief

– are not similarly accessible to my will. I cannot command myself to believe that France is smaller than England, to see a man instead of a table before me, to feel a pain in my finger, and so on. Yet these involuntary ideas seem to be impressed on me with great vivacity. Whence came they? Not from me, for I can neither refuse nor amend them. From nowhere? Their vivacity and compellingness suggest otherwise: they bear the imprint of some other force. But force signifies the active principle – the will – which animates all spiritual substance. I conclude, therefore, that they are produced in me by some other being, some being far greater, and far wiser and far more powerful than I.

The conclusion falls short of what is theologically desirable. Embellished with other arguments, and set in the context of Berkeley's radical scepticism about his own and his reader's powers to transcend the knowledge provided by experience, it might seem persuasive enough. However, the argument involves many a weak step. Its assumption that, because I am passive in respect of an idea, some other being must be active in respect of it, stands, to say the least, in need of justification. It is from this point, however, that Berkeley, like Descartes, begins the laborious task of reconstructing the world of common sense. He considered himself to have effected no genuine change in that world; he had done no more than re-establish the priority of appearance, and so banish the metaphysical superstitions for which 'material substance' was the unholy name.

Conclusion

It is difficult to summarise the achievements or the beliefs of the early British empiricists. But certain threads seem to bind their philosophies together. In particular there is the disposition to put the theory of knowledge before metaphysics. In doing so, they rise to the vantage-point from which metaphysics can be criticised, and even dismissed as nonsense. But, bound up with this same disposition is another, which has been historically central to it. This is the tendency, present already in Descartes, to look for the *foundation* of knowledge, and hence to arrive at a satisfactory theory of what *I* can know and mean, on the basis of the evidence and understanding available to me. Thus we find, in all traditional empiricism, a radical allegiance to the first-person case, a belief that all philosophy must be resolved by appeal to my experience, and by studying the details of how things seem to me.

Out of this preoccupation many confusions arose, but so too did many clarities. It became clear, for example, that certain concepts, previously regarded as subsidiary to philosophical argument, in fact take a central place in all true metaphysics – these are the concepts of cause, of object, of existence and of the distinction between appearance and reality. At the same time the reliance of philosophical argument upon a theory of meaning, and upon a conception of the capacities of the human mind, became more apparent. When Hume was to draw out what he considered to be the true consequences of the empiricist assumptions, he was to put forward what Locke and Berkeley had merely hoped for: a philosophy dedicated to the destruction of metaphysics, and founded in a complete science of human nature.

8

THE IDEA OF A MORAL SCIENCE

The rise of modern science during the seventeenth century shook traditional beliefs in religion, politics and morality, at the same time instilling into those who renounced those beliefs an unforeseen conviction of the power and scope of the human intellect. But science brought with it a new and unfamiliar bridle to the ambitions of thought. It rested its authority at least in part on observation. This gave new impetus to the Cartesian doubt. If what I know of the world I know through observation, then what can I know beyond the fact that I seem to observe things? In other words, what can I know beyond the contents of my own mind? Without the overarching structure of *a priori* truth, philosophy seems to lack the bridge that will take it from subject to object. It lies trapped in the first person, forced either to remain there, or to call, like Berkeley, in some new and less reasonable way, upon the God who had rescued Descartes from solipsism.

Before this radical scepticism could fully assert itself, the optimism of Newton held sway in the minds of less observant philosophers. Because their thought did much to create what has since become one of the fundamental branches of philosophy, we must treat of them here. The purpose of this chapter is to show how the empiricism of Locke gradually worked itself out through theories of ethics – the branch of philosophy which had in modern times been treated systematically only by the profoundly unempiricist Spinoza.

The philosophers that I shall discuss – Shaftesbury, Hutcheson and

Butler – belong to the 'Enlightenment'. In the first flush of scientific confidence, the thinkers of the Enlightenment tried to carry over into every human intellectual endeavour the search for first principles which, in Newton's physics, had been attended with such success. This search brought with it a sceptical attitude towards authority, rejecting everything that had no secure foundation in experience. In history, morals, metaphysics and literature the Enlightenment attitude briefly prevailed, giving rise to the phenomenal ambitions of the French encyclopaedists, and to their materialist, almost clockwork, vision of the universe. It produced the political theories which motivated the French and American revolutions, and the systematic explorations in chemistry and biology that were to find fruition in nineteenth-century evolutionism. It also brought about the technical achievements which precipitated modern industrialism, and while thus preparing the way for the miseries of revolution and factory labour, it infected the minds of the educated classes with a serenity of outlook, and a trust in human capacities, that weathered the assaults of Hume's scepticism, of Vico's anti-rationalism, of the growing introversion and doom-laden mysticism of the romantics. This was the Augustan age of English poetry, the age of Johnson and Goldsmith, of Voltaire, Diderot and Rousseau, of Lessing and Winckelmann. From the point of view of the historian it is perhaps the richest and most exciting of all intellectual eras, not because of the content, but because of the influence, of the ideas that were current in it.

The two major Enlightenment thinkers that I shall discuss – Hume and Kant – are among the greatest of philosophers. But I shall discuss them independently of the intellectual ferment from which they grew, both because they were superior to it, and also because their thought has a philosophical significance that is wholly misunderstood when they are seen merely as manifestations of a spirit which, being common to so many, retains the individual mark of no one in particular. I shall ignore the encyclopaedists, the French materialists and the great tradition of German academic philosophy which created the bridge between Leibniz and Kant. In all these cases philosophical ideas which were elsewhere given complete elaboration found more confused expression. The astonishing fact is not the depth of the thinking involved, but rather the remarkable character of an age that could generate the appearance of depth in so many.

But while it is possible to study the history of epistemology and metaphysics in such a way, concentrating only on the greatest thinkers, it is necessary to stray a little from the path of genius in order to discuss the history of philosophy's subordinate branches. This is particularly true of ethics, aesthetics and political philosophy. I shall touch on the first of these in the present chapter, and the third in chapter 14. In both cases I shall be representing a characteristic aspect of Enlightenment thought.

With the advance of science came the hope for a 'moral' science. This hope achieved early expression in Descartes' *Treatise on the Passions* (1649), a work which profoundly influenced Spinoza. Spinoza's own deductively conceived system of ethics, with its startling conclusions and its remote, noble vision of human things, served as a model for many later thinkers. Its appeal rested not merely in its reinstatement of a Platonic ideal of man as freed and fulfilled in thought, capable of rising above the vicissitudes of nature through understanding alone; but also in the fact that its conclusions seemed to depend on no appeal to revealed religion, or to any other moral authority that was not already contained in human reason. The vision of 'each man his own moralist' was to achieve its most profound and powerful statement in the philosophy of Kant. Before then, other thinkers were radically to change the subject of ethics, by recasting it in empiricist terms. They attempted to combine this outlook with the ideal of a science of human nature from which the precepts of ethics would follow, not as a matter of willing obedience, but as a matter of course. In other words, there arose the general impetus towards an ethical 'naturalism'.* Naturalism is the theory that the ideal of the good life is to be derived not from divine precept but from a description of human nature. Such a theory aims to show that evil is against nature, while good fulfils it.

Ethical naturalism found its most important expression in Britain, giving rise to the school of 'British Moralists', whose modesty of style and lack of metaphysical pretension to some extent conceal the seminal character of their philosophy. Their thoughts began to take shape under the influence of Locke, and in the writings of a man whose family had already enjoyed the intimacy and instruction of that philosopher. Anthony Ashley Cooper, third Earl of Shaftesbury (1671–1713), published his *Inquiry Concerning Virtue or Merit* in 1699 and his *Characteristics* in 1711. The latter was one of the most popular philosophical works of the

---

* This term is also used in ethics in another sense, deriving from G. E. Moore's 'naturalistic fallacy' (*Principia Ethica*, 1905, ch. 1).

eighteenth century and saw eleven editions before 1790. Shaftesbury was the founder of the empiricist 'moral science' and of the modern study of aesthetics. His influence on the French and German Enlightenment was considerable. Even at the end of the eighteenth century Herder could write that 'this virtuoso of humanity . . . has had a marked influence on the best minds of our century, on those who have striven with determination and sincerity for the true, the beautiful and the good'. However, the aspect of his thought which is now of greatest interest is not that which was most immediately influential. In his earlier work Shaftesbury attempted to combine the Lockean theory of the workings of the human mind with many of the arguments of Aristotle's *Nicomachean Ethics*, and it is this aspect of Shaftesbury's philosophy which we need to consider.

In Aristotle the project of deriving an account of the good life from a description of human nature had found its finest ancient expression. At first sight it may seem that Shaftesbury was by no means original in his attempt to revive the outlook (if not all the conclusions) of Aristotle. The few philosophical achievements of Renaissance humanism had been in the field of ethics, and in almost every case the inspiration had been Aristotelian. Even Aquinas had advocated ethical ideas which stemmed directly from the conceptions of Aristotle, and when Count Baldassar Castiglione (1478–1529), in his *Book of the Courtier* (1528), gave to these ideas the humanistic bias which they naturally favour, he changed the morality of scholasticism only in two particulars. He neglected to mention God, and at the same time he shifted the aims of ethics away from a description of the good, towards a description of the noble.

Shaftesbury's Aristotelianism was, however, new. It shared the sceptical temper, and the search for rigorous foundations, which characterise empiricism. It also sought to detach the conclusions of ethics from this or that particular style of life, this or that set of manners, these or those protective institutions. It was, in intention, 'institution-free', in a way that the ethics of the humanists was not. Hence Shaftesbury's description of the good life was derived from qualities of human nature which he regarded as more or less common to all, and definitive of a human norm. Like Aristotle, he was concerned to found his moral system not so much in a conception of the 'right' or 'wrong' of particular actions, as in a notion of the 'goodness' or 'badness' of the characters which generate them. And, again like Aristotle, he regarded good character, or virtue, as the sole and sufficient cause of happiness. Happiness is the state in which our nature is in harmony with itself; the whole character is involved in this harmony, which is a form of proportion in the soul. Our love of beauty is therefore as much excited by the perception of happiness (or virtue) as is our natural sympathy, and it is as much given to human nature to admire virtue in others as to find fulfilment in pursuing it oneself.

But what does virtue consist in? Again Shaftesbury's account is Aristotelian: virtue consists in a certain disposition of character, in which reason has governance over the passions (the 'affections'). This governance is not the *suppression* of passion but the securing of its 'right application'. The virtuous person is not the one who feels no hatred, love, anger or contempt. He is the one who is disposed to feel these passions only towards their appropriate objects – towards those things which are worthy of hatred, love, anger and contempt. Such a disposition requires a steady will and resolution, but it is not a form of unfeelingness, or blind obedience. The whole character is involved in virtue; hence any truly wicked act, since its wickedness displays the vice which was its motive, implicates the character of the agent.

What is this 'reason' that has or should have governance over the affections? Shaftesbury's answer to this question is not clear, but his awareness of the need for an answer, and the terms in which he posed the question, were to provide the structure of moral philosophy as it developed to its culmination in Kant. The principal operation of reason in this respect is connected with 'conscience'. Shaftesbury argued that no morality could be founded in religious obedience, or piety. On the contrary, a person is motivated to such obedience only because conscience tells him that the divine being is worthy of it. Shaftesbury wavered between seeing the origin of conscience in reason, and seeing it in a specific moral feeling. This feeling he also regarded as natural, being a kind of internal reflection of our social sense. It is because we are social beings that we acquire the sense of right and wrong. Conscience therefore reflects the nature not of this or that particular human agent, but rather of our common humanity. The dispositions of the virtuous are the fulfilment of this common nature, and must therefore form themselves in harmony with it. The principle of harmony is sympathy, which is the ability to feel the sufferings and joys of each individual as a part of some greater whole.

This shift in emphasis from reason to sympathy as the ruling principle in moral thought was characteristic. It shows Shaftesbury's reluctance to carry his arguments through, or fully to define his terms. It also shows his awareness of the complexity of the moral and emotional life of human beings. This awareness was to gain strength and vitality in subsequent thinkers. Shaftesbury had perceived two important truths: first, morality is both peculiar to rational beings and also integral to their entire nature; secondly, morality has an intimate relation to the emotions, at the heart of which lies man's perception of his nature as a social being. To which sphere, then, should morality be assigned: the rational or the emotional? Shaftesbury's hesitation is in part an expression of a tardy perception that the distinction between these is as unclear as the definition of either, and that no advance in the 'moral sciences' will be possible without a clearer account of how reason and emotion interact.

As Kant was later to perceive, Shaftesbury's problems arose in the course of an attempt to recapture and delimit the conception of 'practical reason' which had troubled Aristotle. But it was not until Kant that this notion was once again fully to come into the foreground of moral thought. The intervening period, which led from Shaftesbury to Hume, was characterised by further attempts to explore the structure of the 'human nature' from which morality derives. The most interesting of these attempts were those of Hutcheson (1694–1746), Butler (1692–1752) and Adam Smith (1723–1790), to the first two of which I shall devote the remainder of this chapter.

Francis Hutcheson's *Inquiry Concerning Moral Good and Evil* was published in 1725. It shows everywhere the influence of Shaftesbury, adopting a neo-Aristotelian view of human virtue, and directing many of its individual arguments against the seventeenth-century moral sceptics (such as Hobbes and Mandeville) whose writings had equally called forth the opprobrium of Shaftesbury. Nevertheless it is marked by certain important original features. Hutcheson saw in ethics the basis of a new epistemological problem. Putting the point in terms of Lockean empiricism, he notes that, since our language contains terms like 'moral good' and 'moral evil', we ought to be able to locate the ideas which such words stand for, and the qualities in objects which those ideas represent. We must ask ourselves what foundation there is in nature for this distinction of words. As he recognised, such a question generates a problem of epistemology which for the empiricist is particularly acute. What is the experience, or set of experiences, from which our moral ideas derive? If we can say nothing about those experiences, then we have a problem not just about the truth or falsehood of moral judgements, but about their very meaningfulness.

Hutcheson began from the distinction between self-interest and morality. He argued that Shaftesbury's view – that self-interest alone suffices to persuade the reasonable person to virtue – is fallacious. Shaftesbury had ignored the completely different character of the motives of morality and self-interest, and the different manner in which we are affected when we perceive the moral and the non-moral reality of things. Hutcheson now faced a question: how do we know that some action, or character, is morally good, if this is not revealed to us by the calculations of self-interest? He felt that he could not derive an answer by referring merely to ordinary capacities of sense-perception: goodness is not, as one might say, a 'perceivable property' of the world, in the way that redness is. For one thing, as Shaftesbury had also observed, only rational beings have moral views. Yet there is nothing absurd in supposing that a non-rational being should have all the sensory capacities – sight, touch, hearing, etc. – which characterise us. On the other hand, Hutcheson was reluctant to allow that reason alone could determine what is good or bad. He anticipated Hume's view that reason can deliver to us no more than the relations among ideas. Hence it provides no insight into the ends of our conduct, however useful it might be in calculating the means to them. Moreover, Hutcheson was thoroughly persuaded not only of the falsehood of rationalist metaphysics, but also of the falsehood of an implication contained in it. This implication is almost explicit in the ethics of Spinoza (whose 'systematic' approach to ethics Hutcheson nevertheless sought to emulate). It seems that, on the rationalist view, the ordinary unthinking person could only have confused and indefinite moral convictions, and that it is an unlikely accident if the opinions of the normal active majority happen to coincide. This consequence of rationalism was rejected by all the British moralists as palpably absurd.

Hutcheson, despite his empiricist bias and the consequent emphasis on the question 'How do I know?', shared with other eighteenth-century naturalists the view that there is a common body of moral knowledge, and that it is available to everyone whatever the state of their education. It is part of human nature to acquire and exercise this body of moral knowledge. How then is it acquired? Hutcheson's answer is that we each possess a moral sense, which compellingly delivers to us, through experience, the moral ideas that prompt our actions. Hence these ideas are intelligible in the manner of all ideas – by virtue of an intrinsic connection with the experience from which they derive. This postulation of a moral 'sense' explains various facts which would otherwise be mysterious. First, it explains why moral opinions are common to people of all periods and cultures, local variations being explicable not as fundamental differences of outlook but as reflections of the varying circumstances with which the common moral outlook is combined. Secondly, it explains why these opinions are aroused in us spontaneously upon the perception of good or evil acts. They are aroused, as it were, against our will: faced with an outrageous act I am stirred to indignation. This is not something I *do* but something that *happens* to me. ('Passivity' is a feature of sensory perception made prominent by Berkeley and later by Hume.) Moreover it seems that the moral sense cannot be overcome by self-interest or passion: it always tells me what is right or wrong, much as my eyes always tell me what is there, whatever my individual desires, projects or emotions.

It is clear that the moral-sense theory is able to reconcile the objectivity of moral judgement with empiricist conceptions of meaning. Nevertheless it leaves many questions unanswered. For example, it seems odd to speak of a 'sense', when there is no particular organ involved in the perception. Moreover, the problem remains of explaining why only rational beings – beings with certain non-sensory powers – are capable of exercising moral judgement. What is it about a dog that makes it impossible for it to perceive these apparently evident properties of the actions which we call right and wrong? Moreover, how is it that we can engage in and be persuaded by moral argument? We do not argue someone into perceiving the colour of a thing, nor would we try to do so. What is the force, then, of referring to a 'sense' when the rational capacities seem so integral to its exercise?

Hutcheson did not address himself to all those problems: nevertheless, he rightly felt that the moral sense could not be taken as a brute capacity – like the capacity to hear, for example – which we might have lacked while being in every other respect rational. He recognised that the moral sense has a further basis in rational nature, and its fundamental working can be understood only in terms of that basis. Hence Hutcheson, like Shaftesbury, had recourse to a general theory of benevolence. He argued that the disposition of human beings to feel pained at each other's sufferings and to rejoice at each other's delights is, in so far as it exists, the motivating force behind both the perception of moral qualities and the actions which are precipitated by it. The disposition to sympathise in these and all the many other ways with which we are familiar is part of what later philosophers were to call the 'social' nature of humankind. The British empiricists deserve credit for this, if for no other thing, that they so described the moral life as to make it clear that there could be no moral theory, whether sceptical or otherwise, that treated the individual as an isolated unit, in only accidental relation to his fellows. The concepts of 'sympathy' and benevolence became basic to moral theory, until Kant suddenly swept them aside in a theory of ethics that made not only these, but every other variety of emotion, utterly irrelevant.

It is at this point that the moral-sense theory becomes unsatisfactory, however. Benevolence may be a natural disposition, but it is not clear how it can provide the foundation of a *sense*. There are no objects, states of affairs or whatever which it is proper to benevolence to perceive, even though it may be proper to benevolence to act on them. At least, if we do say that there is a perception of right and wrong and it is benevolence which leads us to it, we also need to meet Hume's later charge that this, which we interpret as a 'perception', is but another example of the mind's capacity to 'spread itself upon objects'. There is neither right nor wrong in the world, but only a collective hallucination born of good will. It does not really alter this fact that by nature we all agree on what is right or wrong. That only shows that our sympathies are naturally in tune. It does nothing to persuade those who are out of tune with the spirit of benevolence that there is a respect in which they perceive the world wrongly.

The moral-sense theory waned, was revived, waned again, and still continues its spasmodic life, under the guise of ethical 'intuitionism'. But the immediate contemporary of Hutcheson, and the philosopher who did most to gather together the insights of Lockean moral philosophy into a system, was not persuaded by it. Bishop Butler, whose *Sermons* first appeared in 1726, kept closer to Shaftesbury's strategy. That is to say, he put aside questions of moral epistemology and of the meaning of moral terms in favour of a description of human nature which would show, in Aristotelian fashion, not that the evil perceive things wrongly, but rather that they act and feel against nature. Hence, however we answer such questions as 'To what idea does the word "right" refer?' or 'Is there an objective property of things which constitutes their moral value?', we shall be in a position to argue that there is as much reason to act in accordance with the precepts of morality as there is to act in accordance with any other part of ourselves which is essential to the harmonious functioning of our nature. It was from reflections inspired by this thought – and in particular from those delivered by Butler – that much of the modern philosophy of mind was born. If Butler is admired now it is as much because of his acute understanding of the peculiar philosophical problems posed by the nature of appetite, will and emotion, as on account of his answers to the questions of morality.

Butler argued against a certain species of hedonism. According to this theory, no one does anything unless prompted by desire. Since the satisfaction of desire is pleasure, the ultimate end of all action is pleasure. It does not matter that the original desire was to do good: the fulfilment of the action lies in the pleasure that accompanies its success. Hence it is this pleasure that is *really* wanted. Butler felt that this thought, or some variant of it, lay behind most moral scepticism, as well as behind many accepted accounts of the nature of emotion. Since he also thought that it makes morality either impossible, or at best no more natural or respectable than its opposite, he was led to explore the nature of motivation, in order to refute hedonism in this and every other form. At the same time he developed a subtle and in many ways persuasive theory of rational agency.

First, Butler argued that hedonism rests in a fallacy. Even if it were true that whenever I act, I act from a desire, and true that pleasure is the natural or even essential consequence of the satisfaction of desire, it does not follow that my desire is always for pleasure. On the contrary, Butler argued, pleasure presupposes the existence of desire, and is obtained not because we pursue it, but because we pursue something else. The pleasure of drinking wine comes through the satisfaction of the desire for wine. Had it been pleasure alone that we sought, then the wine would have been replaceable as a means to it. I might have said, to someone who asked for a glass of wine, 'Take this, it will do just as well,' and thereupon handed them some other object – a book, a pistol, a plate of fish – the possession of which brings pleasure. To put the point succinctly, hedonism overlooks the specific nature of the objects of our appetites and passions.

Moreover, Butler argued, hedonism rests on an over-simple view of the nature of desire. It assimilates all desires to those of immediate impulse. It fails to distinguish the desires which are peculiar to reason from those which have their basis in animal nature. A rational being can reflect on his predicament and see that the satisfaction of this or that desire might conflict with his long-term interests, bringing discomfort, restlessness, debility or grief. A modern philosopher might speak here of the rational being's capacity for 'second-order' or 'long-term' desires. Some of my desires involve, as part of their object, that I should or should not act on some other short-term, or first-order desire. Butler spoke in this connection of 'cool self-love'; meaning the general capacity to step outside the sphere of present impulse and reflect on one's existence as it extends through time, to see what kind of disposition or character it would be most satisfactory to acquire, and so to act accordingly, encouraging some appetites and discouraging others, in the interest of one's ultimate well-being.

Shaftesbury had argued that common morality can already be generated by cool self-love, without reference to any other principle. His was the Aristotelian view that, properly considered, reflection on the nature of human fulfilment or happiness will lead us to see that a certain long-term disposition – that of virtue – is uniquely suited to produce it. Butler was not persuaded by Shaftesbury's conclusion, but accepted many of his premises. In particular, he accepted that the motivation of a rational being must be understood in terms of a principle of self-knowledge, which takes long-term satisfaction and fulfilment into account and which may overrule the urgings of more specific appetites or desires. Moreover he accepted the view that the principal objects of this 'second-order' principle are not particular or momentary things, but rather general dispositions of character. And he further agreed that, among these dispositions, benevolence is one of the most, perhaps the single most, important. Hence it is true that cool self-love already points us in the direction of a virtuous life. However, Butler thought that the picture of rational motivation was still too simple. There is a further principle which must be mentioned if rational agency is to be intelligible – the principle of conscience:

> the very constitution of our nature requires, that we bring our whole conduct before this superior faculty; wait its determination; enforce upon ourselves its authority, and make it the business of our lives, as it is absolutely the whole business of a moral agent, to conform ourselves to it.

Butler's description of conscience is extremely interesting, partly because it foreshadows, and to some extent gives content to, Kant's later reflections on the nature of practical reason. It also shows a concern to avoid the usual simplifications of empiricist thought, while remaining free of the contentious claims made in opposition to them on behalf of the powers of reason. As Butler put it, inspired by a remark of St Paul's, man is by his very nature a law to himself. What deters us from evil when we act out of conscience is not the fear of punishment, nor even the natural dispositions which self-love would foster, but something altogether higher, which is the obnoxiousness to us of violating a known obligation. Conscience is steady, immovable, and makes itself felt even in the act of disobedience. It is therefore both the maker of law and the motive to obedience; it has (and here Butler borrows from political thought an old Ciceronian distinction) both power and authority, telling us what is good while at the same time motivating us towards the good. Conscience, unlike self-love, is a motive which can overcome passion. While cool self-love can tell us, in reflection, that we should indeed cultivate the disposition of temperance, say, and while this may be of the utmost consequence in persuading us to amend our lives accordingly, self-love is of little use in the actual moment of passion, and is as soon overcome by lust, gluttony or transient passion, as that passion itself might be overcome by rival affections or desires. Conscience, on the other hand, continues quietly to command us even in the frenzy of desire, and can therefore prevent the *subjection* of human nature to the appetites which conflict with it.

Butler's description of conscience is subtle and distinctive. He remained in part a naturalist, committed to the view that all of ethics, even that part which was the responsibility of conscience alone, was but an exploration of human nature, and of what is necessary for that nature to act in harmony with itself. He was able, therefore, to incorporate into his outlook many of the ancient and interestingly argued doctrines that had appealed to Shaftesbury. For example, he held that

> there is no such thing as love of injustice, oppression, treachery, ingratitude; but only eager desires after such and such external goods; which, according to a very ancient observation, the most abandoned would choose to obtain by innocent means, if they were as easy, and as effectual to their end.

Indeed, it often seems as though the claims that Butler makes for conscience are nothing but descriptive; they derive their authority from that same dispassionate argument about the true nature of rational agency that had surprised and delighted the Greeks with its results – in particular with the result that vice is self-defeating and virtue its own reward. In fact, however, Butler's invocation of this new principle of authority in the moral life represents a departure from naturalism. Even if we attribute to conscience a motivating power adequate to ensure its obedience, we need also to show that what it commands is in fact justifiable. This would seem to raise precisely those epistemological questions which Hutcheson felt he could answer, and which Hume later argued that he could not.

The naturalist's investigation of the moral life was continued by Adam Smith, in an interesting discussion of the moral sentiments. It led eventually to utilitarianism, and to the study of political economy as a natural science, so providing historical foundations to some of the principal traditions of nineteenth-century thought. At the same time – and again under the original influence of Shaftesbury – empiricist philosophers began to interest themselves in the subject of aesthetics. The Lockean theory of the association of ideas seemed to give a new basis to the view that beauty is not a subjective sentiment, but something that precipitates connections of thought which reach into our innermost feelings. Beauty must therefore have a significance which is greater than that of any appetite or sensual delight. The empiricist philosophers began to be aware of the great lacuna left in their philosophy of mind by the failure to speak of beauty, and by their fumbling efforts towards an account that would distinguish true taste from mere sensory preference. This awareness, expressed in the works of Lord Kames (*Elements of Criticism*, 1763), Archibald Alison and Edmund Burke (*On the Sublime and the Beautiful*, 1750), was to provide the concepts from which Kant invented anew the philosophical discipline of aesthetics.

9

HUME

The Scottish philosopher David Hume (1711–1776) was the most important and influential of the eighteenth-century British empiricists. Of good family and comfortable means, he was for some time engaged in the diplomatic profession and held the office of secretary to the embassy in Paris. His philosophical masterpiece – the *Treatise of Human Nature* – was published in 1739, when Hume was 28, and remained unsurpassed by his later writings. However, the book fell, in Hume's words, 'dead-born from the press' – the first of many disappointments.

On returning from his post in France, Hume resumed his literary career in the atmosphere of intellectual activity which Scotland then enjoyed, writing, besides his *Enquiries* (1748–1751) (a shorter and modified version of the *Treatise*), many literary, political and philosophical essays. He also composed a *History of Great Britain* (1752–1777), remarkable for its elegance, scholarship and human insight. A sceptic and freethinker in his intellectual outlook, Hume was nevertheless a staunch and articulate Tory, a man seemingly at peace with the world, who conveyed to his contemporaries a love of life and serenity of outlook which attracted to him the affection and esteem of almost everyone whom he encountered.

Scepticism and naturalism

There are two ways of reading Hume. The first is as a sceptic who defends, from empiricist premises, the view that the standard claims to knowledge are untenable. The second is as the proponent of a 'natural philosophy' of man, who begins from empirical observations about the human mind and concludes that the mind has been wrongly construed by the metaphysicians. The two readings are not incompatible, although the second has been emphasised in recent commentaries, partly because it parallels recent developments in philosophy.

Hume's 'naturalism' is Newtonian: he tries to construct a science of the mind while making no unfounded assumptions and relying only on observation. If he rejects the theories of the metaphysicians, he implies, it is because he has been able to discover no grounds for affirming them. At the same time, he affects not to be a radical sceptic, since radical scepticism is against nature. He is a sceptic only in the moderate sense once defended in Plato's Academy – seeking to curb the pretensions of human reason and to remind us of our true nature as passionate and custom-governed beings. When faced with a sceptical conclusion, therefore, Hume often appears to retreat from it, informing his reader that he has merely been discussing the operations of the human mind and not criticising the beliefs that spontaneously arise in us. However, his ironical style, and the barely discernible twinkle in his eye as he proposes his own 'sceptical solutions', make it difficult to be sure of his intention.

Perhaps the best way of reconciling the two Humes is to take seriously his repeated emphasis on custom and instinct as guides to human life. Those who take reason as their master, he seems to suggest, will always be led into confusion; and from this confusion scepticism will spring. Having relied upon reason to guarantee our beliefs, we are thrown into doubt and consternation when reason proves its incapacity. If we rely on custom, however, we are led by our own nature to the beliefs by which our lives are conducted, and will never find a better guide, since custom is a summary of genuine knowledge – knowledge established by experience.

Nevertheless, even if that irenic Hume sometimes speaks from his pages, he made no impression on Hume's contemporaries, who heard only the radical assailant of received ideas. To his early readers, Hume seemed to be arguing against the existence of God and the truth of religion; indeed, he seemed to reject the very concepts of God and the soul, along with such concepts as substance upon which the rationalist world-view had been constructed. He seemed to be sceptical about the existence of material objects, about the objectivity of moral beliefs and even about the fundamental concepts of science, including – most famously – that of causation.

Meaning and ideas

Hume's philosophy depends, like those of Locke and Berkeley, on a theory of meaning, and the theory is substantially the same, designed to articulate the fundamental empiricist postulate that there can be no concept except where there is experience. Hence there can be neither grounds for believing in, nor adequate means for expressing, the metaphysical theories of rationalist philosophy. Berkeley had taken Locke's theory of knowledge to its logical conclusion (as he saw it), and abolished therewith the belief in a material world, elevating the subject and his own mental states into the premise and the conclusion of his philosophy. Hume took Locke's theory of meaning as his point of departure, and drew conclusions which were at once more radical and more disturbing than those of Berkeley.

As already noted, Hume presented his philosophy as though it began from a natural science of the human mind, being the results of observations which could be confirmed by his readers through direct introspection. He distinguished among the contents of the mind 'impressions' and 'ideas'. The first correspond to what we should call sensations and perceptions, the second to what we should call concepts, or 'meanings'. When I perceive a horse, I have a particular impression (in this case a visual impression); when I think of a horse, I summon up an idea: this idea belongs to a class which together constitute the meaning (for me) of the word 'horse'.

What is the difference between impressions and ideas? For Hume it lies in their respective 'force' or 'liveliness'. The impression is received through the senses, and is vivid and forceful during the moment of its reception. The idea is what remains thereafter, when liveliness and force have dwindled. However, Hume also describes ideas as 'copies', 'representations' and 'images' of impressions: they are 'the faint images [of impressions] in thinking and reasoning'.

Hume follows Locke in distinguishing simple from complex ideas and makes the claim that 'all our simple ideas in their first appearance are derived from simple impressions, which are correspondent to them, and which they exactly represent'. He seeks to prove this important claim by empirical investigation, though his arguments are far from scientific, and he even admits the counter-example of an idea that can be acquired *before* the corresponding impression (the 'missing shade of blue'). This does not prevent him from taking the empiricist principle – *no impression, no idea* – as the starting point of his philosophy.

Complex ideas are built from simple ideas; hence all ideas can be traced to the impressions from which they derived. It follows that no term is meaningful (expresses an idea) unless there is an impression from which its meaning can be learned. The meaning of everything that can be said consists in its sensory or empirical content. Hume also endorses Berkeley's attack on abstract ideas, arguing that a term acquires its generality not through being related to a special kind of 'general' idea, but rather through being related to a class of particular ideas, each being nothing but a faded sensory impression, having no real existence outside the mind of the thinker. It would now be natural to reinterpret Hume as saying, not that ideas necessarily originate in sensory impressions, but that their content must be given in terms of those impressions. But the philosophical significance of the doctrine in either case remains the same.

So far there is little difference between Hume and Locke, and, in following Berkeley's method of pruning away Locke's redundant assumptions, it would not be surprising if Hume were to arrive, like Berkeley, at a form of idealism. However, Hume's theory of meaning leads him in quite a new direction. First, he divides all significant propositions into two kinds: empirical and logical. In the first case they derive what meaning they have from experience; in the second case they speak only of the relations between ideas. Hume explains the distinction thus:

> All the objects of human reason or enquiry may naturally be divided into two kinds, to wit, *relations of ideas* and *matters of fact*. Of the first kind are the sciences of geometry, algebra, and arithmetic, and, in short, every affirmation which is either intuitively or demonstratively certain. . . . Propositions of this kind are discoverable by the mere operation of thought, without dependence on what is anywhere existent in the universe. . . . Matters of fact . . . are not ascertained in the same manner, nor is our evidence of their truth, however great, of a like nature. The contrary of every matter of fact is still possible, because it can never imply a contradiction.

Hume here expresses three fundamental views which, in one form or another, have reappeared as definitive of empiricism from his day to ours. Conclusions established by pure reasoning are certain and necessary only because they are, if true, empty. Even mathematics expresses nothing but the relations among ideas, so that its propositions are true only by virtue of the ideas expressed in them, or, what amounts to the same thing, 'true by virtue of the meanings of terms'. Secondly, the only alternative mode of knowledge, that of matters of fact, does not generate necessary truth, but simply summarises what happens to be true and what might have been otherwise. Thirdly (as Hume goes on to make clear), the only source of any knowledge of matters of fact is experience. The ideas expressed in factual propositions will all ultimately derive their content from the impressions that served to generate them. There can thus be no *a priori* proof of any matter of fact. For example, we could not demonstrate *a priori* that the world either does or does not originate from a God; that either we do or do not survive death; that either there are or are not 'substances' which constitute the reality behind the veil of appearance. In this way Hume raises what is

> the justest and most plausible objection against a considerable part of metaphysics; that they are not properly a science, but arise either from the fruitless efforts of human vanity, which would penetrate into subjects utterly inaccessible to the understanding; or from the craft of popular superstitions, which, being unable to defend themselves on fair ground, raise these entangling brambles to cover and protect their weakness.

From this standpoint Hume is able to adopt and turn to his own sceptical ends the criticisms that Berkeley had offered of Locke's supposed theories of 'material substance' and of 'abstract ideas'. The first, together with the associated distinction between primary and secondary qualities, Hume rejected immediately as superstition, scarcely bothering to examine either Locke's real intention or Berkeley's scant but vivid reasoning against it. (As Hume put it, in the terms of his theory of meaning – a theory to which he held dogmatically despite its intended status as a conclusion of scientific observation – there can be no impression of material substance; it follows therefore that there can be no idea of it, so the very term 'material substance' is meaningless.) The theory of abstract ideas Hume regarded as incompatible with a fundamental premise of his philosophy, referring to Berkeley's 'great and valuable discovery' that, since everything that exists is both individual and determinate in all its properties, the very idea of an existent with the attribute of 'generality' involves an absurdity. In the place of this absurd supposition Hume argued that individual ideas might 'agglomerate' so as to introduce into our thinking the necessary element of generality. This theory – the theory of the 'association of ideas' – he took in essentials from Locke (who had taken it from Harvey). The theory retains in Hume its original status of a refutable empirical hypothesis. This fact eventually caused it to fall in confusion before the onslaughts of Kant's theory of knowledge. Nevertheless from these unpromising beginnings Hume was able to formulate a philosophy that presented a powerful challenge to metaphysics. The first subject of his sceptical attack was the concept of causality, fundamental to every scientific enterprise, including that enterprise in which Hume supposed himself to be engaged.

Causality and induction

The idea of cause is one of 'necessary connection', according to Hume. His argument points in two directions: first, towards the demolition of the view that there are necessary connections in reality; secondly, towards an explanation of the fact that we nevertheless have the idea of necessary connection. The argument undergoes significant alterations in the first *Enquiry* and abounds in subtleties and complexities which cannot here detain us. In essence it is this.

The idea of necessary connection cannot be derived from an impression of necessary connection – for there is no such impression. If *A* causes *B*, we can observe nothing in the relation between the individual events *A* and *B* besides their contiguity in space and time, and the fact that *A* precedes *B*. We say that *A* causes *B* only when the conjunction between *A* and *B* is constant – that is, when there is a regular connection of *A*-type and *B*-type events, leading us to expect *B* whenever we have observed a case of *A*. Apart from this constant conjunction, there is nothing that we observe, and nothing that we could observe, in the relation between *A* and *B*, that would constitute a bond of 'necessary connection'. In which case, given the premise that every idea derives from an impression, it may seem as though there were no such idea as that of necessary connection, and that those who speak of such a thing are uttering empty and meaningless phrases.

Why is Hume so confident that 'necessary connections' between events cannot be observed? His reasoning seems to be this: causal relations exist only between *distinct* events. If *A* causes *B*, then *A* is a distinct event from *B*. Hence it must be possible to identify *A* without identifying *B*. But if *A* and *B* are identifiable apart from each other, we cannot deduce the existence of *B* from that of *A*: the relation between the two can only be a matter of fact. Propositions expressing matters of fact are always contingent; it is only those conveying relations of ideas that are necessary. If there were a relation of ideas between *A* and *B*, then there might also be a necessary connection – as there is a necessary connection between *2 + 3* and *5*. But in that case *A* and *B* would not be distinct, any more than *2 + 3* is distinct from *5*. The very nature of causality, as a relation between distinct existences, rules out the possibility of a necessary connection.

We say that *A* causes *B*, then, because of a constant conjunction between *A* and *B*. This constant conjunction causes us to associate the idea of *B* with the impression of *A*, and so to expect *B* whenever we encounter *A*. Such is the force of habit, that the experience of *A* compels this idea of *B*, which therefore arises in us with the kind of involuntariness and vivacity which, according to Hume, are the distinguishing marks of belief. Hence we are compelled to believe that *B* will follow *A*, and this impression of determination gives rise to the idea of necessary connection. The impression is not an impression of a causal relation – or an impression of anything else in the external world. It is simply a feeling that arises spontaneously within us, whenever we encounter the constant conjunction of events. Nevertheless, we misread the resulting idea, as though it had been derived from an impression of necessary connection between *A* and *B*. Thence comes the idea of cause as necessary connection. This is an instance of the mind's tendency to 'spread itself upon objects' – to see the world as decked out in qualities and relations which have their origin in us and which correspond to no external reality.

This criticism of the common concept of causation was not entirely new,* but it was pursued by Hume at great length and with considerable rigour, and the dispute to which it gave rise remains one of the enduring problems of metaphysics. In addition, Hume presented a further problem to the advocates of scientific investigation. This problem has come to be known as the problem of induction. Since the relationship between distinct objects and events is always contingent, there can be no necessary inference from past to future. It is therefore perfectly conceivable that an event which has always occurred with apparent regularity and in obedience

---

* It is anticipated in Al-Ghazali's *Incoherence of Philosophy* (*Tahafut al-Falsafa*, c. 1100), and also in the writings of William of Ockham and Nicolas d'Autrecourt (see above, pp. 18–19).

to what we call the laws of nature, should not occur. The sun may not rise tomorrow, and this would be entirely consistent with our past experience. What then justifies us in asserting on the basis of past experience either that the sun will rise tomorrow, or that it is even probable that it will do so? This problem can be seen to be general. Since scientific laws state universal truths, applicable at all times and in all places, then necessarily no finite amount of evidence can exhaust their content. Hence no evidence available to finite creatures such as we are can guarantee their truth. What therefore justifies us in asserting them?

The external world

While Hume's most original contribution to metaphysics is to be found in that systematic attack on the Cartesian idea of an *a priori* science, he also added a new dimension to scepticism of a more traditional form. This is the scepticism which arises from reflections on the disparity that exists between our knowledge of ourselves as subjects and our knowledge of an objective world. Hume begins from the idea that things which exist at different times must be both distinct and in principle distinguishable. A fundamental ingredient in our conception of a physical object is that of 'identity through time'. Without identity through time the idea of objectivity is imperilled. In a world of instantaneous things, it would seem impossible to distinguish our fleeting experiences from the objects which occasion them. There would be exactly the same evidence for our judgements about both, in which case the distinction between them (between appearance and reality) would break down. Hume argued that we cannot rely on the concept of identity over time in order to make this distinction. If we could rely on this concept, then we could come to the conclusion that objects endure from one moment to another, and hence that they may exist, in principle, when unobserved.

But how could we have the idea of existence unobserved, when there can be no corresponding impression? Such an idea cannot be referred to the 'outer' world, but only (as Hume diagnoses it) to the workings of our imagination. The imagination constantly constructs from the fragmentary deliverances of sense-perception the images of enduring things. The resulting idea – of 'identity' – is, like that of necessary connection, a product of custom and association. Hume contrasts the idea of 'identity' with that of 'unity'. Whenever we are presented with an impression we are simultaneously presented with an impression of unity. This unity of a thing with itself is indistinguishable from the impression, and therefore from the idea, of an 'object'.

When presented with two impressions at different times, we are presented with an impression not of unity but of duality, and no effort of the imagination can justify, even if it may in some way produce, the thought of 'identity' as a distinct and discriminable experience. Lacking the impression of identity, we lack also the idea, from which it would seem to follow that the whole notion of an external world is thrown in doubt. All that we can legitimately signify by referring to such a world is some element of 'constancy' and 'coherence' among our impressions.

It should be noted that Hume – while he also relied on and to some extent reiterated Berkeley's attack on Locke – has, in this argument, focused on a wholly new aspect of the problem of the external world. In submitting the concept of 'identity through time' to sceptical examination, Hume brought to the attention of later philosophers the fundamental pattern of thought on which all our ideas of objectivity finally rest. The principle of his scepticism – that of the contingent connection between distinct existences – shows the extent to which the concept of causality and that of objectivity are vulnerable to the same doubts and might (as Kant was to argue) be protected by the same anti-sceptical strategies. It was to become increasingly apparent that there are not two problems – one concerning causality and induction, the other concerning the external world – but one, the problem of objective knowledge as such. This problem could be manifest in many ways, but it remained solved or unsolved in accordance with the ability of a philosopher to argue for real connections between separately identifiable objects.

The self

Perhaps the most surprising aspect of Hume's scepticism is to be found in his theory of the self. It might be thought that a philosopher so determined to emphasise the inadequacy of our claims to knowledge when set beside the secure basis of experience would at least be content with the Cartesian position that, being certain of my own experience, I know that I exist. But what, asks Hume, *is* this 'I' whose existence is so audaciously asserted in all thinking? When he looks into his own mind, he finds many separate particulars: impressions, ideas and the activities exemplified in their relations. But he finds no particular, whether impression or idea, which corresponds to the 'I' of which we so confidently assert existence. If I ask myself what I am, then the only satisfactory answer is that I consist, not in this or that impression or idea, but in the totality of my impressions and ideas. This theory, sometimes referred to as the 'bundle' theory of the self, arises by extending into the mental realm the familiar objections to the concept of individual substance. These objections Berkeley had already levelled against Locke's theory of the physical world, and Hume largely approved of them. In the absence of any mental 'substance', there is nothing for me to be identical with, save either an impression, or an idea, or some bundle of the same. With the same spirit that had unearthed what were to become the standard epistemological problems of metaphysics, Hume proceeded to disclose parallel difficulties for ethics. Two in particular serve to cast doubt on the possibility of an objective moral system. The first is introduced thus:

> in every system of morality which I have hitherto met with . . . the author proceeds for some time in the ordinary way of reasoning . . . when of a sudden I am surprised to find that, instead of the usual copulation of propositions *is* and *is not*, I meet with no proposition that is not connected with an *ought* or *ought not*. This change is imperceptible; but is, however, of the last consequence. For as this *ought* or *ought not* expresses some new relation or affirmation, it is necessary that it should be observed and explained; and that at the same time a reason should be given, for what seems altogether inconceivable, how this new relation can be a deduction from others which are entirely different from it.

As in his criticism of induction, Hume is here arguing that the relation between propositions which we accept and the evidence that we adduce for them is not, and cannot be, deductive. In which case, on what do we base our confidence that the 'evidence' provides us with any reason at all for asserting the propositions that we suppose to be grounded in it? Here the difficulty is that of finding a satisfactory relationship between propositions about what is and propositions about what ought to be. That there is no deductive relation between an 'is' and an 'ought' is a proposal which is sometimes known as Hume's law. If true it has seemed to many that this 'law' must jeopardise all claims to moral knowledge and leave ethics at the mercy of subjective whim, against which no arguments can be cogently delivered.

The second difficulty that Hume discerned for the objectivity of morality is more profound and more far-reaching in its implications. This is a difficulty not for the idea of moral judgement, but for the more fundamental idea upon which moral judgement rests, the idea of practical reason. Hume denied that there could be such a thing as practical reason. For reason to be practical it is not sufficient that it be applied to practical matters; it must also be capable of generating practical conclusions. As Aristotle argued in the *Nicomachean Ethics*, practical conclusions are not thoughts but actions. Reason, in its practical employment, must therefore generate actions in just the way that, in its theoretical employment, it generates thoughts and beliefs. But how can this be so?

Actions are generated by motives, but reason alone, Hume argued, can never provide a motive to action. All reason can do is present us with a picture of the means to given ends; it cannot persuade us either to adopt those ends or to reject them. Reason is confined in its operation to matters of fact and the relations among ideas. 'After every circumstance, every relation, is known, the understanding has no further room to operate nor any object on which it could employ itself.' Whatever conclusions we may draw as to the way things are, we are still as far as ever from the motive to action. It is therefore 'not contrary to reason to prefer the destruction of the whole world to the scratching of my finger'. What we take to be practical reasoning is simply the working out of the best means to the satisfaction of desires that have their origin not in reason, but in passion. Indeed, Hume goes so far as to say, 'Reason is, and ought only to be, the slave of the passions.' As a modern philosopher would put it, all practical reasons are relative to some antecedent desire, which is therefore the sole origin of their persuasive power. In which case, no amount of reasoning can persuade evil people (those with evil desires) to any course of action except that which already attracts them. This ethical scepticism can be seen as a further application of the thought that there can be only contingent relations between events identified at separate times. If reason could provide a motive to act, then an action could be determined by the reasoning which precedes it. But the relation between this reasoning and the action would have to be necessary, which contradicts the assumption that the action *follows* the reasoning and is distinct from it.

Why does Hume say that reason *ought* to be the slave of the passions? Surely this is hardly compatible with his far-reaching scepticism about the word 'ought'? The answer to this is to be found in the part of Hume's philosophy which was most obviously a product of the intellectual environment into which he grew: his theory of the moral sentiments, and of their immovable centrality in human nature. Hume insists that, despite apparent local variations, there is a basic uniformity of moral sentiment among human beings. Like the British moralists discussed in the last chapter, Hume thought that in every locality and in every period of history, people have been drawn to favour some things and disapprove of others, through the innate disposition, inseparable from human nature, to sympathise with their fellows. It is from the sentiment of sympathy, the origin and object of which lies in man's social condition, and from the benevolence which alone makes that condition possible, that the world comes to appear to us as decked out in the colours of morality. But we should not therefore think that 'right' and 'wrong' are properties that inhere in things independently of our disposition to approve or disapprove of them. By an extension of the Lockean idea of a secondary quality, Hume argued that there is no *fact* of the matter here, other than our moral sentiments. 'Vice and virtue . . . may be compared to sounds, colours, heat and cold, which are not qualities in objects, but perceptions in the mind.' With the result that, 'when you pronounce any action or character to be vicious you mean nothing but that from the constitution of your nature you have a feeling or sentiment of blame towards it.'

In his description of the moral sentiments Hume drew heavily on the analysis of moral feelings given by Aristotle, Hutcheson and, to some extent, Spinoza. His perception of the complexity of these feelings and his attempt to give a truthful account of their significance led to a system of ethics which mitigated his scepticism about the place of reason in determining human action. Having subverted the 'vulgar' systems of morality, Hume raised in their place a balanced and dispassionate picture of the good life for man. This picture was not wholly dissimilar from that already defended by Shaftesbury and Hutcheson.

Indeed, by extending his naturalism into the realm of ethics, Hume produced a moral philosophy which contains an interesting and to some extent credible answer to moral scepticism. The sceptic supposes that nothing holds sway in the human heart besides its own emotions, and that we each pursue our own goals, resisting those who impede us. Morality is merely a fiction, with which we try to hoodwink those who stand between us and our prize. In fact, Hume argues, this picture entirely misrepresents our nature as social beings. The⟨⟩ when we are not in the grip of passion, when our goals re⟨⟩ and when we contemplate the human world from a positio⟨⟩ curiosity. This happens when we read a story, a tragedy o⟨⟩ history. It happens too when others set their case before us, as ⟨⟩ourt of law, and solicit our judgement. In such cases our passions are stirred not on our own behalf, but on behalf of another. This movement of sympathy is natural to human beings and informs all their perceptions of the social world. Moreover, it tends always in the same direction. Whatever our goals, you and I can agree once we have learned to discount them. If two parties to a dispute come before us, then we shall tend to agree in our verdict, provided the facts are clear and provided neither you nor I have a personal interest in the outcome. This discounting of personal interest leaves an emotional vacuum which only sympathy can fill. And sympathy, being founded in our common nature, tends to a common conclusion.

Such is the origin of morality for Hume: the disposition that we all have, to discount our interests and reflect impartially on the world. Although the resulting passions are faint compared with our selfish desires, they are steady and durable. Moreover, they are reinforced by the agreement of others, so that, collectively, our moral sentiments provide a far stronger force than any individual passion and lead to the kind of public constraints on conduct that are embodied in custom and law.

And here lies the justification for Hume's claim that reason *ought* to be the slave of the passions. For *if* we assign to reason the final authority in matters of moral judgement, we shall be driven to scepticism, upon discovering that reason has no competence in the matter. Here as elsewhere reason must give way to custom, as the final guide to human life and the embodiment of our human nature.

God and free will

In his posthumously published *Dialogues Concerning Natural Religion*, Hume demolishes to his satisfaction what he considers to be the principal arguments for the existence of God. His professed aim is once again to curtail the pretensions of reason and put instinct in their place. But his subdued protestation of a 'faith' that needs to be safeguarded from the absurdities of metaphysical speculation has seldom been read as other than ironical. Hume was well known among his contemporaries for his scepticism towards the idea of an afterlife. He is reputed to have found nothing more absurd in the idea that he should cease to exist on dying than in the idea that he began to exist at birth. Two vast periods of Humelessness stretch before and after him – and why should he be concerned by either?

In a famous essay, and again in the first *Enquiry*, Hume also mounted an argument, of which he was particularly proud, despite the fact that it had been anticipated by Spinoza, to show that belief in miracles is always irrational. The very laws of nature which suffice to summarise our knowledge of reality constitute the strongest possible evidence against the testimony of those who bear witness to miracles. For a miracle is, by definition, a violation of a law of nature, and is therefore ruled out by the *rest* of our scientific knowledge.

In the matter of human freedom, however, Hume appears once again in his irenic character. He held that there is in fact no contradiction between the belief that we are free and the belief that nature (including human nature) is governed by immutable and universal laws. If we examine the idea of freedom, he argued, we shall find in it nothing that supposes the abrogation of natural laws. For freedom does not mean the absence of causation. Rather, it is 'the power of acting or not acting, according to the determinations of the will; that is, if we choose to remain at rest, we may; if we choose to move, we also may.' Even if the universe is a fully deterministic system and human beings are governed by the laws that determine everything else, this does not contradict the belief that we have this power to act, according to the determination of the will. Indeed, the very definition of freedom shows that free will *presupposes* causality and therefore does not deny it. What has been thought to be a philosophical problem is no problem at all, but a metaphysical illusion caused by the failure to define our terms. This 'compatibilist' solution to the problem of free will has been greatly influential, even though few would now adopt it in the simple form put forward by Hume. Hume's 'dissolution' of a traditional metaphysical question shows him attempting to remove rather than to create intellectual perplexity, over a matter where he regarded perplexity to be not natural, but artificial.

Hume and the first person

If Hume's philosophy is purified of its attachment to discredited theories of meaning and outmoded psychology, we can see in it a remarkable derivation of the consequences of the Cartesian doubt. Combining Descartes' emphasis on epistemology and the first person with a rigorous empiricism, Hume found himself successively breaking down our common-sense claims to objective knowledge. The consequent retreat into the confines of the first person was accompanied by no thread of reasoning that would enable him to emerge from there except by appeal to custom and instinct. Even the sphere of the subject is thrown in doubt when, as is almost inevitable for a philosophy which consistently questions all propositions that cannot be translated into empirical terms, the concept of substance is abandoned. Hume finds himself trapped within the sphere of his own experience without even the assurance of a self to whom that experience belongs. The loss of the object seems to bring the loss of the subject in its train. Kant perceived this, and perceived the ultimate incoherence in a philosophy which elevates subjective experience into the sole basis of knowledge, while demolishing the idea of the subject. He therefore sought to reverse Hume's argument and to show that the very supposition of a realm of subjective knowledge already involves the covert affirmation of everything Hume had sought to deny. It is to the Kantian enterprise that we now must turn. We may then see the full historical significance of Hume.

Part Three

Kant and idealism

10

KANT I:
THE *CRITIQUE OF PURE REASON*

We have traced two contrasting philosophical currents, rationalism and empiricism, from their common inception in the 'cogito' of Descartes, to their final divergence in Leibniz and Hume. In the eighteenth century, the century of Enlightenment, it was between those two philosophies that a thinking person had to choose. It was Kant's principal contribution to show that the choice between empiricism and rationalism is unreal, that each philosophy is equally mistaken, and that the only conceivable metaphysics that could commend itself to a reasonable being must be both empiricist and rationalist at once.

Immanuel Kant (1724–1804) lived and taught at Königsberg, then in Prussia (but now part of Russia). His early works (known as the 'pre-critical' writings) were followed by a period of silence (1770–1781) and then by the first of the three great *Critiques* – the *Critique of Pure Reason* (1781, second edition 1787). This dealt in a systematic way with the entire field of epistemology and metaphysics; it was followed by the *Critique of Practical Reason* (1788), concerned with ethics, and the *Critique of Judgement* (1790), concerned largely with aesthetics. Among Kant's other works, the most important are the *Prolegomena to any Future Metaphysics* (1783) and *The Foundation of the Metaphysic of Morals* (1785), the first being a popular exposition of his mature metaphysics, the second of his lifelong stance towards morality. His writings on logic, jurisprudence and political philosophy have been less influential, although Hegel's political transformation of the *Critique of Practical Reason* has had an incalculable effect on subsequent political thought and practice.

Of diminutive stature and austere habits, Kant was nevertheless a gregarious man, a brilliant talker, and a loved and respected member of social and literary circles. He was a founding spirit of the German Romantic movement which was to change the consciousness of Europe, and also the father of nineteenth-century idealism. He was (and remains) the greatest philosopher since Aristotle, and his most important book – the *Critique of Pure Reason* – is of an intellectual depth and grandeur that defy description. Mme de Staël wrote of it thus:

> His treatise on the nature of the human understanding, entitled the 'Examination of Pure Reason', appeared nearly thirty years ago, and this work was for some time unknown; but when at length the treasures of thought which it contains were discovered, it produced such a sensation in Germany, that almost all which has been accomplished since in literature as well as in philosophy, has flowed from the impulse given by this performance.

I shall devote this chapter to a discussion of that work, leaving the ethics, the aesthetics and the vagaries of Kant's immediate influence to the chapter which follows.

Kant's early philosophical inspiration had been the system of Leibniz, as expounded by Wolff (see chapter 6). But despite this influence – which is everywhere apparent in the *Critique of Pure Reason* – Kant's philosophy is unique, both in its methods and in its aims. In order to understand those aims we must again consider the impact, during the seventeenth and eighteenth centuries, of the rise of science. Science presented itself as a universal discipline, the premises of which were certain, and the methods of which were disputable only by the adoption of a stance of philosophical scepticism. No one could engage in science without accepting both the established results of his predecessors, and also the empirical methods that led to their discovery. Science presented a picture of unanimity and objectivity which no system of metaphysics could rival. Forced by this fact into unnatural self-consciousness, philosophy found itself with no results that it could offer as its own peculiar contribution to the fund of human knowledge. The very possibility of metaphysics was thrown in doubt, and this doubt was only exacerbated by Hume's radical scepticism – a scepticism which, according to Kant, aroused him from his 'dogmatic [by which he meant Leibnizian] slumbers'. All philosophy, then, for Kant, must begin from the question 'How is metaphysics possible?'

In answer to that question, Kant attempted a systematic critique of human thought and reason. He tried to explore not just scientific beliefs, but all beliefs, in order to establish exactly what is presupposed in the act of belief as such. He wished to describe the nature and limits of knowledge, not just in respect of scientific discovery, but absolutely: his metaphysics was designed, not as a postscript to physics, but as the very foundation of discursive thought. He hoped to show three things:

1 That there is a legitimate employment of the understanding, the rules of which can be laid bare, and that limits can be set to this legitimate employment. (It is a striking conclusion of Kant's thought that rational theology is not just unbelievable, but unthinkable.)
2 That Humean scepticism is impossible, since the rules of the understanding are already sufficient to establish the existence of an objective world obedient to a law of causal connection.
3 That certain fundamental principles of science – such as the principle of the conservation of substance, the principle that every event has a cause, the principle that objects exist in space and time, can be established *a priori*.

Kant's proof of these contentions begins from the theory of 'synthetic *a priori*' knowledge. According to Kant, scientific knowledge is *a posteriori*: it arises from, and is based in, actual experience. Science, therefore, deals not with necessary truths but with matters of contingent fact. However, it rests upon certain universal axioms and principles, which, because their truth is presupposed at the start of any empirical enquiry, cannot themselves be empirically proved. These axioms are, therefore, *a priori*, and while some of them are 'analytic' (true by virtue of the meanings of the words used to formulate them), others are 'synthetic', saying something substantial about the empirical world. Moreover, these synthetic *a priori* truths, since they cannot be established empirically, are justifiable, if at all, through reflection, and reflection will confer on them the only kind of truth that is within its gift: necessary truth. They must be true in any conceivable world. (Kant's idea of necessity is here weaker than that of Leibniz, for whom necessity meant truth in every *possible* world; see pp. 69–70.) These truths, then, form the proper subject matter of metaphysics; the original question of metaphysics has become: 'How is synthetic *a priori* knowledge possible?'

Kant compared his answer to that question (to which he gave the vivid name 'transcendental idealism') to the Copernican revolution in astronomy, because, like Copernicus, he had moved away from the narrow vision which sees one thing as central, towards a wider vision from which that one thing (in this case the capacities of the human understanding) can be surveyed and criticised. There is an immediate intellectual difficulty of which Kant was aware, and which provides the explanation of the word 'transcendental' (a technical term which has as little to do with 'Transcendental Meditation' as with Liszt's *Transcendental Studies*). Consider the question 'How is logic possible?' What argument could there be for the principles of logic that did not already presuppose them? Analogously, if the synthetic *a priori* principles of the understanding are as fundamental to thought as Kant asserted, then the very attempt to establish their validity must at the same time assume them. It was for this reason that Kant called his philosophical method 'transcendental', since it contained an attempt to transcend through argument what argument must presuppose. Not surprisingly, the possibility of such 'transcendental argument' has been the object of continual scepticism. Nevertheless, the individual conclusions of the *Critique of Pure Reason* are of such interest, and often of such intrinsic plausibility, that Kant's own theory as to the nature of his method has dissuaded only the most fatuously commonsensical from trying to reconstruct his argument.

Kant believed that neither the empiricists nor the rationalists could provide a coherent theory of knowledge. The first, who elevate experience over understanding, deprive themselves of the concepts with which experience might be described (for no concept can be derived as a mere 'abstraction' from experience); while the second, who emphasise understanding at the expense of experience, deprive themselves of the very subject matter of knowledge. Knowledge is achieved through a synthesis of concept and experience, and Kant called this synthesis 'transcendental', meaning that it could never be observed as a process, but must always be presupposed as a result. Synthetic *a priori* knowledge is possible because we can establish that experience, if it is to be subject to this synthesis, must conform to the 'categories' of the understanding. These categories are the basic forms of thought, or *a priori* concepts, under which all merely empirical concepts are subsumed. (For example, the concept 'table' is subsumed under 'artifact', which in turn is subsumed under 'object' and hence under 'substance'; the concept of 'killing' is subsumed under 'action', which falls under 'cause'. The categories are the end-points of these chains of subsumption, points beyond which one cannot proceed, since they represent the most basic operations of human thought.) Thus we can know *a priori* that our world (if it is to be *our* world) must obey certain principles, principles implicit in such concepts as substance, object and cause, and that it must fall under the general order of space and time.

The cornerstone of this anti-sceptical proof occurs in a famous, but extremely obscure, passage of the *Critique of Pure Reason*, known as 'The Transcendental Deduction of the Categories'. This exists in two versions, corresponding to the two editions of the *Critique of Pure Reason*, and it is hard to say which version is to be preferred, since neither is fully intelligible. But the outline of the argument can be displayed, and it can be seen that, if valid, it is one of the most important arguments in the whole of philosophy.

Like Descartes, Kant begins from an examination of an aspect of self-consciousness. But, unlike Descartes, he uses his arguments in order to reject what I have called 'the priority of the first person'. In other words, he removes the privileges from subjectivity, and in doing so destroys the possibility of an empiricist theory of the mind. The immediate result is that epistemology becomes secondary to metaphysics; for without metaphysics the deliverances of the senses become impossible to describe.

Kant's near contemporary Lichtenberg remarked that Descartes should have said not, 'I think', but only, 'It thinks in me'. However, as Kant recognised, there is contained in the idea of a thought, as of every mental content, the notion of a subject. Moreover, this subject has an immediate and intuitive apprehension of its own unity: I know immediately of my present mental states that they are mine, and in the normal case I cannot be wrong about this. (In other words, in the case of the present contents of the mind, the distinction between being and seeming evaporates. This is what is meant by the 'subjectivity' of the first person.) It is impossible that I should be in the position of Mrs Gradgrind (in *Hard Times*), who, on her deathbed, knew only that there was a pain in the room somewhere, but not that it was hers. Nor do I have to *find out* that my pain and my thought belong to a single consciousness. My having these states presupposes my ability to assign them to the single subjective unity of the self.

Kant refers to this unity as the 'Transcendental Unity of Apperception', 'apperception' meaning self-consciousness, and the word 'transcendental' indicating that the 'unity' of the self is not known as the conclusion of an argument but as the presupposition of all self-knowledge. Now this unity is not a mere 'binding force' among mental items; it is what Kant calls an 'original' unity. It consists, in other words, in the existence of a thing (the subject), which bears its mental states not as adjuncts but as properties. The very idea of self-knowledge leads us therefore to the unity of the self, as an entity over and above the totality of its mental contents. It follows that there is more to the self than present self-knowledge can offer. The self has an identity (and in particular, an identity through time) beyond the mere collection of its present thoughts and feelings. Hence, while I may have immediate knowledge of my present mental states, there are other aspects of myself about which I might be mistaken, and about which I might have to find out. I might have to discover the truth about my past and future. Hence the self as subject presupposes the self as object. While there is an area of self-knowledge which is subjective (where the distinction between being and seeming evaporates), this is possible only because the self has an enduring, objective identity, in other words, only because it may also be other than it seems. So a subject of experience, if it is to have knowledge of itself as subject, must inhabit an objective world, a world in which the general concept of an object finds application. Radical scepticism, which can be stated only from the premise of self-knowledge, therefore presupposes its own falsehood.

According to Kant, the Transcendental Deduction establishes the validity (in some sense) of the general concept of objectivity. It remains to discover what that concept contains, and it is here that we must turn again to the theory of the categories. Kant argues that all knowledge involves the application of concepts to experience. Having shown that no knowledge is possible, not even self-knowledge, without the general concept of an object, we can at once conclude that experience must conform to the strictures which that concept contains. In other words, experience must conform to the categories; for these are nothing more than a working out in detail of all that is contained in the abstract concept of objectivity. Thus I cannot think in terms of objects without thinking of entities that endure through change; this requires that I apply to my experience the concept of substance. But substance, in its turn, involves the idea of something that sustains itself in being, and that idea involves the notion of causality (or causal explanation). Causality in turn requires the idea of a law of nature, and hence the notions of necessity, possibility and actuality. And so on. Thus we see that, from the assumption that experience falls under the concept of an object, we arrive at the conclusion that it must fall under all the categories in turn.

There is a further step in Kant's argument. For, having shown (as he thinks) that experience conforms to the categories, he feels that he must show that the categories conform to experience. That is, they cannot denote mere abstractions, but must have their primary application in experience; and that means (as he argues at the very beginning of the *Critique*) in space and time. (Kant's thesis in the first section – the Transcendental Aesthetic – is that space is the 'form' of 'outer sense', time is the 'form' of 'inner sense'. This means, roughly, that the idea of experience is inseparable from that of time, and the idea of an experienced *world* is inseparable from that of space.) In this way, he tries to show that the rationalist view of knowledge is as mistaken as the empiricist view. For rationalism assumes an understanding of such categories as cause and substance independently of any actual or possible experience to which they might be applied. Through the process of 'fit' between concept and experience, Kant argues, the whole of scientific knowledge is generated. And it is through examining the structure of this 'fit' that the synthetic *a priori* principles of the understanding may be expounded and justified. For example, if we are to understand how it is that the category of cause gains application in experience, we must see experience itself as already restricted by a general principle of causality, the principle that every event has a cause. By elaborating the system of 'principles' Kant hoped to establish that the fundamental axioms of science are synthetic *a priori*. In this, while he was partly influenced by the parochial conceptions of Newtonian physics and Euclidean geometry, he was also able to argue in abstraction from those sciences, and to deliver results which might well be accepted by many contemporary scientists. For example, Kant attempted to provide a proof of the unity of science (the theory of all events as falling under a law of mutual influence), of the necessity of a principle of conservation of 'substance' (mass for example, or energy), of the need for both intensive and extensive magnitudes in the formulation of scientific laws. All these proofs carry persuasive weight beyond the limitations implicit in eighteenth-century scientific thought.

What does Kant mean in referring to his philosophy as a form of 'idealism' (albeit 'transcendental')? This is one of the most puzzling questions of Kantian exegesis, in particular since Kant expressly dismisses the philosophy of Berkeley (which he labels 'empirical idealism'), asserts that 'transcendental idealism' is a form of 'empirical realism', and appends to the second edition of the *Critique* a chapter called 'The Refutation of Idealism'. I shall return to this difficult question later. First, however, it is necessary to grasp Kant's important distinction between 'phenomenon' and 'noumenon'. Kant's theory of the synthetic *a priori* depends crucially upon the element of empiricism in his philosophy – the view that knowledge comes through the synthesis of concept and 'intuition'. We can have *a priori* knowledge of reality only as 'phenomenon' – as a possible object of empirical observation. Phenomena are those things which can be *discovered* to be thus and thus; things, in other words, which enter into causal relation with ourselves and our experience. Philosophers like Leibniz had tried to describe reality as 'noumenon' – as the object of pure intellectual apprehension. Kant's theory of the synthetic *a priori* and his refutation of scepticism are meant to establish the reality of the phenomenal world (the 'world of appearance'). To try to establish the reality of the noumenal world is to attempt to achieve knowledge by pure concepts alone; it is to attempt to transcend the limits of the human understanding and so achieve knowledge of a world that could never be empirically discovered. Such an attempt involves the transformation of understanding into 'pure reason', and Kant regarded it as doomed to failure. Part of the meaning of the phrase 'transcendental idealism' is contained, then, in this robust emphasis on the empirical as the legitimate sphere of knowledge, and on the impossibility of knowing a 'noumenon' or 'thing-in-itself'.

But does Kant's 'transcendental idealism' really contain a refutation of scepticism? There is a systematic ambiguity in the actual theory of transcendental idealism which makes it difficult to answer this question. The ambiguity is contained in the phrase, used in the last paragraph: 'the world of appearance'. I have taken Kant's claim that transcendental idealism is a form of realism seriously. I have assumed that he intends to assert that the world of which we have knowledge really *exists independently*. The world is a 'world of appearance' only in the sense that it exists in time, consisting of objects and processes which are either perceived by us, or else causally related to our perception. One might call this the 'objective' interpretation of Kant's theory. It is an interpretation that makes the theory incompatible with Humean scepticism.

However, there is a rival interpretation, which we might call 'subjective'. Until recently this was far more widely accepted, despite being compatible at least with the intentions underlying the Humean point of view. This rival interpretation emphasises not 'empirical *realism*' but 'transcendental *idealism*'. It interprets the Transcendental Deduction as expounding a thesis about the nature of the human mind. It is our finite capacities that are being described, and the attack on empiricism is directed, not against scepticism, but against the impoverished concept of human mentality (and in particular the untenable concept of 'experience') from which empiricism departs. When Kant says that we have knowledge not of the world 'as it is in itself', but only of the world as it appears ('the world of appearance'), this could be read as a complicated way of agreeing with the empiricist's conclusions. The world of appearance marks a limit which we cannot in the nature of things transcend. Knowledge is described in subjective terms – as something generated by the understanding, through the synthesis of concept and intuition. In no sense does it, on this interpretation, reach beyond that synthesis to an independent world (the world of the 'thing-in-itself'). This rival psychologistic interpretation of Kant can find support in the text, and has been profoundly influential. In retrospect, however, it seems to me that only the objective interpretation of the first *Critique* allows us to think of Kant's enterprise as either worthwhile or significant.

In the second part of the *Critique of Pure Reason* Kant diagnoses the failure of 'pure reason', trying to show that the attempt to employ concepts outside the limits prescribed by their empirical application leads inevitably to fallacies – in the form of paradoxes, incoherencies and direct contradictions. The inevitable tendency of reason to transcend the limits of intelligibility Kant called the 'Dialectic' of reason (and this concept was to have a profound influence – through Hegel – on subsequent philosophy, although an influence that was at variance with Kant's intentions). Kant tried to show that all the traditional metaphysical (specifically rationalist) arguments – arguments about the substantiality and immortality of the soul, the infinitude of the universe, the necessary existence of God and the reality of free will – were inevitably grounded in contradiction and paradox. The brilliance of his exposition of these errors, together with the fascination of his diagnosis of them, not as accidental but as inevitable diseases of the understanding, are unsurpassed in the history of philosophy. There is space, however, to mention only the most important of Kant's conclusions, those concerning the soul and God. The account of free will must await the chapter which follows.

Kant's view of the soul is extremely subtle. He begins once again from the notion of 'apperception'. It is clear that there is no thought without a subject. And because that subject must have privileged access to its present mental states it is tempting to think, with Descartes, that its pure 'subjectivity' provides some indication of its essential nature; that the abolition of the distinction between being and seeming licenses the inference to the conclusion that the self has a purely 'subjective' being; hence that the self is not subject to the laws of objects, being indestructible and indivisible. Kant points out that there is a fallacy in this inference. There is no passage from the privilege of self-knowledge to the essence of what is known. The privilege of the first person presupposes the existence of the self as object; it is therefore not for self-knowledge to determine what it knows. The essence of the self remains hidden, even though its accidents are immediately 'given' to consciousness. Kant goes on to connect this view with a theory of practical knowledge, and of the moral being of the self, that I shall elaborate in the chapter that follows.

Just as the understanding has its categories, so does 'pure reason' have its 'ideas'. These are categories that have outrun, as it were, the possibility of cognitive application – permanent delusions of the understanding, which one is constrained always to pursue but never to grasp. Among these ideas is that of infinity, construed not as indefiniteness (as in the perpetual incompletion of a mathematical series) but as a completed infinity (as in the Platonic and Boethian view of time). The principal and most compelling instance of that idea is God, and it is to the refutation of the traditional arguments for God's existence that Kant turned his attention in much of the Dialectic. In particular, he presented a famous refutation of the ontological argument, a refutation which a great many have chosen to regard as conclusive, and also as damaging to the whole enterprise of rational theology. The argument turns on the premise that existence is not a predicate; it is therefore impossible, Kant argued, to advance from the concept of God to the existence of God. No concept can imply its own instantiation, and the logical character of existence is misrepresented by any attempt to make it part of the concept of a thing. Kant's premise contained a premonition of one of the most important results of modern logic. This result was to change the course of philosophy once again.

Kant's dismissal of the claims of 'pure reason' was subject to certain important reservations. For one thing, he regarded the 'ideas' of reason as having an important 'regulative' function. If regarded, not as autonomous instruments of knowledge, but as signposts for the understanding, their theoretical employment would lead not to error, but to the constant stimulation of fresh discovery. There was a more important use of 'pure reason', however, adumbrated already in parts of the Dialectic, but fully elaborated only in the *Critique of Practical Reason*. Reason finds its legitimate employment in the practical sphere, and we can understand the claims of theology, for example, if we see them, not as intellectual truths which could be stated and argued for, but, so to speak, as 'intimations', made manifest to our consciousness when we act in obedience to the moral law.

11

KANT II:
ETHICS AND AESTHETICS

The *Critique of Pure Reason* set out to curb the pretensions of speculative metaphysics while establishing *a priori* those principles which must be assumed if there is to be knowledge of an objective order. These principles enable the fundamental distinction between appearance and reality to be drawn with system and authority. The same concern for objectivity can be seen in Kant's writings on ethics and aesthetics, both of which subjects he transformed entirely. There are two *Critiques* (1788 and 1790) which deal with these branches of philosophy, together with an earlier and in many ways more challenging work, the *Foundations of the Metaphysics of Morals* (1785). These works develop systems of value which not only purport to explore in a definitive way the entire question of the objectivity of moral and aesthetic judgement, but also to bring to completion the metaphysical speculations begun in the first *Critique*. Kant tries to rehabilitate, through the theory of 'practical reason', some crucial metaphysical dogmas which theoretical reason alone is unable to establish.

In his ethics and aesthetics Kant was less concerned with the demolition of speculative pretensions and more concerned with providing positive support for evaluative judgements. He wished to justify fundamental items of belief, and to provide the underpinning of thoughts which seem both vulnerable to philosophical scepticism and at the same time basic to our conception of ourselves. Once again Kant considered himself to be responding to the challenge of Hume's scepticism, in an area where – because moral and aesthetic principles provide obstacles both to the fulfilment of natural inclination and to the exercise of choice – there is a universal motive to welcome scepticism. Moreover, this motive seems well founded. For what else can moral and aesthetic principles amount to, if not the expressions of individual preferences, powerful perhaps in their sovereignty over the mind which conceives them, but unwarranted by any independent order? They seem to be supported, if at all, by sanctions which are as arbitrary as the laws which they uphold.

Hume formulated the fundamental premises of this scepticism in two succinct but complex thoughts. First, there is no derivation of an 'ought' from an 'is', which is to say that moral judgements, since they do not describe how things are, gain no justification from natural science. Secondly, since the sole motive to action is desire, and reason itself is no motive, the only rational justification that can be offered for any action lies in showing that it contributes to the satisfaction of an agent's wishes. All reasoning is reasoning about means, and has no authority beyond that of the desire which compels it. There is no innate power of reason to overrule desire, and hence no power of reason to determine action objectively.

The first great insight contained in Kant's moral philosophy was the realisation that Hume's first source of scepticism was of no real significance. Suppose that the 'is–ought' problem were solved, so that moral judgements could be determined with the objectivity of a natural science. That would not refute scepticism. For to refute scepticism we must also show how such judgements provide reasons for acting. In other words, Hume's second objection would still be sufficient to refute the objectivity of morals. On the other hand, if we can show that there are objective reasons for acting, then the 'is–ought' problem becomes insignificant. It no longer matters that we can or cannot derive an 'ought' from an 'is', for morality will gain its rational basis independently. It seemed to Kant therefore that the ancient distinction between theoretical and practical reason should be revived, and the foundations of the second explored with the same discipline that he had devoted to the exposition of the first. This reintroduction and elaboration of the concept of practical reason was among one of the most influential of Kant's achievements and provided the grounds not only for his own partial repudiation of the metaphysics of the first *Critique* but also for many of the insights of later German idealists.

Theoretical reason guides belief, and practical reason guides action; the first therefore aims at truth, the second at rightness. The first, when employed legitimately, Kant called understanding; when illegitimately, pure reason. Reason can, however, also be employed legitimately, but it must then be subjected to those determinations which transform it into practical reason. Understanding issues in judgements (intellectual acts which might be true or false); practical reason issues in imperatives, which may be acted on, but which cannot be called true. (Hence – though Kant does not derive this conclusion – there is no *logical* argument from an 'is' to an 'ought', no argument which proceeds by the use of principles governing truth alone.) Practical reason consists, therefore, in the justification of imperatives, and the problem is to define and validate a concept of objectivity which will both apply to such imperatives and generate a recognisable system of morality.

The categorical imperative

Imperatives, Kant noticed, are of two kinds, the hypothetical and the categorical. The first kind are distinguished by the presence of a conditional antecedent, an 'if . . . ', which makes reference to some condition of need or desire. 'If you want a drink, then go into the drawing-room'. The consequent of such an imperative states (if the whole is valid) an adequate means to the satisfaction of the want or desire mentioned in the antecedent. Such imperatives can be justified objectively, without assuming any special function of practical reason. It suffices to show that, as a matter of fact, the means referred to are adequate to the end supposed. But in an important sense hypothetical imperatives neither have nor claim objectivity, for they provide reasons for action only to people who have the desire mentioned in their antecedent. Their weight, or motivating force, depends upon the actual desires of the subject to whom they are addressed, and derives purely from the motivating force of those desires. According to Hume, there is no other practical employment of reason than in the generation of imperatives of this kind, that is, in a specific and limited application of theoretical reason to the calculation of the means to our ends.

But there is another kind of imperative – the categorical – which makes no relation to specific desires or needs, and which therefore depends for its validity (should it be capable of validity) on no 'empirical conditions', as

Kant put it. Such imperatives contain no 'if . . . ', no concession to the antecedent interests of the subject. They take the form 'Do this!' or 'You ought to do this!' The presence of the 'ought' indicates that, while they may not obtain validity, they certainly claim it. And the claim here is for a genuine objectivity, independent of theoretical reason. It is a claim to bind the subject irrespective of his actual desires, to lay down, as a dictate of reason, an injunction which must be enforced.

But how is such an imperative justified? It is here that Kant discerned the distinctive task and structure of practical reason. Categorical imperatives are justified by the invocation of certain principles of practical reason, all of which can be shown to be either derivable from, or equivalent to, a single governing principle. This governing principle he called *the* categorical imperative. He formulated it in several ways, the first of which was this: 'Act only on that maxim which you can at the same time will as a universal law.' This imperative is designed to capture in a pregnant philosophical phrase the persuasive force of the moral question to which all rational beings respond, the question 'What if others were to act likewise?' It was represented by Kant as having *a priori* validity. It had the same ultimate status in practical reason that he attributed to the principles of the pure understanding: any further justification of it must be philosophical. It is as much a precondition of practical thought as the law of causation is a presupposition of science.

The categorical imperative was restated in various forms, and Kant claimed that these forms were all equivalent, different formulations of the same philosophical insight. Two that are of particular importance are these: 'Act so as to will the maxim of your action as a universal law in a Kingdom of Ends,' and 'Act so as to treat every rational being, whether in yourself or in another, never as a means only but always also as an end.' The first of these means, roughly, that in formulating a principle of conduct, a rational being is constrained to postulate an ideal. In this ideal, or Kingdom of Ends, what is, ought to be and what ought to be, is. In positing such a realm, and himself as part of it, the agent sees himself in relation to other rational beings as one among many, of equal importance with them, deserving and giving respect on the basis of reason alone, and not on the basis of those empirical conditions which create distinctions between people.

The second principle implies that a rational being is constrained by reason not to bend others to his own purposes, not to enslave, abuse or exploit them, but always to recognise that they contain within themselves the justification of their own existence, and a right to their autonomy. The principles between them constitute the vital Kantian idea that the moral law is founded in, and expressive of, the 'respect for persons'.

Kant's claim that the three principles given are simply separate versions of a single principle is difficult to understand: the principles do not seem the same, and indeed involve different terms in their formulation. However, Kant clearly thought that any philosophical justification of the one would be adequate to ground the others too, perhaps because they each involve some fundamental aspect of a single cluster of concepts: rational agency, autonomy, will, end. These concepts could plausibly be considered to provide the basic ideas of practical reason. It is clear that the three principles (and the various modifications of them which Kant from time to time gave) contain the seeds of a powerful and also common-sensical moral point of view. They enjoin respect for others; they forbid slavery, fraud, theft, violence and sexual misuse; they provide a systematic and plausible test against which the pretensions of any particular morality could be measured. Kant's claim, therefore, to have discovered the funda-mental presuppositions of morality may not be entirely unfounded.

The objective necessity of the categorical imperative

The objectivity of the categorical imperative consists in three separate properties. First, it makes no reference to individual desires or needs, indeed to nothing except the concept of rationality as such. Hence it makes no distinctions among rational agents, but applies, if at all, univer-sally, to all who can understand reasons for action. (It therefore governs reasoning about ends and not about means.) Secondly, the rational agent is constrained by reason to accept the categorical imperative: this imperative is as much a fundamental law of practical reason as the law of non-contradiction is a law of thought. Not to accept it is not to reason practically. Like the law of non-contradiction, therefore, it cannot be rationally rejected. Thirdly, to accept such a principle is to acquire a motive to act – it is to be persuaded to *obedience*. Since the imperative makes no reference to any desire, but only to the faculty of reasoning as such, it follows that, if all those three claims can be upheld, practical reason alone can provide a motive for action. Hence the ground of Hume's scepticism – which is that reason is inert, and that all practical reasoning is subservient to desire – is cut away. The moral law becomes not just universal, but necessary, for there is no way of thinking practically that will not involve its explicit or implicit affirmation. The categorical imperative has 'objective necessity', and achieves this by abstracting from all needs and desires, all 'empirical determinations'. It represents the agent as bound by his rational nature alone.

How can this claim to objectivity be upheld? It is here that Kant's moral philosophy becomes difficult and obscure. While he affirms that we know the validity of the categorical imperative *a priori*, he recognises that it is no more sufficient in the case of practical reasoning than it is in the case of scientific understanding to make such a claim. It also stands in need of proof – the kind of proof that the Transcendental Deduction was supposed to provide in the case of the presuppositions of scientific thinking. But Kant did not provide this Transcendental Deduction; instead, he devoted the second *Critique* to an examination of metaphysical questions which, while enormously influential, left the gap between his metaphysics and his morals unclosed. This examination, perhaps intended as a kind of substitute for a Transcendental Deduction, concerns the concepts of freedom, reason and autonomy.

Freedom and reason

Kant argued that no moral law, and indeed no practical reasoning, is intelligible without the postulate of freedom; he also argued that only a rational being could be free in the sense that morality requires. In what then does freedom consist? Not, as Spinoza, Hume and many others had adequately proved, in mere randomness, nor in freedom from those laws that govern the universe. The free agent, as soon as we examine the question, we see to be distinguished, not by his lack of constraint, but by the peculiar *nature* of the constraint which governs him. He is constrained by reason, in its reception of the moral law. Freedom is subjection to the moral law, and is never more vivid than in the recognition of the necessity of that law and its absolute authority over the actions of the moral agent.

To clarify this thought we must distinguish action *in accordance with* the law from action *from* the law. A person might act in accordance with the law out of terror or coercion, or in the hope of reward. In these cases the law is not his motive, and the maxim governing his action, while it may seem to be categorical, is in fact hypothetical. To act from the law is to act out of an acceptance of the categorical imperative itself, and to be motivated by that acceptance. Since this motivation is itself intrinsic to the categorical imperative, it arises from the exercise of reason alone; in acting from the law, therefore, a rational agent at the same time expresses what Kant called 'the autonomy of the will'. His action stems from his own rational reflection, which suffices to generate the motive of his act. His act is, in a deep sense, his own, and the decision from which it springs reflects his whole existence as a rational being, and not the arbitrary (empirical) determination of this or that desire.

Opposed to this autonomy is the 'heteronomy' of the agent who acts not in obedience to the commands of reason, but, for example, out of passion, fear, or the hope of reward. The 'heteronomous' agent is the one who has withdrawn from the exactions of pure morality and taken refuge in slavery. He acts in subjection, either to nature or to some superior force. He may disguise his a-morality by religious scruples, which lead him to act in accordance with the moral law out of hope or fear. But in himself, having failed to achieve the autonomy which alone commands the respect of rational beings, he stands outside the moral order, unfree, subservient, diminished in his very personhood, and in his respect for himself.

The antinomy of freedom

Having established a connection between freedom, reason and autonomy, Kant approaches the problem of free will. In the course of doing so he begins the partial retraction of his strictures against speculative metaphysics. In the 'Antinomy of Pure Reason', contained in the Dialectic of the first *Critique*, Kant had purported to show the various ways in which pure reason tries to reach beyond the limited, 'conditioned', time-dominated world of empirical observation, so as to embrace the unconditioned, eternal world of 'noumena'. Kant sought to demonstrate that each of these ways of pursuing the 'unconditioned', 'intelligible' order generates a contradiction.

One of the 'cosmological' contradictions seemed to him, however, to demand a resolution. This was the contradiction between free will and determinism. The category of cause, and its attendant principle that every event has a cause, orders the empirical world in such a way as to leave no room for the unconditioned event. And yet human freedom seems to require us to think of ourselves as in some sense the 'originators' of our actions, standing outside the course of nature. This freedom is something of which we have an indubitable intuition. The antinomy troubled Kant. He could not accept Hume's view, that there is, here, no genuine contradiction. Nor could he accept his own official theory, that such antinomies are the inevitable result of human reason's attempt to think beyond nature, to aspire towards the absolute and unconditioned, instead of confining itself to the phenomenal world. He therefore sought to develop, both here, and in the second *Critique*, a solution to the problem of free will. The solution took the following form:

The intuitive knowledge of our freedom is primitive and original. It is the presupposition of any practical problem and of any practical reasoning that might be brought to solve it. It stands to practical reason much as the Transcendental Unity of Apperception stands to the theoretical understanding: it is the unquestionable premise without which there would be neither problem nor solution. But practical knowledge is not like theoretical knowledge. It aims not to understand nature, not to explain and predict, but to find reasons for action, and to lay down laws of rational conduct. In thinking of myself as free I am thinking of myself, so to speak, 'under the aspect of agency'. That entails seeing myself, not as an object in a world of objects, obedient to causal laws, but as a subject, creator of my world, whose stance is active, and whose laws are the laws of freedom, knowable to reason alone. (To some extent, this distinction can be understood through another that we all intuitively grasp, that between predicting and deciding. It is one thing to predict that I will get drunk tonight, another to decide to do it. In the first case I look on myself from outside, in the context of the laws of nature to which I am subject, and I observe myself as I would another, trying to arrive at a prediction of my likely behaviour. In the second case I respond as determining agent, and make it my responsibility to bring a future event into being. In one case I give myself reasons for believing something about my future behaviour (theoretical reasons), in the other I give myself reasons for acting (practical reasons).)

It seems then, said Kant, that I know myself in two ways, theoretically, as part of nature, and practically, as agent. And bound up with these two forms of knowledge are two forms of law which I discover through them: the laws of nature and the laws of freedom, the latter being, not surprisingly, the versions of the categorical imperatives. Kant then took the step which was both to undo the conclusions of the first *Critique* and also to inspire succeeding generations of German philosophers to undo likewise. He asserted that in the first form of knowledge I know myself as phenomenon, in the second, practical knowledge, I know myself as noumenon. Despite Kant's seemingly established theory that noumena are in essence unknowable to the understanding, he has, through invoking the ancient idea of 'practical' knowledge, presented a picture of how they might nevertheless be known:

> the will of a rational being, as belonging to the sensuous world, recognises itself to be, like all other efficient causes, necessarily subject to laws of causality, while in practical matters, in its other aspects as a being-in-itself, it is conscious of its experience as determinable in an intelligible order of things.

In other words, the world of noumena is made open to reason after all, but reason not in its theoretical employment, but in its legitimate form, the form of practical reason. Kant goes on to argue that, even in this form, it provides us with knowledge. Whether or not the postulation of the self as noumenon resolves the problem of free will I leave for the reader to judge. The question we must now consider is the status and content of this knowledge which practical reason yields.

The postulates of reason

We find, in fact, that practical reason leads us precisely to those crucial metaphysical theories that the first *Critique* had purported to refute: the existence of a noumenal realm, the immortality of the soul, the affirmation of positive freedom, and the existence of God (the last three being known by Kant as 'Postulates of Reason'). The positive freedom of the rational agent lies in the fact that he

> is conscious of his own existence as a thing-in-itself, [and] views his existence so far as it does not stand under temporal conditions, and . . . himself as determinable only by laws which he gives to himself through reason. In this existence nothing is antecedent to the determination of his will.

The immortality of the soul is supposed to be a necessary consequence of the thought (in some way derivable from the categorical imperative) that human beings are indefinitely perfectible, and therefore able to endure for as long as infinite perfection requires. The existence of God is vouchsafed in turn by the same categorical imperative, as a kind of guarantee without which the necessary idea of a Kingdom of Ends would be logically inconceivable.

Nobody, I think, has been able to give a satisfactory account of this aspect of Kant's philosophy, and the reason is not hard to find. Having separated theoretical and practical reason, in such a way that the province of the former is judgement and the latter action, it seems inevitable that claims to truth belong to the first, whereas the second must deal with claims to right, obligation and duty alone. Practical reason cannot therefore postulate the existence of God or the immortality of the soul, as theoretical conclusions. It cannot lead us to say that this is how things *are*. The best it can say (and this, of course, is not enough) is that this is how things *ought* to be.

One way to make Kant's thought accessible, however, is this: the existence of God and the immortality of the soul cannot be proved as theoretical judgements, since it lies beyond the power of the human understanding to conceive or conjecture them. Nevertheless, when acting in obedience to the moral law we know these things not as truths, but in some other way. We 'know God' as a noumenal presence; we possess an intimation (in Wordsworth's sense) of our immortality. But these feelings of familiarity, forced on us by the very perception of the moral order, cannot be translated into the language of scientific judgement, and so can be assigned no value as literal truths.

Aesthetics

No philosopher has argued more firmly than Kant for the view that moral judgements are objective, rational and universally binding, and his exposition of morality is the starting-point from which all subsequent scepticism began. But even Kant, for whom the objectivity of rational enquiry constituted the fundamental philosophical problem in all realms of human thought, felt that he must, in treating of aesthetics, make some concessions to subjectivism.

Aesthetic judgement, Kant argued, concerns itself with particular objects, and is both 'disinterested' (outside the demands of practical reasoning) and 'free of concepts' (outside the rules of the understanding).

Its aim is neither scientific knowledge nor right action, but rather the contemplation of the individual object for its own sake, as it is in itself, and in the light of the particular sensuous experience that it generates. Nevertheless, aesthetic contemplation is not the same as animal enjoyment. It is a rational pursuit, and issues in judgements which, while they can never be supported by objective or universal principles, do lay claim to objectivity. This claim is unavoidable. For to the extent that our enjoyment of something stems from our rational nature, so do we feel that beings similarly constituted ought to share in it, and so do we look in the object for the grounds that will persuade them to enjoy it too. This pursuit of objectivity, while hopeless, is inevitable. It is indispensable to aesthetic enjoyment, which is founded in critical understanding and never reducible to mere sensuous indulgence.

Kant's theory of aesthetic judgement was complex, and obscurely worked out. While the third *Critique* is undeniably the most important work of aesthetics to have been produced since Aristotle, it was the product of a mind exhausted by its labours, still pregnant with unformed thoughts, but unable to give to them their full elaboration. For example, Kant suggests, in a famous phrase, that the aesthetic judgement seeks in nature and in art for 'purposiveness without purpose'. Here he gestures not only towards a theory of aesthetics, but also towards a larger vision, which shows the role of aesthetic judgement in intellectual enquiry as a whole. Aesthetic judgement is given an indispensable place in forming a picture of the relation of the human mind to the world of experience. It was left to other thinkers, notably to Schiller, to give elaboration to this thought, and in doing so to lay the foundations of a philosophy of art that has been the most influential in intellectual history.

Transcendental idealism

The *Critique of Judgement* argues, then, not for the objective validity of aesthetic values, but for the fact that we must *think* of them as objectively valid. This immediately leads us to ask how Kant can distinguish in general between the actual objectivity of a mode of thought and the innate need that we feel to construe it as though it *were* objective. Consider moral judgements (understood in the Kantian way, so that the intimation of God and immortality is an immovable part of moral understanding). Is it the case that Kant has argued for their objectivity? Or has he merely argued that we must *treat* moral judgements as though they were objective? Many philosophers who accept the second thesis (believing, indeed, that this 'pressure of reason' is what is distinctive of the moral point of view) nevertheless reject the first: the thesis of the objectivity of morals.

As I have already suggested, this doubt as to the nature and scope of Kant's enterprise can be extended even into the first *Critique*. Has he argued for the actual objectivity of science, and for the existence of objects that may be other than they seem? Or has he merely advanced a thesis concerning human mental capacities, the thesis that we are constrained to think as though this were true? To put it in more idealistic terms: has he argued simply that we impose (through the organising principles of the understanding) an order on our experience which we then interpret in the familiar terms of object, cause, space and time? Modern philosophers have tended to interpret Kant as arguing for the actual objectivity of science. The world is as science describes it to be. We ourselves are no more than observers of it, whose peculiarities are not to be discovered by introspection, but rather by adopting the point of view of the objective world of which we form a part. Kant's immediate successors, however, interpreted him differently. To them he had not so much laid the foundations of a true objectivity as explored the reaches of subjectivity. Far from demoting the first person from the privileged place which it had, until then, assumed in epistemology, he had elevated it to the single principle not only of epistemology but of metaphysics itself.

Three features of Kant's philosophy give grounds for this interpretation. First, there is his own description of the philosophy of the first *Critique* as 'transcendental idealism'. Secondly, Kant, in referring to the capacities of the human mind, speaks always of 'our' experience, 'our' understanding, 'our' concepts, 'our' will, etc., leaving open the crucial question whether this 'our' is to be taken in a general sense. Does it mean all human beings conceived impartially? Or is it to be interpreted in the specific sense of idealism, in which it refers to the abstract subject, the 'I' that is engaged in the intellectual construction of a 'world'? This ambiguity is crucial, since, depending on its interpretation, we seem drawn either towards an impersonal metaphysics, or towards a highly solipsistic epistemology. Finally there is the confusion introduced by the second *Critique*, which seems to reject the view that the world of 'phenomena' is the actual world, within which the distinction between appearance and reality must be drawn, and asserts in its place the view that all 'phenomena' are mere appearance, with the reality consisting in the thing-in-itself that lies behind it. At the same time it is argued that the thing-in-itself is knowable after all, through the postulates of practical reason.

Fichte, Schiller and Schelling

Kant's immediate followers adopted the framework and the language of transcendental idealism, the principal achievement of which, they believed, was to have demoted the thing-in-itself from its metaphysical eminence, and elevated the self and its mental faculties in place of it. Henceforth the first study of philosophy was to be the 'faculties' – known by their Kantian names as intuition, understanding, reason, judgement, and so on – through which the self orders the world of appearance, and knows self and world together. The ground of all that exists is the subject of consciousness – unknowable to the understanding, but revealed to practical reason as freedom and will.

But if the self is the source of knowledge, something has been left unexplained. How can a merely subjective entity, beyond the reach of concepts, construct an objective world and endow it with the order of space, time and causality? This is the question that motivated the tradition known on the Continent as 'classical German philosophy', but which could be more accurately described as 'romantic German philosophy', not only for its association with romantic literature, but also on account of its manifest preference for lofty visions over valid arguments. The tradition was founded by Fichte and Schelling, and I shall conclude this chapter with a brief summary of their leading ideas, in order to show the profound impact on German philosophy of the Kantian agenda.

Johann Gottlieb Fichte (1762–1814) was appointed (thanks to the influence of Goethe and Schiller) to the chair of philosophy in Jena at the age of 32. His lectures were immensely popular, and he published them in 1794. Known as the *Wissenschaftslehre* (Science of Knowledge), they were reworked in later editions, and were prefaced by Fichte with the claim that 'my system is nothing other than the Kantian'. According to Fichte, Kant had shown that there are but two possible philosophies: idealism and dogmatism. The idealist looks for the explanation of experience in intelligence, the dogmatist in the 'thing-in-itself'. Kant had shown that idealism can explain everything that dogmatism explains, while making no assumptions beyond the reach of observation. The dispute between the two concerns whether 'the independence of the thing should be sacrificed to that of the self, or, conversely, the independence of the self to that of the thing'. The starting-point of idealist philosophy is therefore the self (*das Ich*).

The task of such a philosophy is to discover the 'absolutely uncon-ditioned first principle of human knowledge'. Logicians offer an instance of necessary and indisputable truth in the law of identity: $A = A$. But even in that law something is presupposed that we have yet to justify, namely the existence of A. I can advance to the truth of $A = A$, once A has been 'posited' as an object of thought. But what justifies me in positing A? There is no answer. Only if we can find something that is posited in the act of thinking itself will we arrive at a self-justifying basis for our claims to knowledge. This thing that is posited absolutely is the I; for when the self is the object of thought, that which is 'posited' is identical with that which 'posits'. In the statement that I = I we have therefore reached bedrock. Here is a necessary truth that presupposes nothing. The self-positing of the self is the true ground of the law of identity, and hence of logic itself.

To this first principle of knowledge, which he calls the principle of identity, Fichte adds a second. The positing of the self is also a positing of the not-self. For what I posit is always an *object* of knowledge, and an object is not a subject. That which comes before my intuition in the act of self-knowledge is intuited as not-self. This is the principle of counter-positing (or opposition). From which, in conjunction with the first principle, a third can be derived, namely, that the not-self is divisible in thought and opposed to a 'divisible self'. This third principle (the 'grounding principle') is supposedly derived by a 'synthesis' of the other two. It is the ground of transcendental philosophy, which explores the 'division' of the self by concepts, whereby the world is constituted as an object of knowledge.

The self is 'determined' or 'limited' by the not-self, which in turn is limited by the self. It is as though self-consciousness were traversed by a movable barrier: whatever lies in the not-self has been transferred there from the self. But since the origin of both self and not-self is the act of self-positing, nothing on either side of the barrier is anything, in the last analysis, but self. In the not-self, however, the self is passive. There is no contradiction in bringing this passive object under such concepts as space, time and causality, so situating it in the natural order. As subject, on the other hand, the self is active, spontaneously positing the objects of knowledge. The self is therefore free, since the concepts of the natural world (including causality) apply only to that which is posited as object, and not to the positing subject.

All activity in the not-self (including that which we should describe as causation) is transferred there from the self. But transference of activity is also an 'alienation' (*Entfremdung*) of the self in the not-self, and a determination of the self *by* the not-self. This self-determination (*Selbstbestimmung*) is the realisation of freedom, since the not-self that determines me is only the self made objective in the act of self-awareness.

Fichte's philosophy rests not so much in argument as in impetuous explosions of jargon, in which that fabricated verb 'to posit' (*setzen*) kaleidoscopes into a thousand self-reflecting images. Schopenhauer described Fichte as 'the father of *sham philosophy*, of the *underhand* method that by ambiguity in the use of words, incomprehensible talk and sophisms, tries to . . . befool those eager to learn'. This harsh judgement (characteristic of its author) may be deserved; but it does nothing to deny Fichte's enormous influence: an influence that can be seen in the writings of Schopenhauer himself. For what Fichte bequeathed to his successors was not an argument at all, but a drama, the outlines of which may be summarised thus:

Underlying knowledge is the free and self-producing subject. The destiny of the subject is to know itself by 'determining' itself, and thereby to realise its freedom in an objective world. This great adventure is possible only through the *object*, which the subject posits, but to which it stands opposed as its negation. The relation between subject and object is dialectical – thesis meets antithesis, whence a synthesis (knowledge) emerges. Every venture outwards is also an alienation of the self, which achieves freedom and self-knowledge only after a long toil of self-sundering. The self emerges at last in possession of a 'realised' self-consciousness, which is also consciousness of an objective order. The 'process' of self-determination does not occur in time, since time is one of its products: indeed the order of events in time is the reverse of their order in 'logic'.

That drama, give or take a few details, remains unchanged in Schelling and Hegel, and remnants of it survive through Schopenhauer, Feuerbach and Marx right down to Heidegger. What it lacks in cogency it amply supplies in charm, and even today its mesmerising imagery infects the language and the agenda of Continental philosophy.

But there was another input, besides Fichte's drama, into the post-Kantian agenda. This was the aesthetic theory of Kant's third *Critique*, as refined and polished by the poet Friedrich von Schiller (1759–1805). In a series of *Letters on Aesthetic Education* (1794–1795) Schiller gave special content to the Kantian view of the aesthetic sense as 'disinterested'. While Kant had paid little attention to art, Schiller attempted to describe it as the highest of man's activities. Art is the activity in which, being 'disinterested', man is at once wholly free and wholly at rest. Art is a form of 'play'. It therefore has a privileged place, not only in human self-knowledge (of which it forms the highest example) but in the life of the state. It is through 'aesthetic education' that the moral and cognitive faculties of man achieve their free expression, and so develop in accordance with their innate principles of harmony. The good state must therefore both encourage and embody that aesthetic understanding which brings the greatest intuition of unity between man and man and between man and nature.

Schiller was followed by Friedrich Wilhelm Joseph von Schelling (1775–1854), in the attempt to incorporate into the critical philosophy a comprehensive account of the nature and value of art. Schelling began as a disciple of Fichte, arguing, in his *System of Transcendental Idealism* (1800) for the same view of the world as self-creative ego, and the same view of knowledge, as a progression from subject to object, in which the subject plays the active and determining role. But like Schiller he was deeply influenced by the prevailing romantic attitude to art and to the creative imagination. He therefore sought to describe the aesthetic mode of understanding as an indispensable part of human consciousness. In the course of doing so, he invented the subject of art history as we know it and placed aesthetic experience at the pinnacle of human knowledge.

From the point of view of aesthetics Schiller is both more original than Schelling and of greater contemporary interest. And from the point of view of the history of philosophy Schelling is now entirely eclipsed by his colleague and rival Hegel, who nevertheless would not have thought as he did had Schelling, Fichte and Schiller not prepared the ground for him. All three of these last-named philosophers remain honourably situated in the history of ideas, being part of that great burgeoning of literary activity known as the *Goethezeit*. Had Hegel not existed, Fichte and Schelling would be studied as avidly now as they were by their contemporaries. But Hegel, the most powerful of the German idealists, towered above these lesser figures, presenting a philosophy which has been not only one of the most influential that the modern world has known, but also the greatest in range and imaginative grasp, the clearest in its understanding of the consequences that ensue when philosophy takes practical and not theoretical knowledge as its central interest, and the boldest in its contempt for any mode of thought that is not both *a priori* in method and infinite in ambition.

12

HEGEL

G. W. F. Hegel (1770–1831) was influenced by three separate intellectual movements: first, and most importantly, by post-Kantian idealism and by Kant himself. Secondly, by Christianity, and in particular by New Testament theology, to the subject of which much of Hegel's early writing was devoted. (Hegel sought to give the complete exposition of the thought that 'in the beginning was the Word'.) Finally, in his outlook and manner, by the literature of late German romanticism, for which he provided an elaborate philosophical justification. Hegel was a highly cultivated man of letters, and a friend of many of the artistic figures of his day, notably of the poet Hölderlin. Despite his bohemian entourage, however, he did not allow the fashion for romantic despair to overcome his will for success and establishment, and ended his life as the revered and comfortable official philosopher in the Prussian state which, by a happy but characteristic turn of thought, he had foretold as the highest expression of the political life of man.

Hegel's lectures, published after his death, contain influential works on aesthetics and the philosophy of history; while the *Encyclopedia* (1817, enlarged 1827) adumbrates an entire system in which science, logic, mind, art, morality and religion are given their respective situations, and in which the whole of the world, as it appears to reason, is blessed, as it were, by an act of philosophical recognition. There are three specific works which will concern us, all published in Hegel's lifetime: *The Phenomenology of Spirit* (1807), *The Science of Logic* (1812–1816) and

The Philosophy of Right (1821), which will be considered in chapter 14. The first two are notorious for their difficulty, in despite of which they have spawned interpretations and rival philosophies by the thousand. To many of Hegel's contemporaries it did indeed seem true that the key to the mysteries of the universe had been found, and that Hegel's implicit claim to utter the ultimate truth about everything should be upheld. Since his death the course of philosophy has been, to put it roughly, a process of steady disillusionment with Hegel, culminating in the vigorous rejection of his thought and method by analytical philosophers in the early years of the twentieth century. But even in our century his influence is felt. His philosophy of 'being' survives in amended form in the writings of Heidegger, and his theory of self-knowledge is present, in some version or other, in most of the major works of phenomenology, and in most theories of art. In this chapter I shall try to sketch certain central Hegelian themes in order to show why Hegel must still be seen as a towering presence in modern philosophy.

In one sense it was unfortunate that Hegel sought to found his philosophy in a general theory of logic, and particularly unfortunate that he should have advanced the theory of the 'dialectic' as containing the whole of metaphysics, thus illustrating, in Bertrand Russell's words, 'an important truth, namely, that the worse your logic, the more interesting the consequences to which it gives rise'. Hegel imagined himself to be replacing the empty formalism of the neo-Aristotelian logic with a new science, which has both form and content, and from which the nature of metaphysical truth can be derived. He therefore invented a new starting point for logic, which was to deal, not with the formal structure of argument, but with the nature of Being itself. Logic deals with truth, not merely in the formal sense of telling us which arguments *preserve* truth, but in the substantive sense of telling us what truth is, and hence what is true (the 'is' here being an 'is' of identity).

That ambitious project is apt to look eccentric in the light of the development of modern logic. This logic has removed from its subject matter not only the metaphysics of Hegel, but also the particular brand of formalism advanced by Aristotle. It is therefore now necessary to read Hegel with more attention to detail, and less respect for system, than he himself would have countenanced. The surprising thing, however, is that his 'dialectical' philosophy still seems both important and often acceptable.

The term 'dialectic' was used by Plato to describe the method of Socrates, who sought philosophical truth through disputation. Kant had given a far more precise meaning to the term, and it was this meaning which Hegel adopted, to make use of it in a manner wholly antipathetic to the Critical philosophy. The second – negative – part of Kant's *Critique of Pure Reason* had been devoted to exploring the fallacies which attend the attempt to pass from the circumscribed realm of the 'understanding' into the limitless space of 'pure reason'. In its desire for absolute truth, human reason commits itself only to the absolute falsehood of self-contradiction. Kant's diagnosis of the fallacies of pure reason contained a section called the 'Antinomy of Pure Reason' (see p. 150). Here Kant had tried to describe certain contradictions into which reason strays in its ambition to pass from the circumscribed viewpoint of empirical knowledge to the realm of absolute cosmology, in which the 'whole' of things is grasped as it is in itself, independently of the limitations imposed by our perceptual capacities. I have already referred to an ambiguity in Kant's conclusions: it is not entirely clear whether he is saying that the limits of human understanding and the limits of truth are one and the same, or whether, on the contrary, he is gesturing towards a world of 'things-in-themselves' about which we can at least know that we do not know them. Because of this ambiguity it was possible for Hegel to interpret Kant's 'critique' of pure reason as heralding its eventual celebration. The Kantian contradictions, Hegel thought, were only contradictions from the limited point of view of the understanding. They therefore provided a kind of logical impetus to transcend that point of view into the world of pure reason itself, from the perspective of which these and many other contradictions could be resolved. (To take an analogy: sitting in a railway carriage moving away from a station I suffer the illusion that the station is slipping backwards. I also believe that the station is motionless and that I am going forward. These two judgements form a contradiction which is 'resolved' when, in ascending to the impartial standpoint of scientific discourse, I recognise that they both presuppose a fallacious, egocentric view of motion. The truth of the matter consists in a relative movement whose nature can be fully grasped only by a scientific theory that assigns no importance to my limited personal perspective.)

Thus while Kant had used the word 'dialectic' to refer to the propensity to fall into contradictions, Hegel used it to mean the propensity to transcend them. This process of transcendence is the true course of logic, and 'dialectic' is the name for the intellectual pursuit whose endpoint is not limited or partial, but on the contrary, absolute truth itself. 'A deeper insight into the antinomies or, rather, into the dialectic nature of Reason shows us . . . that *every* concept is a unity of opposite moments, which could therefore be asserted in the shape of an antinomy.'

What then is the structure of reason's dialectic? It should be recognised that the terms of Hegel's logic are not propositions or judgements, but rather concepts: and it is *concepts*, in his view, that are true or false. Falsehood is a form of limitation or incompleteness, whereas truth is a form of wholeness, a transcendence of all limitation. (Here and elsewhere we see the influence of Spinoza.) Dialectic is the method of progression among concepts, whereby a 'more true' (or, as Spinoza might say, 'more adequate') concept is generated from inadequate beginnings, through overcoming the oppositions intrinsic to them.

The dialectical process is, then, as follows: a concept is posited as a starting-point. It is offered as a potential description of reality. It is found at once that, from the standpoint of logic, this concept must bring its own negation with it: to the concept, its negative is added automatically, and a 'struggle' ensues between the two. The struggle is resolved by an ascent to the higher plane from which it can be comprehended and reconciled: this ascent is the process of 'diremption' (*Aufhebung*), which generates a new concept out of the ruins of the last. This new concept generates its own negation, and so the process continues, until, by successive applications of the dialectic, the whole of reality has been laid bare.

The metaphor is attractive, but how do we interpret it? Hegel's logic is in stark contrast with traditional theories, which see logical relations as timeless, determined not by content but by structure. A thought does not need time, one feels, in which to generate its consequences; indeed it is the essence of a *logical* consequence that it is inseparable from the thought itself: a logical consequence can be neither lost nor acquired. Yet Hegel thinks of concepts as *moving towards* a greater grasp of reality, and he speaks of the 'working through' of the dialectic as being necessary both to the truth and to the meaning of the result. He refers to the successive stages as 'moments', which have to be 'overcome', in the act of 'diremption' whereby a new concept is born.

These temporal similes would be less puzzling if it were not also the case that Hegel thought of historical processes in dialectical terms – as the successive generation and overcoming of contradictions. And it is this aspect of Hegel, put forward overtly in the lectures on the philosophy of history, but covertly elsewhere, that has been the most influential, perhaps because the most intelligible, of his theories. It often seems that the whole of Hegelian metaphysics points towards a logical and historical interpretation at once. To some extent this reflects a confusion on Hegel's part, between logic conceived as a science of the relations among ideas, and logic conceived as the intellectual operation whereby those relations are discovered. Clearly, if it is true that we must undergo some dialectical process in order to know logical relations, this is a fact about *us*, and not about logic. But even this confusion can be glimpsed only obscurely, since Hegel writes at a level of abstraction so great as to attribute the process of thinking not to any particular subject, but rather to a *general* subject of thought. Logic becomes, in the end, the history, or perhaps the anatomy, of an eternal, impersonal 'concept'.

This notion becomes a little clearer if we examine the beginning and the end of the dialectical process, and say something about the course between them. The starting-point of logic is, for Hegel, not arbitrary. Modern conceptions of logic have tended to the view that logic is an instrument whereby the consequences of some premise are derived. Logic is powerless to give knowledge until the premise is determined. This was emphatically not Hegel's view, who thought that the premise of logic is determined by logic itself. The premise of logic is 'pure indeterminate being' – being conceived without any of the particular determinations through which it makes itself manifest to the understanding. Being is the single great *a priori* concept, from reflecting on the nature of which we arrive at an *a priori* theory of reality. (The modern logician will be reluctant, as we shall see, to admit that there is any such concept as that of pure being: this only shows that Hegel's metaphysics can no longer be so easily disguised as a logic, with all the incontestability which that label implies.)

Logic begins, then, from 'being', and advances towards its conclusion, which is the 'absolute idea or truth itself' . This absolute idea is thought and reality at once: it is like the God of Spinoza, who comprehends the whole of things and, being identical with that whole, exists thinking Himself. Each concept in the dialectical process that leads to this supreme conception is obtained from that of being by a sequence of dialectical transformations.

Imagine a kind of impersonal dialectical 'thought', or thinker, attempting to understand the world. It has nothing available to it but thought and so must put forward, as its sole instrument of knowledge, the 'concepts' which enlighten it. Of necessity it begins from the single most indeterminate concept – that which is contained in all concepts and yet which is logically precedent to them, the concept of being. But what is being, considered as 'unmediated' by reflection, and as free from extraneous determinations? It is, surely, nothing, or (as the English translators of Hegel prefer to write it) Nothing. (Cf. Berkeley's arguments against the Lockean substratum.) Hence the concept of being contains within itself its own negation – nothing – and the dialectical opposition between these two concepts is resolved only in the passage to a new concept. This concept is 'becoming', which captures the truth contained in that previous opposition, the truth of the *passage* of being into nothing and nothing into being. To our impersonal thinker the world now appears as becoming rather than as being, and this perception is 'truer' than the preceding one, although as yet far short of that absolute truth in which all such oppositions will be resolved.

Becoming seems to be a specifically 'temporal' characteristic, but we cannot assume at this stage that the 'temporal' character of Hegel's logic is anything more than a metaphor. From the point of view of logic 'becoming' suffers from the same defects as 'being'; it generates its own contradiction out of 'the equipoise of arising and passing away'. So it gives way to a higher truth, which is that of 'determinate being', in which being and nothing are finally reconciled. Determinate being is that more familiar, less abstract, form of existence of which our world presents us with examples: being becomes determinate by being limited and so, as it were, incarnate in a certain identity. From this 'limitation' further oppositions arise and the process continues, until our 'thinker' is brought by a seemingly ineluctable process to the absolute idea itself, so perceiving the whole of reality as 'coming forth' from that indispensable concept from which all thinking must begin.

It would not be unfair to say that Hegel's metaphysics consists of an ontological proof of the existence of everything. The character of this, as of any ontological proof, is that it proceeds from concept to reality, arguing moreover that the discovery of reality and the 'unfolding' of a concept are one and the same. In Hegel's metaphysics this aspect is to some extent concealed by his reluctance to specify the nature of the abstract 'thinker' for whom the dialectical succession of concepts unfolds. His genius for abstractions leads us always away from the subject of thought, to thought itself. And the nature of the resulting metaphysics is such as to abolish the distinction between thought and reality altogether, thus displaying the principal characteristic of idealism.

It is not to be expected that such a logic can readily be made intelligible, or that a philosophy which is able cold-bloodedly to announce (for example) that 'Limit is the mediation through which Something and Other is and also is not' should be altogether different from arrant nonsense. Nevertheless, a *picture* of the dialectic is not hard to form, and this picture is important to bear in mind as we turn to that part of Hegel's philosophy – the philosophy of mind and of politics – which seems now to be most worthy of study and most likely to contribute to the pursuit of knowledge. The picture I have in mind is one that can be seen at its clearest in Leibniz's theory of time. According to Leibniz, ours could be the best possible world only if it were also the richest – the richest in the number and variety of monads that it contains. For this to be possible some monads must contain predicates which cannot – from our limited point of view – co-exist. For example, a thing cannot be both red and green at once: these two attributes seem to contradict each other. But it *can* be red and green successively. So that, in the order of phenomena, the dimension of time enables monads (whose reality is timeless), as it were, to display their abundance of predicates in succession. In perceiving the world under the aspect of time we thereby reconcile what might otherwise have seemed to be contradictions pertaining within it. As Leibniz put it (*Réponse aux réflections de Bayle*): 'Time is the order of possibilities which are inconsistent, but which nevertheless have some connexion.' In some such way it is the dialectic of contradiction which squeezes the Hegelian concept out of its logical changelessness into the order of succession, replacing being by becoming, and logical stasis by ontological evolution.

The constant slide between logical and temporal relations is of the very essence of Hegel's philosophy and preceded the official formulation of his doctrine of logic, exemplified in what is probably the greatest, and certainly the most intricately suggestive of his works, *The Phenomenology of Spirit*. This was written in 1806 and completed in Jena on the eve of the Napoleonic battle outside that town. The complexity and range of the *Phenomenology* defy description: it covers all subjects from art to theology, from science to history, and contains some of the most suggestive examples and intellectual parables in the whole of literature and philosophy. I shall content myself with a résumé of what I take to be its central argument.

It will be remembered that Kant's positive philosophy in the *Critique of Pure Reason* was delivered by the 'Transcendental Deduction'. According to this, the pure 'subject' of Descartes and the empiricists is capable of knowing itself as subject only because it also knows the world as object, disciplining its experience in accordance with the *a priori* categories of the understanding. From the epistemological point of view Hegel did not so much advance beyond as dance around this master thought of Kant's, but he danced in a fascinating way. In the Hegelian whirlwind epistemology melts into ethics, metaphysics into the philosophy of mind, and theoretical understanding into practical reason. This amalgamation of practical and theoretical reason partly explains the temporal emphasis of Hegel's logic. For it is of the essence of practical reason to *advance* towards *decisions*, and not to be detachable from the circumstances of the reasoner. Conclusion and argument are here inseparable, yet neither can be represented in the wholly a-temporal manner demanded by traditional theoretical logic.

Let us allow ourselves, then, as Hegel allows himself, full use of the temporal metaphor. We explore the relation between subject and object in the manner laid down in Fichte's primeval drama (see pp. 156–8). We show how the pure subject *advances towards* self-consciousness through successive postulations of the objectivity of his world. Now Hegel's 'pure subjectivity' is an abstraction, and he goes on to argue, both in the *Phenomenology* and elsewhere, against any view of the 'I' that does not grant universal status to its subject matter. Nevertheless, we can without distortion regard him as referring also, and primarily, to the individual subject, and laying down, in parabolical, quasi historical terms, the conditions which must be fulfilled if that subject is to rise to the self-consciousness that fulfils his nature.

Like Kant, Hegel recognised that the existence of the self in any form brings with it a peculiar immediacy – the immediacy of Kant's Transcendental Unity of Apperception. And Hegel took over from Kant one of the major conclusions of the *Critique of Pure Reason* (established in that part of the Dialectic called the Paralogisms, where the rationalist theory of the soul is demolished). This is that the 'immediacy' with which our mental states are presented to us can provide no clue as to the nature of those states. It is the mere surface glow of knowledge, wholly without depth. The immediacy of the pure subject is, as Hegel would put it, undifferentiated, indeterminate and so devoid of content.

It follows that the pure subject we have imagined can gain no knowledge of what he is, and still less any knowledge of the world which he inhabits. Nevertheless, as Kant saw, his existence presupposes a *unity*, and that unity requires a principle of unity, something that holds consciousness together as one thing. Spinoza had spoken in this regard of the *conatus*, or striving, that constitutes the identity of organic beings. Hegel has recourse to a similar notion, the Aristotelian *orexis*, or appetite. Through this, the subject is launched forth in a manner which is void of knowledge and uninformed by the prospect of success. Consciousness exists only as the primitive 'I want' of the infant, the contumacious screeching of the fledgling in the nest.

But desire cannot exist without being desire *for* something. As Hegel puts it, adopting Fichte's jargon, desire *posits* its object as independent of itself: our primitive subject has already made a step towards the conception of another, and hence towards a conception of itself as differentiated from the other. Its 'absolute simplicity' is on the point of being sundered. But consciousness is not yet an *agent*: it has no conception of the nature of itself, or of the value of its primitive desire. It remains the slave of appetite and impulse. This is, roughly, the state of animal consciousness, which explores the world purely as an object of appetite, and which, being nothing *for* itself, is without genuine will. At this stage the object of desire is conceived only as a lack (*Mangel*), and desire itself destroys or consumes the thing desired.

There follows a peculiar 'moment' in the consciousness of the primitive subjectivity. This is the moment of opposition. The world is not merely passively uncooperative with the demands of appetite: it also actively resists them. The otherness of my world forms itself into opposition. It seems to remove the object of my desire, to compete for it, to seek my abolition as a rival.

The self has now 'met its match', and there follows what Hegel poetically calls the 'life and death struggle with the other', in which the self begins to know itself as will, as power, confronted with other wills and other powers. Full self-consciousness is not the result of this – for the struggle is one that arises from appetite, and brings no conception of the value of what is desired. Hence it does not create the consciousness of the self as standing in definite relation to the world, fulfilled by some things, denied by others. As Hegel would put it, it does not generate the concept of the self *in its freedom*. On the contrary, the outcome of this struggle is the mastery of one party over the other. Conflict is resolved only in the unstable relation of master and slave.

This new 'moment' of self-consciousness is the most interesting, and Hegel's account of it was destined to exert a profound influence on nine-teenth-century ethical and political philosophy. One of the parties has enslaved the other, and therefore has achieved the power to extort the other's labour. By means of this labour he can satisfy his appetites without the expenditure of will and so achieve leisure. With leisure, how-ever, comes the atrophy of the will; the world ceases to be understood as a resistant object, against which the subject must act and in terms of which he must labour to define himself. Leisure collapses into lassitude; the otherness of the world becomes veiled, and the self – which defines itself in contrast to it – becomes lost in mystery. It sinks back into inertia, and its newly acquired 'freedom' turns into a kind of drunken hallucina-tion. True freedom requires self-consciousness, without which there can be no conception of how one is bettered by an action, and therefore no conception of its value. But the self-consciousness of the master is fatally impaired. He can acquire no sense of the value of what he desires through observing the activities of his slave. For the slave, in his master's eyes, is merely a means; he does not appear to pursue an end of his own. On the contrary, he is absorbed into the undifferentiated mechanism of nature, and endows his petty tasks with no significance that would enable the master to envisage the value of pursuing them.

But now let us look at things through the eyes of the slave. Although his will is chained, it is not removed. He remains active towards the world, even in his submission, and while acting at the behest of a master, he nevertheless bestows his labour on objects, and imprints his identity upon them. He makes the world in his own image, even if not for his own use. Hence he differentiates himself from its otherness, and discovers his identity in the act of labour. His self-consciousness grows, and although he is treated as a means, he unavoidably acquires both the sense of an end to his activity and the will to make that end his own. His inner freedom intensifies in proportion with his master's lassitude, until such time as he rises up and enslaves the master, only himself to 'go under' in the passivity that attends the state of leisure.

Master and slave each possess a half of freedom: one the scope to exercise it, the other the self-image to see its value. But neither has the whole, and in this toing and froing of power between them each is restless and unfulfilled. The 'dialectic' of their relation awaits its resolution, and its resolution occurs only when each treats the other not as means, but as end: which is to say, when each renounces the life and death struggle that had enslaved him, and respects the reality of the other's will. In doing so they accept the categorical imperative of justice – to treat others as ends and not as means. They are forced then to see themselves as they see others. Each man sees himself as an object to be respected, standing outside nature, bound to a community by reciprocal demands upheld by a common moral law. This law is, in Kant's words, the law of freedom. And at this 'moment' the self has acquired a conception of its agency; it is autonomous yet law-governed, partaking of a common nature and enacting universal values. Self-consciousness has become *universal* self-consciousness.

But the progress of our undifferentiated subject is not complete. Hegel explores the development, from the primitive conception of right so far established, to the religious world-view (the 'unhappy consciousness') in which the exercise of self-discovery oversteps the limit of personal autonomy. The unhappy (or alienated) consciousness endows the objective world with the power that belongs to itself alone, and so becomes forlorn, guilt-ridden and anxious for redemption. Hegel describes the overcoming of this religious consciousness, and the growth of the ethical life (or *Sittlichkeit*), the ultimate end of which is the development of the free citizen in the protective state. Some of these later developments will be discussed in chapter 14. They contain important psychological insights and amazing leaps of imagination. But it would be too great a labour to express their full philosophical significance. I shall conclude this discussion of the *Phenomenology* by saying something about its methods and the status of its results.

First of all what are we to make of the story-like form which the *Phenomenology* takes? Although Hegel expressly says that the *Logic* simply lays out the general principles of the *Phenomenology*, it is fairly clear that a temporal interpretation is, in the latter case, far more plausible and could be attempted by someone for whom the method of the 'dialectic' was strictly nonsense. It is interesting to note that there are *two* temporal interpretations of the 'moments' of consciousness. The *Phenomenology* contains a parable of the subject, launched with its infantile 'I want' into a world that it gradually reduces into possession, so giving both itself and the world objective form. It also contains a covert history of the human race. Such was the astonishing intellectual effrontery of Hegel, that he made no efforts to deny that mankind *as a whole* must evolve in accordance with the pattern of the *Phenomenology*. We have already shown the episodes corresponding to the pre-historical state of nature, to the undifferentiated 'species' being of the animal, to the episode of primitive combat among tribes, to the Roman *imperium*, with its need for slavery and autocratic rule. (We are also led to understand, furthermore, that the states of mind described in the passage referring to the master and slave are those of the emperor Marcus Aurelius, and of his intellectual master, the stoic slave Epictetus.) Not surprisingly we find that the later stages of the evolution of consciousness fall one by one into the successive periods of history, and by a miracle of predestination, self-consciousness reaches its apogee in that free, protestant, Germanic *Wissenschaft* of which Hegel was both prophet and exegete.

But these historical interpretations are both fanciful and misleading. There is a deeper, logical point that emerges from the argument. To discover it we need to interpret the 'moment' of consciousness not as a stage on the way to self-consciousness, but rather as a state contained within self-consciousness. In saying that the religious consciousness is somehow higher than the primitive recognition of a moral law, Hegel could be taken to refer not to a temporal but rather to a conceptual priority. But this conceptual priority in fact reverses the 'temporal' ordering, in the following way.

Just as Kant had argued that my knowledge of myself as subject presupposes knowledge of an objective world, so Hegel seems to argue that the 'earlier' moments of consciousness presuppose at least the possibility of the latter. The immediate knowledge of self (the Cartesian premise) presupposes the activity that constitutes the self, and this presupposes desire, and hence the knowledge of objects. This in turn presupposes the struggle with the other and the reciprocal dealing which stems from that. Eventually we are driven to the conclusion that the 'self' or 'subject' is not possible except in the context of the political organism which 'realises' it.

The process of 'self-realisation' may admit of degrees, but these degrees do not mark 'stages on the way'. However fragmentary my self-consciousness, it exists only because I participate in that collective self-transcending activity which constitutes the full elaboration of the human mind. I may participate in it only waywardly or spasmodically; to that extent will my self-understanding and freedom be shattered or impaired. But if I am even to *exist* as a subjectivity (as a being that knows itself immediately) I must acknowledge and participate in the claims of the objective arrangements which transcend me.

Construed in this way, as an analytic rather than a genetic theory of rational self-consciousness, the thesis of the *Phenomenology* can be seen as an extension of the Transcendental Deduction. Hegel tries to show that knowledge of self as subject presupposes not just knowledge of objects, but knowledge of a public social world, in which there is moral order and civic trust. Moreover he tries to show from whence arises the *a priori* claim of that most contentful and contentious of the Kantian imperatives – the imperative to treat rational beings as ends and not as means. Whether the argument is valid is not in point: what we should notice is the extent to which it transcends in ambition anything envisaged by Kant. For it aims to defeat epistemological and moral scepticism simultaneously. It also abolishes the distinction between practical and theoretical reason (since the constraint on the subject to acknowledge the existence of the other stems always from the exercise of activity and will). It thus gives cogency to that peculiar logic, the workings of which we have already discussed, which treats reasoning in dynamic terms.

Having offered that interpretation of the *Phenomenology*, however, I must now express a hesitation. For the self-realisation described in the *Phenomenology* is not, despite what I have implied, a realisation of the individual. The individual 'I' is, for Hegel, only a metaphor. No philosophical argument can proceed from the cognisance of an individual, for in that very act of cognisance the individual becomes universal. Every thought is the subsumption under a concept. It is for this reason that Hegel put forward, in the *Logic*, the view that the true subject matter of thought is the concept itself. I may think, in my own case, that I am directly acquainted with some individual thing, but, just as soon as I begin to utter this thought to myself, I must designate that thing – I must employ the concept 'I'. And 'I', like any concept, is a universal. Hence Hegel feels quite justified in abstracting so far from the first-person viewpoint of Descartes and the empiricists as no longer to regard their puzzles as intelligible. The real subject matter of the *Phenomenology* is not the concrete, sceptical, solipsistic self, but the universal, affirmative spirit (*Geist*), whose progress towards realisation in an objective world is something in which you or I may participate, but which transcends every merely local manifestation of its implacable movement.

Much of Hegel's metaphysics thus develops independently of any epistemological basis. He avoids the first-person standpoint of Descartes not through any rival theory of knowledge, but by a process of abstraction which, because it abolishes the individual, leaves no evident room for the theory of knowledge at all. This makes Hegel's metaphysics so vulnerable to sceptical attack that it is often thought to have little to bequeath to us but its poetry.

The dialectic of reason advances from pure, immediate being, through all the determinations of being which in sum constitute reality, so as to consummate itself in the absolute idea. As I have said, this absolute idea is the whole of reality, the truth of the world, and God Himself. Nothing exists in actuality that is not some determinant of pure being, and whose existence is not derived from the dialectical working out of that concept. Reason, because it generates everything, comprehends everything; hence, in a famous phrase, 'the real is rational and the rational is real'. Everything which exists, exists of necessity; but it exists not in virtue of some eternal essence, but in virtue of the struggle of reason to constrain its successive concepts to give birth to their ever more detailed progeny. Hegel calls this struggle the 'labour of the negative'. And the world thus generated, being the product of reason, shows 'the cunning of reason' – it reveals itself to reason, so that the apparently contingent can be seen to be really necessary, and the arbitrary and diffuse as directed and whole.

For Kant, the thing-in-itself was an 'infinite resistance principle' – it stood proxy for the idea that our knowledge has a limit. For Hegel, the thing-in-itself is actual and knowable, being nothing but the absolute idea and its successive revelations. There cannot be more than one such transcendent thing: but nor can there be less than one. The absolute idea is the single immortal substance of Spinoza. It has, in Hegel's view, only one nature, and that nature is revealed to us in consciousness. In our advance towards it, we 'posit' the world of nature (seeing the idea as 'force' and hence as 'matter', the locus of force) and the world of 'spirit'. These are modes of realisation, which the absolute undergoes in us, but in which it does not exhaust itself. How, then, do we know the absolute? Hegel's nearest approach to an answer to this lies in his theory of the concrete universal, according to which the world as *given* is both known (because it is universal) and also sensuously known (because it is concrete). Hence, in moments of pure observation we see it as it eternally is, while seeing it transfixed in time, beleaguered by all its determinations, clothed in attributes, specified to a comprehensible point of being. Philosophy shows the world thus, but philosophy is a lingering occupation: art shows it more immediately, since art is the sensuous *shining* of the idea.

From the obscure but tantalising theory of 'the concrete universal' (a theory which, announcing itself in blatant contradiction, drew a prolonged breath of admiration from the intellectual world) grew the idealist philosophies of art, of history and of the state. All these have been profoundly influential, and their outline is sufficiently known. The poetic appeal of the doctrine that the real is rational and the rational real, combined as it was with a theory of history that represented events as proceeding with whatever inevitability had seemed proper to the proofs of logic (history being nothing more than the 'march of reason in the world'), has had consequences so disastrous in politics, in history and in the criticism of art, that it is not surprising if Hegel has recently been execrated as the greatest intellectual disaster in the history of mankind. Rightly understood, however, he was the true philosopher of the modern consciousness, and those who, like Russell, see only the pretentious exterior of his thinking, show themselves to be blind to the profound spiritual crisis that Hegel was striving to describe – the crisis of a civilisation that has discovered the God upon whom it depended to be also its own creation.

13

REACTIONS: SCHOPENHAUER, KIERKEGAARD AND NIETZSCHE

Hegelian idealism so dominated philosophical thought in early nineteenth-century Germany, and in the states which depended upon German literature for their intellectual life, that the local reactions against it were not at first taken seriously. The so-called 'Young Hegelians', who had given to Hegelian philosophy its varied popular colourings, constituted an intellectual movement of almost unprecedented power, in which the most abstruse and difficult of philosophies was made the foundation not only for vigorous moral, religious and aesthetic doctrines, but also for imaginative literature and organised political life. The movement, which culminated in the historical materialism of Marx, was so influential that the history of ideas must accord to it an important place in nineteenth-century thought. The history of philosophy, however, can afford to pass it by with a glance or two, and turn its attention to the far more impressive thinkers that the Hegelian flurry of self-advertisement concealed from their contemporaries. The first of these, increasingly recognised over the last hundred years as one of the great philosophers of his time, was Arthur Schopenhauer (1788–1860). Schopenhauer was a younger contemporary of Hegel who, partly out of bitterness at the latter's capacity to eclipse him, and partly out of a genuine distaste towards the intellectual self-indulgence of the Hegelian system, dismissed Hegel as a 'stupid and clumsy charlatan'.

Schopenhauer's philosophy takes the transcendental idealism of Kant as its starting-point. Like most of his contemporaries Schopenhauer construed this theory in what I have called the 'subjective' version (see p. 141). He held that Kant had proved that the world we experience through the senses is a construction out of appearances (or 'representations', as he called them), and, while ostensibly repudiating the Kantian idea of a category, he nevertheless saw these 'representations' as the creative embodiment of the intellect, which orders the world of knowledge in accordance with concepts of space, time and causality. It was this simplified Transcendental Idealism that Schopenhauer opposed to the elaborate system of Kant. As the title of his principal work – *The World as Will and Representation* (1818) – implies, he thought that there is more to the world than the system of appearance. The world contains not only representations and their systematic relationships, but also will; and it is on account of his philosophy of will that Schopenhauer is now principally studied. This philosophy bears a relation to that of Fichte. It is, however, extraordinarily ambitious, deriving from the single dichotomy between will and representation the whole of metaphysics, epistemology, ethics and the philosophy of mind, and providing both new answers to old problems, and a new consciousness of the problems themselves.

The philosophy of will begins from the well-known paradox of the thing-in-itself. Transcendental idealism, Schopenhauer argues, implies that the empirical world exists only as representation: 'every *object*, whatever its origin, is, as *object*, already conditioned by the subject, and thus is essentially only the subject's *representation*.' A representation is a subjective state that has been ordered according to space, time and causality – the primary forms of sensibility and understanding. So long as we turn our thoughts towards the natural world, the search for the thing-in-itself behind the representation is futile. Every argument and every experience leads only to the same end: the system of representations, standing like a veil between the subject and the thing-in-itself. No scientific investigation can penetrate the veil; and yet it *is* only a veil, Schopenhauer affirms, a tissue of illusions which we can, if we choose, penetrate by another means. He lavishly praises the Hindu writers for perceiving this.

The way to penetrate the veil, according to Schopenhauer, was stumbled upon by Kant, though he did not see the significance of his own arguments. In self-knowledge I am confronted precisely with that which cannot be known as appearance, since it is the source of all appearances: the transcendental subject. To know this subject as object is precisely not to know it, but to confront once again the veil of representation. But I can know it *as subject* through the immediate and non-conceptual awareness that I have of the will – in short, through practical reason. This leads Schopenhauer to the following conclusion:

> on the path of *objective knowledge*, thus starting from the *representation*, we shall never get beyond the representation, i.e. the phenomenon. We shall therefore remain at the outside of things; we shall never be able to penetrate into their inner nature, and investigate what they are in themselves . . . So far I agree with Kant. But now, as the counterpoise to this truth, I have stressed the other truth that we are not merely the *knowing subject*, but that we *ourselves* are also among those entities we require to know, that *we ourselves are the thing-in-itself*. Consequently, a way from *within* stands open to us to that real inner nature of things to which we cannot penetrate *from without*. It is, so to speak, a subterranean passage, a secret alliance, which, as if by treachery, places us all at once in the fortress that could not be taken from outside.

My essence is will (Kant's 'practical reason'), and my immediate and non-conceptual awareness of myself is awareness of will. But I can know the will, even in my own case, only as phenomenon, since all my knowledge, including inner awareness, is subject to the form of time. At the same time (Schopenhauer does not really explain how) the true nature of will as thing-in-itself is revealed to me. I know that will is one and immutable, embodied in the transient will to live of individual creatures, but in itself boundless and eternal.

What then is the relation of the will to the individual subject? Schopenhauer's answer is framed in terms taken from Leibniz. I am an individual, and identified as such by means of a *principium individuationis* (a principle of individuation). It is only in the world of representation that such a principle can be found: things can be individuated only in space and time, and only when understood in terms of the web of causal connection. The thing-in-itself, which has neither spatial nor temporal nor causal relations, is therefore without a principle of identity. In no sense, therefore, am I *identical* with the will. All we can say is that will is *manifest* in me, trapped, as it were, into a condition of individual existence by its restless desire to embody itself in the world of representation. The will in itself is timeless and imperishable. It is the universal substratum from which every individual arises into the world of appearances, only to sink again after a brief and futile struggle for existence.

Will manifests itself among phenomena in two ways: as individual striving and as Idea. An Idea is something like a complete conception of the will, in so far as this can be grasped in the world of representation – it corresponds to the universal, not the particular, and it is therefore only in the species that the Idea is truly present to our perception. In the natural world, therefore, the species is favoured over the individual, since in the species the will to live finds a durable embodiment, while the individual, judged in himself, is a passing and dispensable aberration. Schopenhauer expresses the point in one of his many beautiful images:

> Just as the spraying drops of the waterfall change with lightning rapidity, while the rainbow which they sustain remains immovably at rest, quite untouched by that restless change, so every Idea, i.e. every *species* of living beings remains entirely untouched by the constant changes of its individuals. But it is the *Idea* or the species in which the will-to-live is really rooted and manifests itself; therefore the will is really concerned only in the continuation of the species.

From this premise Schopenhauer derives a masterly portrait of nature's indifference to the individual, in terms that anticipate evolutionary biology. His pessimism, which keenly inserts itself into every niche where people seek comfort and consolation, stems in part from his sociobiology. And it is in sociobiological terms that he spells out one of the most impressive theories of sexual love in the philosophical literature. However, Schopenhauer's pessimism has other and more metaphysical roots. According to Schopenhauer individual existence is really a kind of mistake, yet one into which the will to live is constantly tempted by its need to show itself to itself as Idea. The will *falls* into individuality and exists for a while trapped in the world of representation, sundered from the calm ocean of eternity that is its home. Its life as an individual (my life) is really an expiation of original sin, 'the crime of existence itself'.

Although intellect is in most things the slave of the will, helplessly commenting on processes that it cannot control, it has one gift within its power – the gift of renunciation. The intellect can overcome the will's resistance to death, by showing that we have nothing to fear from death, which cannot extinguish the will, but only the veil that covers it. And though the thing which survives death is not an individual but the universal, this should not worry us, since it was the mistake of existing as an individual which caused all our suffering in the first place. In such a way Schopenhauer justifies suicide, a step that he himself showed no inclination to take.

The will infects all our thoughts and actions. Nevertheless, we can stand back from it, hold it in abeyance and see things objectively, independently of our transient goals. Then and only then can we be content with the world, having freed ourselves from the restless desire to change it. This detachment from the will comes through art and aesthetic experience. These must therefore be accorded the highest place in man's self-understanding. Indeed, it is through one art in particular, that of music, that we comprehend what is otherwise permanently hidden from us, namely, the objective presentation of the will itself (as opposed to its subjective presentation in me). In music I hear not *my* will or *your* will, but the will detached from all individual striving, from all objects of desire and fear, and rendered objective and intelligible. Melodies and modulations present us with a movement that is purely *ideal*, and through which we glimpse the ocean of eternity. That is why, even in the stormiest symphony of Beethoven, we hear only the resolution of contending forces and the achievement of sublime consolation. In music the will plays with itself, like the waves above the ocean's calm.

Schopenhauer's many applications of his philosophy are worked out with imagination and panache, and in his essays he shows a remarkable ability to conjure from his system new, surprising, but always apt and penetrating observations of the human lot. His system was for daily use: not the abstract jargon of Fichte, but a weapon against the 'unscrupulous optimism' by which he saw himself surrounded. He enjoyed his pessimistic conclusions too much to convince the reader that he really believed in them; and his sardonic assaults on popular prejudice reveal a far greater attachment to life than to the renunciation that he officially favoured. He was certainly arrogant and overbearing in his manner, with a morose streak that led him always to keep a loaded pistol beside him when he slept. But his character was gregarious: he loved wine, women and song and lived the normal life of a selfish academic. He was bitterly distressed by the favourable reception accorded to Hegel. Yet his own philosophy too had far-ranging influence. Not only did Schopenhauer present the Kantian system in easily digestible form; he made it coincide with the prevailing mood of nineteenth-century Germany, which was one of baffled hope and romantic resignation. By his philosophy of will and renunciation he gave new forms of life (or at any rate new forms of death) to Christian culture. Without Schopenhauer there would have been neither Wagner nor Nietzsche as we know them, and it was Nietzsche's final choice of will against renunciation that brought German romantic philosophy to an end.

It might be thought that, having located the essence of reality in the will, and having conceived this will on the model of the thing-in-itself of Kant, Schopenhauer would have found himself with a ready answer to the problem of freedom. On the contrary, however. He recognised that men are praised and blamed only for their actions, and that these actions belong to the world of representation. Hence human action cannot be vindicated by the freedom (which is in any case no more than a universal waywardness) of the underlying and unknowable will. A person's phenomenal character is the origin of all his acts, and is also determined in every particular. Hence there is freedom only in the qualified, common-sense form: a person can do things, and is not always constrained or obstructed in his immediate aims. The 'transcendental' subject of Schopenhauer's philosophy therefore drops out of consideration even in the discussion of that problem which Kant had introduced it to solve. It is to be wondered whether or not any further philosophical reasoning can be found in favour of this thing which, while represented as the single ultimate reality, remains none the less (to borrow a phrase of Wittgenstein's) a 'something about which nothing can be said'.

Schopenhauer was not the only one of Hegel's opponents to rest his faith in the unsayable. Søren Kierkegaard (1813–1855), in his attack on the prevailing Hegelian rationalism, sought to undermine the claim that 'the real is the rational and the rational the real', and so to reaffirm the value of that which, while real, lies beyond the reach of reason. But, lacking Schopenhauer's gift of argument, and being indeed more literary than philosophical in his inclination, he did not set up any elaborate system of ideas whereby to postpone the recognition of his ultimate refuge. There is, in Kierkegaard, no attempt to address the traditional philosophical problems and present a partial answer to them, no attempt to explore the observable (if transient) world, in order to renounce it more confidently for the realm of the unknowable. On the contrary, the whole order of post-Kantian philosophical argument was dismissed, and while the result was a species of irrationalism which, by its very nature, defies philosophical defence, there is no doubt that, in retrospect, Kierkegaard must be seen as a significant thinker, if only because he grasped the fact that the philosophical systems of his day could not be established by argument, and therefore contained no authority that he was constrained by reason to accept.

Kierkegaard wrote much. His style was humorous, vivacious and often highly poetical, although marred by the acute self-consciousness which led him also constantly to hide behind pseudonyms, and to write long and tedious polemics (often against himself). His principal interest was the vindication of the Christian faith, and he wrote always directly or indirectly towards this end, inventing in the process the name, if not the philosophy, of 'existentialism', for which achievement he is now chiefly known. His philosophy is a clear example of a reaction against idealism which is not also a form either of empiricism or scepticism. In the course of this reaction, it is once again the *subject* that is reaffirmed, as the ground of all philosophical thought. The first-person case comes to acquire just the same over-bearing significance that it had for Descartes and Hume. The main difference is that Kierkegaard's interest lies not in the properties of the individual, nor in the knowledge of the world that might be derived from them, but in the sheer *fact* of individual existence, conceived independently of all our attempts to bring it under concepts.

Kierkegaard's first and principal target was Hegel. He attacked the idea of 'universal' spirit, and the associated Hegelian attempt to describe the nature and development of spirit *in abstracto*, without reference to the individual. It is in the individual, according to Kierkegaard, that the true essence of spirit – its essence as 'subjectivity' – is revealed. He was particularly hostile to the Hegelian philosophy of history, which he rightly saw as inviting both the deification of history and the loss of the sense of individual responsibility towards events. This sense he sometimes describes as 'subjectivity', sometimes as 'existential pathos', and sometimes as 'anxiety'; without it, all freedom, all ethical life, and all hope of religious salvation are cancelled.

Many of the Young Hegelians – such as Bruno Bauer (1809–1882) and David Strauss (1808–1874) – were already in the process of developing a theology of history that, in paving the way for Marxist materialism, made possible the realisation of Kierkegaard's fears concerning the transference of religious faith from God to the world. This transference Kierkegaard saw as irremediably evil. Yet for him it was the inevitable outcome of the renunciation of individual existence as the premise of philosophy. Kierkegaard criticised the Hegelian logic as a tissue of illusion, arguing in *Concluding Unscientific Postscript* (1846), his principal philosophical text, that the 'introduction of movement into logic is a sheer confusion of logical science'. The 'logical system' of Hegel, in attempting to regiment the world and its history within the conceptions of a universal science (*Wissenschaft*), must inevitably be self-defeating. Logic, as the science of inference, cannot provide its own premises. These must therefore be obtained from some other source. Moreover, the Hegelian 'universal subject' is nothing but the absence of a subject. The only legitimate subject is concrete, individual and in some deep sense inaccessible to the laws of thought. Logic is timeless, empty of content, whereas the individual finds his essence in time, and enacts in time the drama which uniquely defines him. The movement that Hegel wished to see in logic lies in the individual alone.

Kant once said that he had criticised the pretensions of reason in order to make room for faith. How seriously he meant this I do not know: the contrast between reason and faith belongs to medieval conceptions which are too far from Kant's transcendental idealism to cast any obvious light on it. It is certainly true, however, that there is much affinity between Kierkegaard and those thinkers who had first presented the contrast as central to the Christian vision of the world. Indeed Kierkegaard's philosophy can be seen as a peculiarly modern, as well as a peculiarly Protestant, exposition of the famous '*credo quia absurdum*' of Tertullian.

Kierkegaard's philosophy begins and ends with the individual. This individual is, very crudely, the Cartesian subject; his predicament is described by Kierkegaard as one of 'subjectivity'. In order to characterise it more completely, Kierkegaard thinks it is necessary to develop a philosophy of existence. But, as he argues, an existential system is impossible, since any system, in abstracting from the individuality of what it describes, must ignore that which is important, namely existence itself. Like almost every philosopher who has located his subject in the unsayable, Kierkegaard goes on to say a great deal about it. He seems to accept at one point (namely in the famous *Either/Or* (1843)) the Hegelian conception of the 'moment of consciousness'. There he argues that the essence of the individual is temporal, but that this existence in time is conditioned by an ineradicable longing for the eternal. The 'aesthetic' way of life, which is that most evidently available to the romantic consciousness, unites the subject with what is temporary, and fixes his soul in the immediate. The aesthetic consciousness finds its paradigm of personal life in that which is most determined by the passage of time – the erotic. 'The essential aesthetic principle' is 'that the moment is everything, and in so far again essentially nothing'. The ethical consciousness by contrast recognises the destiny of the individual outside time. From the ethical point of view, individual life is an aspiration towards eternity. It therefore foreswears allegiance to the temporal. For all that, it does not lose itself in the abstractions of logical thinking, even though these represent the world, in some sense, *sub specie aeternitatis*. To have recourse to abstraction is simply to abrogate existence. It is impossible to conceive existence without movement, and therefore impossible to convey its eternal reality. The ethical consciousness finds the subject suspended between time and eternity, rejecting the former, but unable to grasp the latter without losing his identity. What then can the subject do in order both to reach to eternity and at the same time to keep hold of – and indeed establish – his reality as an individual existence?

It is here that Kierkegaard invokes his idea of faith. Reason, which produces only abstractions, negates our individual essence. This essence is subjectivity, and subjectivity exists only in the 'leap of faith', or 'leap into the unknown', whereby the individual casts in his lot with eternity in the only manner that will also guarantee his present being.

Kierkegaard was a convinced Christian, despite his lifelong reaction against the mingled bleakness and hypocrisy of his native Protestant church. He therefore devoted much of his writing to the somewhat self-defeating task of showing that the Christian faith is precisely the one which best calls forth this existential leap. In his efforts to establish this he came up with the doctrine that 'truth is subjectivity'. The traditional conceptions of truth – either as correspondence with reality or as coherence with the system of true ideas – he regarded as equally empty, not because false, but because tautologous. Truth, like everything else, ceased to be empty only when related to the subject. And 'for a subjective reflection the truth becomes a matter of appropriation, of inwardness, of subjectivity, and thought must probe more and more deeply into the subject and his subjectivity'.

As a literary idea, and as an invitation to exalt the individual to a position of eminence that he had never achieved before, this is fairly comprehensible. But as a philosophical theory it has the obvious weakness that the distinction between appearance and reality disappears. For truth, the concept in terms of which that distinction has ultimately to be made, has been absorbed into the realm of appearance, resulting in the following obscure definition: truth is 'an objective uncertainty held fast in an appropriation-process of the most passionate inwardness', hence 'the mode of apprehension of the truth is precisely the truth'. We could put this more simply by saying that there is, for Kierkegaard, no longer any distinction between subject and object. The leap into subjectivity and the leap of faith are ultimately one and the same, and while Kierkegaard supposes that the individual finds himself, at the end of this vertiginous process, emerging into the full reality of the 'ethical life', certain of his own eternity, and yet living in time with true 'existential pathos', it is difficult to see how he is supposed to achieve this. The best that he can do, in his state of subjectivity, is to believe that the world is larger than himself, perhaps with that 'romantic irony' which Hegel described so well in his *Lectures on Aesthetics*. But to believe is not to know, and irony is no substitute for conviction.

Kierkegaard's brilliance as a writer and critic more than makes amends for his magnificent philosophical failure. A study of a philosopher with whom he has often been compared suggests that this ethic of 'subjectivity' will always require literary gifts of a high order. These Friedrich Wilhelm Nietzsche (1844–1900) certainly possessed. Far from using his gifts in the defence of Christianity, however, Nietzsche was guided in part by a hostility to that religion which some have considered to reflect the insanity which in later life overcame him. In retrospect, this hostility is likely to seem obsessive, if not tedious. But fortunately it is not the most significant aspect of Nietzsche's thought.

Nietzsche was a moralist, but one capable of considerable metaphysical ingenuity. He took as his starting-point the famous apophthegm, 'God is dead'. This remark was first given philosophical significance by Max Stirner (1806–1856), in a striking book called *The Ego and His Own* (1845). Stirner belonged to that group of 'Young Hegelians' who reacted against the Hegelian thesis that the individual achieves freedom and self-realisation only in the institutional forms which 'determine' and therefore limit his activity (see p. 205). Stirner was the most extreme among them, rejecting all institutions, all values, all religion, and indeed all relations, except those which the individual ego could appropriate to itself. Stirner, a kind of atheistical Kierkegaard, found, like Kierkegaard, the capacity to generate many words out of the inexpressible state of isolation which he extolled. Nietzsche, by contrast, was more succinct and more subtle.

Nietzsche's philosophy begins, like Kierkegaard's and Stirner's, in the individual; but unlike his predecessors, Nietzsche remained profoundly sceptical that anything significant remained to the individual when the veil of appearance had been torn away. He accepted the doctrine that all description, being conceptual, abstracts from the individuality of what it describes. Moreover, he regarded the description and classification of the individual as peculiarly pernicious, in that it attributed to each individual only that 'common nature' which it was his duty to 'overcome'. Nietzsche tried to avoid the paradoxes involved in this stance by adopting a scepticism towards all forms of objective knowledge. He repeated Hume's arguments concerning causality, and Kant's rejection of the thing-in-itself. (The thing-in-itself is a fabrication of that vulgar common sense with which every true philosopher must be at war.) Nietzsche sought for a 'life-affirming scepticism' which would transcend all the doctrines that stemmed from the 'herd instinct', and so allow the individual to emerge as master, and not as slave, of the experience to which he is condemned.

Nietzsche affirmed, then, the 'master' morality against the 'slave' morality. This idea was directed both against the orthodox Christian and egalitarian outlook of his day, and against the conclusion of the 'master and slave' argument given by Hegel (see p. 170). In *Beyond Good and Evil* (1886) Nietzsche argued that there are no moral facts, only different ways of representing the world. Nevertheless one can represent the world in ways that express and enhance one's strength, just as one can represent it under the aspect of an inner weakness. Clearly it is appropriate for a person to engage in the first of these activities, rather than the second. Only then will he be in command of his experience and so fulfilled by it. This thought led Nietzsche to expound again the Aristotelian philosophy of virtue, or excellence, but in a peculiarly modern form. Like Aristotle, Nietzsche found the aim of life in 'flourishing'; excellence resides in the qualities that contribute to that aim. Nietzsche's style is of course very different from Aristotle's, being poetic and exhortatory (as in the famous pastiche of Old Testament prophecy entitled *Thus Spake Zarathustra* (1892)). But there are arguments concealed within his rhetoric, and they are so Aristotelian as to demand restatement as such.

First, Nietzsche rejects the distinction between 'good' and 'evil' as encapsulating a theological morality inappropriate to an age without religious belief. The word 'good' has a clear sense when contrasted with 'bad', where the good and the bad are the good and bad specimens of humanity. It lacks a clear sense, however, when contrasted with the term 'evil'. The good specimen is the one whose power is maintained, and who therefore flourishes. The capacity to flourish resides not in the 'good will' of Kant (whom Nietzsche described as a 'catastrophic spider') nor in the universal aim of the utilitarians. ('As for happiness, only the Englishman wants that.') It is to be found in those dispositions of character which permit the exercise of will: dispositions like courage, pride and firmness. Such dispositions, which have their place, too, among the Aristotelian virtues, constitute self-mastery. They also permit the mastery of others, and prevent the great 'badness' of self-abasement. One does not arrive at these dispositions by killing the passions – on the contrary the passions enter into the virtuous character in a constitutive way. The Nietzschean man is able to 'will his own desire as a law unto himself'. (Aristotle had argued that virtue consists not in the absence of passions but in a right order among them.)

Like Aristotle, Nietzsche did not draw back from the consequences of his anti-theological stance. Since the aim of the good life is excellence, the moral philosopher must lay before us the ideal of human excellence. Moral development requires the refining away of what is common, herd-like, 'all too human'. Hence this ideal lies, of its nature, outside the reach of the common man. Moreover the ideal may be (Aristotle), or even ought to be (Nietzsche), repulsive to those whose weakness of spirit deprives them of sympathy for anything which is not more feeble than themselves. Aristotle called this ideal creature the 'great-souled man' (*megalopsuchos*); Nietzsche called it the '*Übermensch*' ('Superman'). In each case pride, self-confidence, disdain for the trivial and the ineffectual, together with a lofty cheerfulness of outlook and a desire always to dominate and never to be beholden were regarded as essential attributes of the self-fulfilled man. It is easy to scoff at this picture, but in each case strong arguments are presented for the view that there is no coherent view of human nature (other than a theological one) which does not have some such ideal of excellence as its corollary.

The essence of the ' new man' whom Nietzsche thus announced to the world was 'joyful wisdom': the ability to make choices with the whole self, and so not to be at variance with the motives of one's action. The aim is success, not just for this or that desire but for the *will* which underlies them. (In Nietzsche we find the Schopenhauerian will re-emerging as something positive and individual, with a specific *aim*: that of personal dominion over the world. Nietzsche's early admiration for and subsequent passionate attack on Richard Wagner express the same ambivalent relationship to Schopenhauer.) This success is essentially the success of the individual. There is no place in Nietzsche's picture of the ideal man for pity: pity is nothing more than a morbid fascination with failure. It is the great weakener of the will, and forms the bond between slaves which perpetuates their bondage. Nietzsche's principal complaint against Christianity was that it had elevated this morbid feeling into a single criterion of virtue; thus it had prepared the way for the 'slave' morality which, being founded in pity, must inevitably reject the available possibilities of human flourishing.

To some extent we can see all this as a restatement in modern language of the Aristotelian ideal of practical wisdom. When combined with Nietzsche's theoretical scepticism, it led to the view which is sometimes called pragmatism, according to which the only test of truth is a 'practical' one. Since there are no facts, but only interpretations, the test of the truth of a belief must lie in its success. The true belief is the one that augments one's power, the false belief the one that detracts from it. This made it easy for Nietzsche to recommend belief in a metaphysical theory which presents considerable obstacles to sober thought – the theory of eternal recurrence. For, however difficult it may be to justify the assertion that everything happens again and again eternally, this belief is certainly something of an encouragement to the 'will to power'. If you believe in eternal recurrence, it becomes easier 'so to live that you desire to live again'. But why, in that case, stop short of that most heartening of all beliefs, the belief in an omnipotent deity of whom it is said, 'Ask and thou shalt be given'? One cannot help feeling that Nietzsche's passionate extension of his egoism into the realm of metaphysics leads to more confusion than even his rhetorical gifts were able to hide. Moreover, a philosopher who says, 'There are no truths, only interpretations,' risks the retort: 'Is that true, or only an interpretation?'

In recent years, nevertheless, considerable interest has been expressed in Nietzsche's metaphysics and epistemology, which have partially eclipsed the ethical theory for which he was earlier renowned. Nietzsche was acutely aware of the peculiar predicament of modernity. Hitherto, he argued, our beliefs and the concepts used to formulate them, have had the transcendental backing of religious faith. At no point in the conceptual scheme of civilisation has the void been fully apparent behind the thin paste of our conceptions. Now, however, everything is changing. People come into a world without certainties, and between the torn shreds of our inheritance the abyss is always visible. In such a condition human life becomes problematic; without a radical re-construction of our world-view, which will permit the will to power on which our enterprises depend, we shall enter a peculiar spiritual desert, in which nothing has meaning or value – the world of 'the last man'. Nietzsche has been accused of nihilism, but more recent commentators tend to the view that he is trying – perhaps against the odds, given his sceptical epistemology – to forestall nihilism and to provide us with the weapons against it. Moreover, his acute social criticism, and his ability to sniff the 'will to believe' behind all our ordinary beliefs and attitudes, have endeared him to radical critics of Western society, and caused him to be conscripted to secular causes – feminism, socialism, egalitarianism, 'multiculturalism' – which he himself would have greeted with cavernous laughter. For such reasons Nietzsche, despite the brevity and impatience of his philosophical reasoning, is now as influential as any nineteenth-century philosopher.

Part Four

The political transformation

14

POLITICAL PHILOSOPHY FROM HOBBES TO HEGEL

Modern writers have tended to regard epistemology and metaphysics as the central areas of philosophy, and to treat political thought as an implied branch of the subject. Of the two greatest modern philosophers – Kant and Wittgenstein – the first wrote in a scattered and fragmentary way about politics, while the second ignored it altogether. Plato's most famous work consists in a sustained account of political life, in which philosophical problems are shown to arise from the business of living together in a community; few modern philosophers would give so central a place to questions of politics, and of the exceptions the most prominent are often regarded, like Marx, as pseudo-scientists rather than philosophical thinkers in the strict sense of the word. There is, however, one modern philosopher who conceived the entire subject matter of politics in philosophical terms, and who saw political applications in almost every philosophical argument – Thomas Hobbes (1588–1679), whose *Leviathan* and *De Cive* set the agenda for modern political philosophy.

Published in Paris in 1651, two years after the execution of King Charles I, the *Leviathan* bears the mark of a civil war in which Hobbes and his contemporaries had been made aware of the terror and evil-doing which stem from anarchy. The book aims to justify the power and authority of the sovereign and to show that rebellion is seldom if ever justified, not only because of the chaos that it brings, but also because it involves a breach of a deep and self-contracted obligation. Many of Hobbes's arguments are *ad hoc*, part of his own personal response to the tragic conflict which he had witnessed, rather than arguments from first principles. Nevertheless, his wide influence over his contemporaries is due at least in part to his attempt to provide a metaphysical foundation for political institutions, and to rise above the contingencies of history so as to view human community as it must be, in every age. He was a monarchist, but he inspired the republican Spinoza, whose *Tractatus Theologico-Politicus* (1670) displays the same realistic view of human nature, and the same lofty disdain for political fashion, that are characteristic of Hobbes. The fact that Hobbes was an empiricist of a crudely formulated but uncompromising kind shows the extent to which empiricism lies at the basis of modern political philosophy, being the generating principle of major theories of the state, even when these issue from the pen of a philosopher like Spinoza, for whom reason is the ultimate court of appeal.

Hobbes's principal concern was with the concept of sovereignty, and with the rights and powers associated therewith. He conceived civil association as a 'commonwealth', arranged in rank and influence around the sovereign power, much as the parts of an organism are arranged around a single active principle of life. The organic analogy was very important to Hobbes, and enabled him both to describe the nature of the sovereign power, and also to separate it intellectually from any particular person, assembly or constitutional process that might be thought – in this or that political arrangement – to embody it. Hence his ideas about sovereignty were to prove acceptable to many who did not share his conviction that, unless the sovereign power finds concrete expression in a monarch, it neither commands the allegiance of the citizen nor supports the cohesion of the state. Hobbes's extremely crude empiricism led him to a philosophy of mind that gave little persuasive power to that thought, or to the analogy between the life of a commonwealth and the life of an individual. But this analogy was later to be reinstated by Hegel, with all the philosophical benefits that Hobbes had been unable to provide for it. It then certainly did begin to seem persuasive.

For the purposes of this chapter, the single most important thought to be found in Hobbes lies in his assertion that there can be 'no obligation on any man which ariseth not from some act of his own'. The history of political philosophy in the eighteenth century is largely the history of that thought, and the rising conviction either that it is false, or that it serves to conceal something far more important. If the thought is right then it follows that no one is born into the world encumbered by obligations, and that no state has a right to allegiance unless it arises from some act of 'consent' – however tacit, unreflecting or spontaneous – on the part of the citizen. (It has to be understood that when Hobbes speaks of an 'act' he means an intentional act of a kind that could be seen as bearing within itself the creation and acceptance of an obligation. Promising is a clear example of this; so too is the knowing engagement in business according to the common laws of contract and trade.)

Hobbes finds his paradigm of obligation in contractual or quasi-contractual relations between 'consenting adults' (to use the modern term). This is naturally an odd starting point for the defence of monarchical government, in which the sovereign usually has rights over the citizen that transcend anything the citizen himself can either contract or even understand. Nevertheless, Hobbes believed that in acquiescing in the benefits of government the citizen does thereby accept, and so put himself under an obligation towards, the established order of the commonwealth. The sovereign, who is nothing but the embodied will of that order, therefore acts with the authority of all those who have overtly or covertly sought his protection.

The philosophical basis of Hobbes's quoted remark is important for what follows. Political philosophy has been preoccupied since its origins by an all-important distinction – that between rights (which are enforced only in the name of justice) and powers (which are enforced come what may). Plato's *Republic* opens with an argument that purports to reduce the first to the second; Marx's historical materialism regards the first as a mere institutional reflection of the second, and allows *material* reality to powers alone. Hobbes, preoccupied by legitimacy, saw how fragile are our human conceptions of justice when not supported by material power. What therefore makes the exercise of justice possible? It cannot exist in the 'state of nature', in which the life of man is 'nasty, poor, solitary, brutish and short': it is therefore an artifact, made possible by the power of the state. So the sovereign power creates the possibility of a just order. At the same time, Hobbes recognised, we distinguish legitimate from illegitimate sovereign power. Is this merely – as the 'vulgar' Marxist would persuade us – an ideological illusion? Or does it have some independent basis in reality – independent, that is, of the evident motive that we all have, out of greed or cowardice, to believe that where might is, there right is also?

Clearly rights exist only between persons, and a distinguishing mark of persons is that they can engage in voluntary transactions and thereby acquire at least a *sense* of obligation towards one another. It therefore seemed clear to Hobbes that we can make sense of 'rights' if we trace them back, through the complex history that surrounds them, to those acts in which the sense of obligation is first aroused. Rights can be seen as *conferred* by one person on another. They have their objective foundation in a habit of reflection that informs and is indispensable to the friendly commerce between rational beings. Their origin is wholly different from the origin of power, and hence they can stand in judgement on the exercise of power, even when power seeks to overthrow them. The happy commonwealth is clearly the one in which right and might are in consort, so that the sense of obligation confers its authority upon those *de facto* powers which seek its allegiance. Such thoughts raise enormous philosophical questions about the nature of rational agency, and about the relation between fact and value. But they serve in part to explain why so many moral and political philosophers have concentrated on the act of promising as a starting-point for their investigations. They also show the philosophical basis of a doctrine which was to develop through Locke and Rousseau to become one of the most influential of all political ideas, the doctrine of the social contract (or 'compact' as Locke called it).

In the state of nature, Hobbes believed, rights cannot be enforced: instead there is a war of all against all, which can be brought to an end only by some agreement to cease fighting. This agreement is rational, to the extent that each person benefits from it. What form would such an agreement take? Surely, Hobbes argued, people would contract together to establish, first of all, a sovereign power supreme over every citizen, and capable of enforcing the law and maintaining the peace. The sovereign so established lies outside the contract which creates him, and therefore is not bound by its terms. Hence rebellion can never be sanctioned by the contract, unless the sovereign acts in such a way as to undermine the whole basis of the civil order, and so to bring the contract to an end.

John Locke's *Two Treatises of Civil Government* (1689–1690) were written, like the *Leviathan*, in defence of political forces which were active in the England of his time. Locke wrote in defence, not of absolute monarchy, but of a constitutional settlement, such as was established in 1688, in which a compromise of social forces dictated the structure of government institutions. Locke believed that Parliamentary rule had been threatened by the Stuart court, and he followed his patron, the first Earl of Shaftesbury, into exile during the difficult years of King James II. His first treatise was a polemic against the doctrine of the divine right of kings, upon which the Stuart kings had depended for their legitimacy, and which had been vigorously defended by Sir Robert Filmer. This somewhat parochial work is irrelevant to our concerns, except in so far as it shows that the dispute which animated Locke was the very same that had animated Hobbes – the dispute over the nature and ground of legitimate government. In the second *Treatise* Locke gave what is perhaps the first extended account of the logic of the social contract.

Locke had a less bleak vision of the state of nature than Hobbes. Even in a state of nature, he argued, there is a law which all people recognise, and which they would uphold if their interests did not conflict with it. This law is implanted in us by reason (which is in turn the medium through which God's will is manifest to us). This 'law of nature' generates the 'natural rights' which are commonly recognised by all rational beings, whatever the particular political constitution which might have been imposed upon them. In subscribing to the existence of these 'rights' Locke showed the influence of the ecclesiastical philosopher Richard Hooker (1553–1600), who in his turn had adopted and reworked the mediaeval idea of 'natural law' in order to endow the Church with an authority which could transcend, regulate, and also take part in the practice of government. The theory of 'natural rights' – variously stated and defended – still has its following. It is characterised by its 'international' character; it specifies rights which are supposed to be independent of, and antecedent to, the rights generated by any particular political arrangement. It can therefore provide a court of appeal against the particular laws which provide a grievance to the citizen. It is for this reason that the notion of 'human rights' (the latest form of the theory) has seemed to provide American liberalism, which has its constitutional foundation in the philosophy of Locke, with an international creed to rival the ideals of socialism.

The question, 'How can there be natural rights?' appears throughout the history of philosophy in many forms and disguises, but Locke deserves credit for his clear formulation of the question and his uncompromising answer to it. It seemed to him that we are compelled by reason to acknowledge the existence of rights independently of any convention, agreement or contract which might have served to create them. To use an ancient distinction: there are rights which stem from nature and not from convention. There are, for example, natural rights to life and limb, and to the freedom which is presupposed in the exercise of choice. There is also a natural right to property, in defence of which Locke offers interesting and influential arguments. By 'mixing' his labour with an object, as when he cultivates a field, or transforms a raw material, a worker makes it his own. Thereby he transforms a relation of power into a relation of right. Nobody else can now make exclusive use of the object in question without denying this right. Yet the right arose quite naturally. It involved the intercession of no agreement or conventional usage which might have served as its 'ground'. It is given to reason to see that this 'mixing of labour' generates ownership. A person owns the fields that he has tilled as much as he owns the parts of his body. However, as Locke recognised, rights of this kind will be open to qualification. Two people may till the same field; or I may owe the opportunity to 'mix my labour' with an object to you, who have already, through your own labour, placed me, or it, in the appropriate relation. Furthermore, I have the rights to the fruits of my labour only if I leave 'enough and as good' for others. Nevertheless, Locke thinks, such qualifications and provisos do not destroy the reality of private property as a natural right.

How persuasive is Locke's argument? Its historical importance can hardly be denied. Not only does it give clear application to the mediaeval ideas of natural law; it also provides a vivid terminology with which to describe the essence of material property. This terminology brings the concept of abstract human labour perhaps for the first time, though certainly not for the last, into the centre of political thinking. Moreover it implies a connection between a person's freedom and his control over the product of his labour. This was later to occupy the attention of political philosophers of every persuasion.

Despite this historical importance, however, it is extremely difficult to accept either Locke's exposition of the doctrine of a natural right, or the particular examples that he gives of it. Just what is it about human reason that enables it to perceive natural rights? Does Locke suppose that there are *a priori* laws of practical reason like the categorical imperative of Kant? Or does he suppose that there is some notion of justice which can be given a clear exposition without reference to the particular political conflicts in which it is permanently embroiled? Locke provides no answer other than a theological one. Nor does he say what it is about the 'mixing of labour' that enables us to pass from a mere fact of nature (that people do things) to a law of right (that people own things). All the same, there is an intuitive power in the conception which called philosophers back to it again and again.

Even if there are natural rights, it is not to be supposed that all people in a state of nature will observe them. Hence society and its institutions are necessary, and these institutions will demand forms of obedience and create forms of obligation which surpass what can be regarded as merely 'natural'. The question therefore arises: what criterion of right and legitimacy will operate outside the realm of 'natural law'? Locke's answer recalls that of Hobbes. The criterion of legitimacy is mutual consent, and the resulting civil constitution is to be construed in contractual terms: it arises from an 'original compact'. The reason for this is as follows: all social order requires the restriction in untold ways of the freedom which a rational being enjoys in a 'state of nature'. By what title, then, can a rational being be deprived of his freedoms? The only title must be that he himself has, through whatever impression of the advantage which accrues to him, contracted not to enjoy them. In return, therefore, the civil order has a benefit which it is obliged to confer on him – the benefit for which he contracted. This benefit is difficult to describe, but we know at least that it includes a measure of security in matters of life, limb, and property, together with such other comforts of human society and material well-being as the efficient order of a commonwealth might bring. The 'original compact' is not, however, made with a sovereign power, since the existence of such a power is, conceptually speaking, the end result and not the foundation of the compact. This compact is made between free beings in a state of nature, as they mutually relinquish their freedom and join forces for the common good.

In normal cases, a contract may involve a surrender not merely of freedoms, but of rights – in exchange for rights of another kind. It is therefore open to someone to argue that the citizens of Locke's community have bargained away many of their rights in exchange for civil protection – perhaps even the rights to life, limb and property. Locke wished to avoid such a result – for he believed that natural rights *set limits* to government, thereby giving grounds for rebellion should they be violated. He argued, therefore, on grounds that are none too clear, that natural rights are *inalienable*: even if you seek to bargain them away, you cannot succeed, since they are not the kind of thing that can be bargained.

There is another difficulty for social contract theories of Locke's variety. On what grounds do we infer the existence of a social contract in any given society? Certainly there is seldom, if ever, an *explicit* contract; and how can we infer an *implicit* contract in so complex a case? Locke's answer is that a civil society, when legitimate, is made so by the 'tacit consent' of its citizens, a consent which could be represented, for clarity's sake, in the form of an explicit 'compact' defining the rights and duties of the parties in the manner of a contract at law. Unfortunately, as Hume pointed out in an essay on the 'Original Contract', the metaphor begins to look precarious. For what is the criterion of tacit consent? Locke was prepared to say that a traveller who passes through a country tacitly consents to the civil order there prevailing – otherwise how could he be bound by its laws? This seems counter-intuitive. Even more counter-intuitive, Hume argued, is the suggestion that ordinary people, born into a situation from which they lack the means to escape, have tacitly consented to all the burdens which they inherit.

Locke found less difficulty than we might in postulating a means (namely migration to a 'vacant place') whereby a citizen's consent to the arrangement which surrounds him might, on becoming conscious, also be withdrawn. We now know that there are very few 'vacant places', and hence that there is a great problem in describing what it would be for a single citizen to withdraw his consent from the arrangement which surrounds and (if he is lucky) protects him. But then, *pari passu*, there must be precisely the same problem about making sense of what it is not just to *live* in a political order, but also to consent to it. In which case the metaphor of a social contract becomes fraught with genuine obscurity.

Locke introduced into political thought another highly influential conception, that of the separation of powers. Hobbes's sovereign is the single autonomous fount from which all the actions of the commonwealth take their origin. His powers are legislative, military and domestic at once. Locke argued that, even if such powers are, in practice, exercised together or by a single authority, they are separable in theory, and can be both exercised and justified independently. He went further, arguing that these powers were in fact already separated – at least to some extent – in the constitution of England, and that they *ought* to be separated if that constitution were to command the consent of its subjects. He proposed that the powers which sometimes are, and always ought to be, so separated are the following: the legislative (involving the creation of laws), the executive (involving the execution of those laws and the business of government), and the 'federative' (involving the making of treaties and the waging of war).

The theory of the separation of powers is familiar from the American Constitution, which explicitly acknowledges it as one of its foundations. It was adopted and refined by the eighteenth-century political theorist Charles Baron de Montesquieu (1689–1755), in his *Esprit des lois* (1748), a vivid celebration of principles which he thought to be enacted in the English constitution and which he recommended as the only certain salvation for a society adapted to the complex pursuits of contemporary man. Such a society must combine the strongest possible safeguards of liberty with the greatest internal cohesion, and it was through the separation of powers, Montesquieu argued, that this could be achieved. Such a separation (in Montesquieu's theory, between the executive, the legislative, and the judiciary) guarantees the individual liberty, by ensuring that each power can be curtailed by the others. It also ensures cohesion, through the internal relations between the powers, which make it impossible that any one of them should be exercised without the elaborate co-operation of the other two. Discussion of this intriguing conception has continued unabated to the present day, so much so that it is now very difficult to separate the basic philosophical ideas from the manifold prejudices which have woven themselves into them. Nevertheless it is another of the achievements of Locke's varied genius that he should have discovered the way in which to decompose, so to speak, the Hobbesian conception of sovereignty, and to give to it at least the semblance of a reasoned basis.

The theory of the 'social contract' is perhaps most familiarly associated with the great eccentric Jean-Jacques Rousseau (1712–1778), who threw to the winds the common sense and political sagacity which motivated Hobbes and Locke. He found in the contractual theory of politics, not only a philosophical basis for legitimacy, but also a pretext for his admiration of the 'noble savage' and a political elaboration of his grossly sentimental vision of human nature. Rousseau believed that man is good by nature and made bad only by institutions. (A view which most people hold during their adolescence, and which some continue to hold, with varying degrees of hysteria, as they grow older.) Rousseau extracted from this prejudice an influential philosophy of education (*Émile*, 1762), and a beautiful celebration of romantic love (*La Nouvelle Héloïse*, 1761). He wrote the famous *Social Contract* (1762) under its influence. In this work the contractual basis of society is offered as the only possible excuse for it, and an extreme democracy (as opposed to mere representative government) is advocated as the best way of making sense of Locke's theory of 'tacit consent'. But the book also shows, and to some extent confronts, the paradoxes of extreme democracy. For the theory of the social contract compels Rousseau to favour what many individual participants in it could only regard as tyranny.

In Rousseau's version the contract's terms are very explicit. It involves 'the total alienation of each associate, together with all his rights, to the whole community'. The reason for this is that nobody may, under the terms of such a contract, obtain a personal advantage, so that the only interest in assenting to it must be an interest in the common good. Hence in Rousseau's version the contract creates an association with almost absolute rights over its members. The association thereby created is called, when passive, the 'State' and, when active, the 'Sovereign'. In its active manifestation it has both personality and will. Rousseau calls this will the 'general will'. The details of Rousseau's theory need not here detain us – although we should note the idea, famous in his day, and murderous in the aftermath of revolution which Rousseau's thinking did not a little to precipitate, that he whose will conflicts with the general will must be constrained by the general will, since his own participation in the social contract ensures that thereby he will merely be 'forced to be free'. What is important from the philosophical point of view is the assertion that the general will is not to be thought of as the sum of individual wills. As Rousseau puts it, there is a distinction between the 'general will' and the 'will of all'. The original contract does not merely aggregate the wills of those who subscribe to it: it brings into existence a new order of volition. This 'general will' is a separate entity, attached to the sovereign power, which is itself conceived in personal terms. It was this part of Rousseau's analysis that was to inspire Hegel.

Why should one speak of the state as a person? Hegel in *The Philosophy of Right* (1821) confronts this question directly, and tries to reconcile it with intuitions concerning legitimacy which – while he pays lip-service to the theory of the social contract – are fundamentally anti-contractual. Kant had presented a picture of personality which involved the following features. A person is an agent; he is autonomous; he has will and reason. He also has rights, obligations, and duties, and it is of his nature to be treated as end and not as means, any other treatment being simply a way of denying his personhood. Whether or not he is also of necessity an organism was a question which Kant obscured, by replacing the distinction between animal and rational being by the more obscure (although in the context equally suggestive) distinction between the empirical and the transcendental self. Now it is clear that Hobbes's 'commonwealth' *is* a kind of organism. It is born, it flourishes, it dies. It can be injured and healed, and its parts bear a relation to the whole which could fairly be called organic. (Admittedly, the concept of ' organism' is a deep and difficult one, subject of much philosophical debate from Aristotle to the present day. It would be too distracting at this juncture to do anything more than assume that we intuitively understand it.) What then can be meant by asserting that the commonwealth is also a person?

The Hegelian answer is this: first, the commonwealth has a will of its own, which is shown by the fact that there are acts of state, such as the declaration of war or the passing of a statute, which are the acts of no other person. Secondly, the state has reason. It acts for reasons, and can be persuaded and dissuaded – through constitutional processes – into doing this or that. Thirdly, the state has rights (against its citizens, and against other states). It also has obligations (for example, to provide for the well-being of its members). Fourthly, the state is to be treated not as means only, but as end. Its rights are to be respected, and it is to be regarded with those interpersonal attitudes, ranging from love to resentment, which we reserve for beings which have the nature of ends in themselves.

Note that I have introduced a new conception – that of the state. One of the most important advances in Hegel's political philosophy lies in his distinction between state and civil society and in his attempt to demonstrate that it makes sense to speak of the latter, but not of the former, in contractual terms. In making the distinction Hegel was to some extent influenced by Roman law, which distinguishes the true legal 'person', who has legal rights and obligations, from the various forms of association which arise out of voluntary contractual or quasi-contractual bonds between their members, but achieve no legal personality thereby. (An example of the former: a company – of the latter: an amateur football club.) But the basis of the distinction is much deeper than jurisprudence reveals. I will therefore try to reconstruct it in different terms.

Hegel's politics have their roots in his conception of the individual self. It is a presupposition of all contractarian theories of the state that the rational being in a state of nature has autonomous choice. How else can he enter into a bargain of such a momentous kind ? Hegel denied this autonomy, not because of its historical impossibility, but because of its logical impossibility. He regarded autonomy as a kind of artifact. It is not, and cannot be, given to the subject in a state of nature, but is, rather, acquired by him through that process of dialectical interaction with his kind, a part of which we have already seen in the parable of the master and the slave. In the state of nature the subject exists as pure subject. He has will of a kind, but neither self-consciousness nor the freedom which expresses it. He emerges from this darkness at the end of a struggle (and since the contractarian allows himself an historical myth, so much the more can Hegel, who regarded history as 'the unfolding of the concept'). Only then, in the light of mutuality, when he recognises himself as a social being, bound by a moral law which constrains him to recognise the selfhood of others, and to see them as ends and not as means, does the individual acquire his freedom. By then society already exists. Society could not, therefore, have been based in any contract, since the individual autonomy, without which no contract can be made, presupposes the society which is supposedly formed through it.

The objection is a profound one. It makes clear that political philosophy cannot proceed independently of the philosophy of mind, and that the notion of individual autonomy which is assumed in social contract theory (and which still has its advocates in modern liberalism) may in fact beg all the political questions that it is supposed to answer. But if we accept the Hegelian conception of the subject, what can we say about the concept of legitimacy? Again in Roman spirit, Hegel draws our attention to the concept of piety (*pietas*). This is the ability to recognise and act on obligations which are not the product of individual choice. Such obligations surround the individual at birth, forming his self-consciousness, and invading his freedom, even before he has fully acquired either. These obligations are those of the household. (Hegel refers to the Roman domestic gods, or *penates*.) Disloyalty to the household is disloyalty to self, since it involves the rejection of the force without which freedom, will and reason would be empty gestures in a moral void. Hence it is an essential part of rationality to recognise obligations which are not self-imposed, or 'contracted'. All the arguments for thinking that a rational being must recognise a legitimacy in contractual rights are therefore arguments for saying that he must also recognise legitimacy in something else. It is this 'something else' which it is the business of political philosophy to describe.

Having introduced a concept of legitimacy which transcends individual contract, the way is open for Hegel to expound and defend the conception of the state as an entity, the authority of which transcends anything that might have been conferred on it by 'tacit consent', much as its historical reality transcends the life of any individual subject. This great 'person' clearly has rights that no small person could have (for example, the right to demand the death of an individual citizen). Hegel has reversed, in one stroke, the whole doctrine of the 'natural right', and replaced it by one of 'artificial obligation'. The individual has no natural rights which transcend his obligation to be ruled by the state which has determined his autonomy. This thought may be attacked as a tyrant's charter: Hegel thought that it was not, and he based his rejection of the charge in an account of the nature of individual freedom.

The individual finds his freedom only in the process of self-discovery. This process implicates every institution by which the individual is surrounded. The first of these institutions (both historically and conceptually) is the family. It is one of the important advances of Hegel's political thought that he recognised, what until then had so seldom been acknowledged, that the political being derives his social sense from an arrangement which is private. It is private in the sense of depending on obligations of piety, and these could never have been contracted. (Could I have contracted with my parents that they conceive and nurture me in return for my later love and protection? The very suggestion is nonsense.) The family and its obligations are therefore deeply implicated in the individual's initial rise to freedom. But his freedom cannot be completed in these relations of 'natural piety'. The individual requires a sphere of free action in which he can try out his will against others and achieve a resolution in just relations. This sphere is the sphere of consent, and hence of contract. Hegel calls it 'civil society': it is the nexus of unformed association which surrounds and gives identity to the family. This unformed association can be described in contractual terms, since it has its essence in the mutual recognition of obligations arising out of individual choice.

However, no social contract can fulfil the freedom which it generates. It will always remain vulnerable to the tyranny of individual will, and so can break down at any moment. It adds to the agent only an imperfect sense of the *objective* reality of social order. It is an association of subjects, but not yet an independent objective being. The individual rises to full self-consciousness only in confronting the social object. Only then does he have a conception of the limits of his action. When he perceives these limits, he will see how to express his freedom within them. In short, civil society stands in need of institutions which protect and foster it, and which enshrine the objective reality of the body politic. The sum of these institutions is the state, and if the state is to have the objective reality which individual freedom requires, it must have the status of a person, with rights, obligations, reason and will. Hence the full flourishing of individual freedom is only possible if the individual can 'realise' himself in institutions which circumscribe his rights. What seemed like tyranny is nothing but freedom in its highest, most self-knowing, form.

To give the full philosophical content of those ideas is hard. They become a little clearer if related to the idea of 'self-realisation' described in chapter 12. But it is perhaps worth mentioning the fact that they are not the sum of Hegel's political thought, but rather the framework within which he conducts arguments of great interest and complexity, all designed to overthrow the simplifications of Enlightenment politics. Hegel replaced the theories of 'natural right' and 'social contract' with something more plausible as a description of political reality, less murderous as an ideology, and above all more able to take account of the fact that man is an historical being, who creates himself and his institutions through a continuous process, the legitimacies associated with which can be fully understood only in historical terms.

Among Hegel's arguments there is a complex defence of private property as an indispensable instrument of freedom. The right to property is indeed a genuine right. It is created by institutions which, as it were, instil the world with the relations of ownership, and so make objects into the focal points of rights and obligations. Ownership humanises the world. It makes it intelligible, by imprinting on it the distinctive features of personality. It is a part of the stage-setting for that individual autonomy which is the end of politics. Hegel showed some disposition to be moved by Locke's conception of the 'mixing of labour'. However, this process creates, not property rights, but a kind of self-image in the labourer (a 'Bildung'), and a self-striving of which property is the natural fulfilment. The institution of property thereby becomes integral to the process of politics, even though there may be no 'natural right' to its benefits.

The Philosophy of Right, perhaps the most succinct work of political philosophy ever written, contains many such arguments, and succeeds, if not in answering, at least in asking almost all the important questions of modern political philosophy. It therefore set the stage for the flowering of political interest among philosophers which was to reach early expression in the writings of Karl Marx.

15

MARX

Hegel would have been less influential had he not answered to the spiritual needs of his generation. He offered absolute truth to an age divested of religious faith; his style is at once abstract – and therefore seemingly unpolluted by parochial trivialities – and yet vividly imagistic, descending to the concrete details of politics, art and the moral life with a grace and an air of profundity that have never ceased to be awe-inspiring. The spirit of late romanticism inhabits Hegel's system, and even his most abstruse utterances have a kind of melancholy poignancy. To his contemporaries this characteristic, and the authority that was acquired through it, were most evident in the philosophy of history. This was the part of the Hegelian system which seemed best to explain the peculiar position of the new nineteenth-century man. History had replaced eternity as the key to our salvation, and a philosophy which accorded to history and the human all those dignities which had previously been conferred on the timeless and the divine, recommended itself instinctively to the dis-orientated conscience of the German romantics. The 'Young Hegelians' were philosophers many of whom, like Hegel, had begun their careers in the study of theology. They brought to philosophy all the seriousness of religion, and lost their innocence one by one in the varying ways towards which Hegel enticed them. (Nietzsche was later to characterise the entire post-Kantian philosophy as 'concealed theology', thinking of it as an attempt to keep the religious spirit alive in secular clothing.) Some sought to extend the philosophy of history into areas of thought that had yet to be assimilated into it; others tried to restate it without the religious and metaphysical theories that they found in Hegel. All attempted, in one way or another, to hold on to the new notion of history as a distinctive philosophical idea, while in various ways and to varying degrees abandoning the idealist metaphysics which had created it. The most important philosopher to emerge from this Hegelian aftermath, and perhaps the most influential philosopher of modern times, was Karl Marx (1818–1883), several of whose early works consist in vituperative criticisms of the Young Hegelians to whose circle he at first belonged.

Marx was a man of prodigious intellect, but to a great extent self-educated. As a result of being forced into exile, first in France, and then in England, by his support for revolutionary activity, his works were neither written nor published in the conditions of serenity or intellectual recognition that would have imposed upon them a satisfactory discipline. His masterpiece, *Capital* (vol. 1, 1867), was never completed, and some of his most suggestive and important writings remained unpublished at his death. His deep commitment to the cause of social revolution led him to read and write at length about subjects that would not now be considered philosophical, and his polemical attacks on the philosophy of his day – such as *The Holy Family** and *The Poverty of Philosophy* – often suggest that he would have preferred to be remembered as a social scientist rather than as a philosopher. Nevertheless, so great has his philosophical influence been, and so interesting in themselves are his conceptions, that the underlying philosophy which guided him deserves detailed attention. We find in Marx an attempt to synthesise the German philosophy of human nature – that philosophy of the 'rational agent' which arose from Kant's *Critique of Practical Reason*, and passed through Schiller and Hegel to the minor figures of Marx's student days – with the common sense of the English political economists, to the critique of whose work Marx eventually addressed himself. Out of this mixture of Hegelian philosophy of mind and empiricist economics, to which was added an influential theory of history, arose the school of contemporary thought which we now know as Marxism.

Among Marx's writings, the most important from the philosophical point of view are, first, the Manuscripts of 1844 and the *German Ideology*,

---

* For bibliographical details of these and other texts mentioned, see the bibliography, p. 293.

both of which represent Marx's early use and critique of Hegelianism; secondly the *Preface to a Critique of Political Economy* and the *Grundrisse*, both of which show the increasing dominance of the theory of history; and finally *Capital* (now supplemented by *Theories of Surplus Value*) in which the theory of history is united with an elaborate economics. The seeds of the theory of history were present in the Manuscripts of 1844, but it achieved its final form only after the research into the science of political economy which Marx undertook during his years of exile in England. In addition to these writings there are the more polemical utterances – such as the *Communist Manifesto* (1848) and *The 18th Brumaire of Louis Bonaparte* – some of which were written in conjunction with Marx's lifelong friend and posthumous editor, Friedrich Engels (1820–1895), himself a prolific and influential writer on social, political and philosophical themes.

Marx inherited the familiar Hegelian picture of human destiny: history has a movement that in some way mirrors the development of the human soul. But from the beginning Marx wished to break with the idealist metaphysic in terms of which this vision had been expressed and so, in a famous phrase, to 'set Hegel on his feet'. This desire led him, first, to a metaphysical materialism, and later, in the *Preface* and *Capital*, to a developed scientific theory. The later theory represents the progressive movement of history in terms which do not depend on the favourite Hegelian parallel, between the development of history and the development of consciousness. The best way to make sense of the synthesis of history, economics and philosophy which Marx attempted is to begin from his early work, much of which remained unpublished in his lifetime.

The early Marx

For the young Marx, the Hegelian philosophy of history and Hegelian theory of self-consciousness were inextricable. In the Manuscripts of 1844, Marx wrote that the 'outstanding achievement of Hegel's *Phenomenology* is first, that Hegel grasps the self-creation of man as a process . . . and that he, therefore, grasps the nature of labour, and conceives of objective man (true, because real man) as the result of his *own labour*.' This idea of 'human nature' as an artifact is apt to seem puzzling, especially when detached from the great 'drama of the spirit' which idealist philosophy had presented.

Hegel had spoken in terms of the necessary development of spirit towards the idea. While it is true that this spirit and this 'idea' were abstract things, and not to be confused with any individual consciousness, nevertheless it is impossible to conceive them in other than spiritual terms. Marx's lifework consisted in the attempt to overcome the intellectual difficulties that stood in the way of expressing Hegel's vision 'materialistically' (Marx's philosophy was later to be called 'dialectical materialism'). Initial encouragement in this task came from the work of Ludwig Feuerbach (1804–1872), a Young Hegelian whose sophisticated iconoclasm was later to recommend him (through his translator, George Eliot) to a generation of sceptical and anti-authoritarian Englishmen. Feuerbach, Marx wrote, 'founded genuine materialism and positive science by making the social relationship of "man to man" the basic principle of his theory.' This social relationship Feuerbach called the 'species-life' of man (*The Essence of Christianity*, 1841). Only man has species-life, since only man *finds* his nature, through the recognition of himself as a social, and therefore socially determined, being. It is this conception of 'species-life' (*Gattungswesen*) that created a materialist version of Hegel's philosophy of man.

The theory of self-consciousness emerges in Marx in the following form: the self has three stages, or 'moments'. (Marx makes it explicit that these 'moments' are not to be construed as historically sequential.) These are the stages, first, of primitive self-awareness, of man immersed in his 'species-life'; secondly, of self-alienation, or alienation from species-life; and thirdly, of self-realisation, or fulfilment in free creative activity. As in Hegel, the theory is profoundly anti-individualistic: at every stage, the self is constituted only through its social activities, in which lies its essence. Marx wished to argue that the social essence was also, as it was for Feuerbach, a material and not a spiritual reality. He did not regard this social essence as residing in any Hegelian 'idea', or spiritual substance. It lies rather in the collective activity which Marx was to identify as 'labour'. It is this 'labour' which generates the language, customs, and institutions – in particular the economic institutions – through which consciousness arises.

Corresponding to the three 'moments' of human consciousness, are the three stages of history, each manifesting a specific stance of man towards his world. These stages of history are constituted by the forms which social activities take. Now it is only in labour that man transforms the world and so defines himself in relation to it. Already, therefore, in his early philosophy, before he had developed his critique of political economy, Marx wished to describe the movement of history in economic terms. The first historical stage – that of natural man – is one in which nature dominates man, and the institutions of property, through which nature becomes an *object* for man, have not been developed. During the second stage, with the flourishing of private property, the separation between man and nature becomes dominant. But dominant along with it is the separation of man from man. Private property (which generates the institutions of exchange and therefore the mode of production which we know as capitalism) is the institution through which man's self-alienation finds expression. This stage is due to be replaced by communism, in which man's mastery of nature is so complete that the institution of private property, and the consequent separation of man from man, are transcended. Man will then be realised, free, in command of nature, and at one with his 'species-life'.

Marx was later to detach the theory of history from the philosophy of mind. It is nevertheless true that his attempt to give a material basis to the 'dialectic' of self-discovery retained, even in its later version, the marks of the 'drama of subject and object' which had been scripted by Fichte. And its moral significance resides in the concept which came to him from Fichte via Hegel – the concept of alienation. It is Marx's treatment of 'alienated labour' that has been at the origin of much of the more recent philosophical interest in his writings.

According to Marx there is some kind of 'internal' relation between alienation and the institution of private property. In order to illustrate Marx's meaning, it is necessary to understand what 'liberal' economists had attempted. Such economists were less interested in the 'natural' right which, according to Locke, underlies the institution of property, than in the 'contractual' rights which stem from it. That is, they were interested in the movement of property under the laws of contract and exchange. Adam Smith, in his famous essay *The Wealth of Nations* (1776), had summed up a century of liberal and empiricist thought by attempting to demonstrate that the free exchange and accumulation of private property under the guidance of self-interest not only preserves justice, but also promotes the social well-being as a whole, satisfying existing needs and guaranteeing stability.

In order to establish that conclusion, Smith considers human nature to be something settled. The *homo economicus* of liberal theory is not thought of as a historical being. However, he is motivated by desires and satisfactions which, while represented as permanent features of the human condition, may in fact be no more than peculiarities of the eighteenth-century market economy, which is in turn to be explained by something deeper than the operation of economic laws. If the nature of man is not fixed, we must see obedience to these economic laws as neither ineluctable nor necessarily advantageous. Marx wished to argue that the laws of liberal economics, while they may govern the movement of property, represent the institution of property as permanent. Hence they discourage an examination of other arrangements in which property, and the alienation that stems from it, might disappear. In these other circumstances the rewards and fulfilments of human nature will also change. And if alienation is overcome, they will change for the better. It could be said that there is something objectionable in this idea: namely, that it represents the nature of man as self-created, and yet also argues that there is a state of man 'restored to himself' which has some kind of supreme and distinctive value. In other words it seems both to reject and to accept the idea of a permanent human 'essence'. Nevertheless, it is undeniable that the charge levelled against liberal economic theory demands an answer. No theory of economic activity can make sense without a philosophy of human nature.

Marx argues that the institution of private property only *seems* to create that freedom of movement and expression, that power over nature, which the liberal economists had ascribed to it. In fact it creates a deeper form of subjection. In his attachment to property man is 'self-alienated'. The institution and the state of mind are related not as cause and effect, but inherently. What exists objectively as features of ownership, is felt subjectively as the alienation of the individual from himself and his species-life.

What is meant, in this context, by self-alienation? Historically speaking the origin of the idea is not difficult to trace; similar observations can be found in Aristotle's critique of the mercantile way of life, in Christian doctrines of the destructive nature of worldly attachments, and in the medieval attacks on usury. But for the purpose of philosophical evaluation it is necessary to detach Marx's conception from all but two of its antecedents.

The first is the concept of the 'fetish', introduced into Enlightenment thought by De Brosses (*Du culte des dieux fétiches*, 1760), and given philosophical content by Kant in his incidental discussions of the philosophy of religion. Kant argued that there is a distinction between genuine religious thought, which aims at the understanding of God, of the self and of the true relation between them, and spurious religious thought – or 'fetishism' – which involves the outward projection onto the world of principles which represent only subjective characteristics of the idolator, and therefore serve to instil his world with mystery. Fetishism obscures the subject's relation to the world, absorbing his human life into the vain worship of objects, and cutting him off from the true under-standing of himself, as an autonomous being in intrinsic relation to others of his kind and to a transcendent God. Fetishism does not make the transcendent personhood of God immanent in the world. It endows the world with a false aura of immanence, painting phenomena in the subjective colours of a finite will. It therefore creates an impassable barrier between the self and God.

The term 'alienation' (*Entfremdung*) became attached to that of fetishism, in something like the following way. Hegel argued that the religious spirit is a spirit which, because it sees itself detached from and in opposition to the sphere of perfection, is a spirit in self-alienation, essentially unhappy in the consciousness that it is not what it is naturally destined to be. (It is 'fallen', as the Christian doctrine puts it.) This applies not only to the Kantian fetishism but also to any religion, in so far as religion reflects man's sense of his own imperfection, of his absolute solitude in the world of creation, and of his dependence on a being that lies beyond the sphere of objective knowledge. In a bold step that had an immediate *succès de scandale*, Feuerbach argued that this alienated character in religion is simply proof that all religion is nothing *more* than fetishism. Christianity itself is a species of self-projection. Men project out of themselves, and make into properties of a divine being, the perfections which are really theirs. These perfections have no objective reality outside man's social life, but there they can have real existence. In removing his perfections from himself, and installing them in a transcendent world, man makes his own perfection seem unobtainable, since it now lies outside the sphere of his social action. Hence he becomes estranged from his own nature, and conscious of himself as an incomplete and limited being. Religion alienates man from the 'species-life' in which his perfec-tion is possible, and hence from himself as constituted by that life.

The Marxist theory of alienation can only be understood if we also add to it a second Kantian idea, one with which we are already familiar. According to one formulation of the Kantian categorical imperative, a rational being is constrained to treat all others of his kind as ends and never as means only. We have seen, in Hegel, the attempt to found this imperative in an analysis of lordship and bondage as necessary 'moments' in the self-consciousness of a rational being. To the extent that a man treats another as a means, so does he become a means to himself. In exploiting the other he exploits himself, losing his freedom in a form of subservience all the greater for his inability to recognise it as such. It is this theory that lends support to Marx's contention that alienation, being a form of isolation from social life, is *experienced* as alienation from self.

We might put the developed forms of the two original ideas thus:

1 A man is an object for himself to the extent that he invests objects with human powers, and so ceases to see those powers as having their origin in himself.
2 A man becomes an object for himself to the extent that others are objects for him (where X is an object for Y = X is only a means for Y).

The combination of 1 and 2 is the state of self-alienation. The true realisation of oneself as subject requires and is required by two things: first, the recognition of others as ends, and secondly the rediscovery through social life of one's actual human potential. But any lapse into self-alienation must also precipitate an alienation from species-life, and vice versa.

The difficult philosophical claim, never properly established by Marx, and in itself contentious, is that this state of alienation is directly connected with the institution of property. Marx hoped to make the connection in the following way. Under the rule of private property, objects become the focus of individual rights, and thus take on the character of human life. There is a sense in which, through the institution of property, we endow objects with a soul. Since the only origin of this soul must be in us, it follows that there is an element of systematic 'fetishism' in the process. This fetishism develops as property develops from use-value (which is intelligibly related to human need) to exchange-value, in which the commodity begins to acquire life and autonomy of its own. With the arrival of pure exchange-value in the form of money, the transformation of objects into fetishes is complete; and with this transformation – effected only under the rule of the free market, which is itself the consummation of property relations – we have the establishment of capitalism. Under capitalism it is not only objects, but also men, who are bought and sold. And in this buying and selling, under the regime of which one party has nothing to dispose of but his labour power, we reach the ultimate point in the treatment of men as means. Men have become objects for each other, and whatever remnants of their human (social) life remain will be dissipated, being projected outwards onto the world of commodities. To summarise all this in Marx's colourful 'Young Hegelian' style:

> Money is the universal, self-constituted value of all things. Hence it has robbed the whole world, the human world as well as nature, of its proper value. Money is the alienated essence of man's labour and life, and this alien essence dominates him as he worships it ('On the Jewish Question').

The later Marx

We have already moved closer to the reformulation of Marx's philosophical critique of the institutions of private property. This reformulation attempted to separate the theory of history from the theory of human nature and endow both with the scientific character suggested by their 'materialist' pretensions. The aim is to give substance to the claim, made in *The German Ideology*, that 'consciousness does not determine life, but life determines consciousness'. Hence Marx wishes to give a systematic theory which will both explain, and in explaining undermine, the illusions which uphold the moral and political order of capitalism.

In his later writings Marx made little use of the concept of alienation, and, although the theory of fetishism was to survive in *Capital* (in the ideas of commodity and capital fetishism), the immediate connection with what one might call the 'unhappy consciousness' was broken. The term now becomes part of a scientific theory which ostensibly disdains all reference to the happiness or misery with which economic relations are experienced by those who participate in them. That experience is criticised not as happy or unhappy, but as true or false. The concept of alienation gives way to that of 'false consciousness', a false consciousness being one that makes, not particular errors of judgement, but universal errors in its perception of the social world. The burden of Marx's critique of capitalism comes to rest on an ingenious and scientifically phrased theory of exploitation. This theory only tangentially makes contact with observations as to how the state of man under capitalism is experienced. False consciousness may not be a form of unhappiness: but its evil lies in the fact that it inevitably endorses exploitation, through its inability to perceive the exploitation that is there.

Part of the reason for this shift of emphasis was the important insight that Marx was able to obtain into the theory of history, once he had replaced the Hegelian representation of its movement by a theory that was more scientifically inspired. This new theory of history, in a version due partly to Friedrich Engels, has been called 'dialectical materialism' (by G. V. Plekhanov (1856–1918), one of the founding fathers of Russian Marxism). It is unclear whether the word 'dialectical' is correctly used to describe it: for this seems to imply that Marx, like Hegel, believed that history proceeds by the successive resolution of 'contradictions'. What is undisputed, however, is that the theory is a form of 'materialism'. Hegel had seen history as the development of consciousness. Marx argued that the fundamental things that develop, and so bring about the movement of history, are not features of consciousness at all, but 'material' forces. The development of consciousness is to be explained in terms of the material reality, and does not explain it. Thus, in the famous phrase of Engels (*Ludwig Feuerbach and the End of Classical German Philosophy*) quoted above, Marx's theory of history 'sets Hegel on his feet'. Moreover, the theory was held to validate, as a prediction, the original view that capitalism would be superseded by a more humane social arrangement. Having faith in this prediction, it seemed less important to Marx to provide a description of man's unhappiness. For it is redundant to give reasons for bringing about what is inevitable.

The theory of history begins from the distinction between 'base' and 'superstructure'. Marxist philosophers who have wished to hold on to the Hegelian antecedents of the theory (for example, George Lukács and certain philosophers of the so-called 'Frankfurt School') have criticised or underplayed this distinction, believing that a truly *philosophical* Marxism must found itself, like the theory of alienation, in an understanding of human consciousness. The purpose of Marx's distinction, on the other hand, was to show human consciousness as an offshoot of a deeper social and economic reality. Consciousness is something to be explained, in terms that may not be recognisable to the conscious being himself. One may say that, in moving to the scientific theory of history, Marx also takes a step from the first-person to the third-person point of view, a step which inevitably takes him away from the standpoint of the agent, towards that of the observer.

The base of all human institutions is that upon which the forms of consciousness are built, and in terms of which institutions (and the consciousness which derives from them) are to be explained. This base consists, for Marx, in two parts: first, a system of economic relations, secondly, certain active 'productive forces'. The existence of any particular system of economic relations is explained in terms of the level of development of the productive forces. These forces consist of labour power, and accumulated knowledge. As man's mastery over nature increases, the productive forces will inevitably develop. At each level of development a particular system of economic relations will be most suited to contain and facilitate their operation. Hence we can explain, rather in the manner of Darwin (with whose theory of evolution early Marxists compared the theory of Marx), the existence of any given economic system in terms of its suitability to the productive forces which, were they at a different stage of development, would either not require, or else actively destroy it.

Upon the system of economic relations rises the superstructure of legal and political institutions. These serve to consolidate and protect the economic base, and are therefore similarly explicable in terms of their sustaining and protective function. Finally, the political institutions generate their own peculiar 'ideology'. This is the system of beliefs, perceptions, values and prejudices, which together consolidate the entire structure, and serve both to conceal the changeability, and to dignify the actuality, of each particular arrangement.

There are roughly five economic arrangements: primitive communism, slavery, feudalism, capitalism and communism. The last is distinguished by the fact that the necessity for a legal, political and ideological superstructure now vanishes, and the state, together with all its apparatus and the 'false consciousness' which surrounds it, finally withers away. Under communism, men live in a state of unmediated fellowship, on equal terms, neither exploited nor exploiting in a world where each gives according to his ability and each takes according to his need. This state of communism Marx saw as inevitable, simply because productive forces were bound to develop beyond the point where capitalism could contain them. Having developed to that point, the 'fetter' of capitalism is broken asunder, and communism, which is the only economic arrangement suitable to the enormous level of development which will by then have been achieved, must necessarily come in place of it. This transition, however, will be impossible without a violent revolution, such as had supposedly attended the transition from feudalism to bourgeois mercantilism in eighteenth-century France.

In the course of developing this theory, Marx provided various elaborate descriptions of the capitalist and feudal arrangements. He tried to show the essential differences between them, and the precise way in which they generate contrasting systems of law. His investigations led him towards the vexed problems of political economy, in particular the problems of value (or price). Nothing can have value except in relation to human activity. Use-values can be explained simply as the relations which hold between objects and the needs which they satisfy. But what about exchange-value? What accounts for the fact that a particular commodity exchanges at the particular price that it commands? Secondly, how does surplus-value arise, in other words, how is it that a particular person (the capitalist) is able to *accumulate* exchange-value through the operation of the market?

In order to explain the two features of exchange- and surplus-value (which he believed to be mutually dependent, and together definitive of capitalism) Marx took over from the political economist David Ricardo (1772–1823) the so-called 'labour theory of value'. This explains the exchange-value of a commodity in terms of the socially necessary hours of labour required to produce or reproduce it. The accumulation of surplus is then explained in terms of the extortion of labour from the labourer, by exchanging his means of subsistence (which serves to reproduce his labour power and is therefore the true 'price' of labour) for hours of labour in excess of those needed to produce those means. Marx was thus led to a theory of exploitation. It seems that the production of surplus-value must necessarily proceed through the extraction of hours of unpaid labour. Hence capitalistic relations are necessarily exploitative.

It might seem, in retrospect, that there is little in common to the various philosophies associated with the name of Marx. In fact, however, the three aspects mentioned – the philosophy of man, the theory of history and the conception of value – can be seen as separate attempts to articulate an abiding intuition. Whether we consider the nature of man, the move-ment of history or the structure of economic values, we are studying, if

Marx is right, a single basic thing. This thing is not consciousness; it is what creates and determines consciousness. It is material, since its essence lies in the transformation of nature; it is also social, in that it exists in the relations between men. In describing this all-important thing as 'labour' Marx sought to return to the heart of political philosophy the concept which describes the condition not of the sovereign, the clerk, the lawyer or the property owner, but of the common person whose activity supports the 'superstructure' upon which they feed. Labour is the human essence, and the driving force of history. It is labour which appears in the fictive forms of market value. And it is labour which can be alienated from and restored to itself, determining thereby the happiness and misery of mankind.

Such a synthetic picture is attractive, but its parts are logically independent. Moreover they are far from uniformly persuasive. It has often been pointed out that both the labour theory of value and the theory of history have serious flaws. The first purports to explain something which it does not in fact explain; the second makes predictions which have turned out to be false. But enough of the theory of history remains to render its image persuasive. There is something almost irresistible in the idea of a social 'superstructure' propelled and destroyed by the movement of an economic 'base'. Many who find themselves unable to accept the details of the theory are still driven to find the movement of history else-where than in the movement of human consciousness. With this outlook has come the 'third personal' approach to political action. This approach sees 'ideology', 'false consciousness' and economic determination where the agent himself finds values, sanctions, laws and the stuff of social life. It is paradoxical that this withdrawal from human affairs should arise from a philosophy which brought to its culmination the theory of the Kantian subject, and which attempted, in its earlier stages, to make sense of the condition of modern man in ways which would both remain in touch with his actual experience, and yet be respectful of his reality as part of the material world.

Marx's *philosophy* recognised as the basis of all political thought the intuition that man is both object and subject for himself. From this intuition came the doctrine of 'praxis', according to which theory and practice must be one. The only theory that will remove the mystery from human things is the theory which can be incorporated into the practical reasoning of the agent. But this philosophy, in borrowing the credentials of science, finds itself renouncing the viewpoint which makes it intelligible, creating a barrier between theory and practice that has come to seem impassable. The attempt to show the social reality behind the tissue of human illusion 'demystifies' consciousness. Almost inevitably, therefore, it ends by removing the values which are the sole stimulus to social action, and so generates a new mystery of its own.

16

UTILITARIANISM AND AFTER

Marx's philosophy is of lasting value, largely because of its attempt to reconcile the Hegelian vision of consciousness with an empiricist political economy. There emerged from this attempt a distinctive view of human nature which has been transformed and adopted by many who would regard the quest for a theory of history as a delusion, and who would scorn the study of political economy as pseudo-science.

The emergence of Marxism from political economy partly coincided with that of another school of thought, deeply rooted in the traditions of empiricism. This school is memorable, if at all, not for a theory of human nature, but for its attempt to describe the whole of morals and politics without one. Utilitarianism represents the will of the eighteenth century to survive into the nineteenth, and the determination of empiricism to resist for as long as possible the attempt to represent the peculiarities of the modern spirit. When this modern spirit finally prevailed, it was with the weapons of an intransigent scepticism. These weapons, devastating in the hands of Bradley and the English idealists, were soon to be turned against idealism itself, and indeed against every form of constructive metaphysics, leaving that desert-land of philosophical agnosticism, over which the logical positivists briefly ruled in empty triumph. In this chapter I shall not discuss all the aspects of the renewed struggle between empiricism and idealism. However, no history can give a picture of nineteenth-century philosophy without discussing the transference of this struggle into the spheres of ethics and politics.

Hume, in a famous essay, dismissed the idea of the social contract as a superstition, and, suggested that there could be no criterion of legitimacy in the public realm other than utility. It was a reading of this that inspired Jeremy Bentham (1748–1832) to write his *Fragment on Government* (1776), a piece which attempts to introduce common sense and scientific method into the discussion of the affairs of state. At the same time Adam Smith, a philosopher deeply influenced by the moral psychology of the British empiricists, wrote his *Wealth of Nations*. This is the treatise which laid the theoretical foundations for laissez-faire capitalism, arguing that self-interest, within the confines of a constitutional government, must inevitably adjust the balance of politics; in acting for his own good, a man would act automatically for the good of the whole. Smith's subtle work was the pioneer study in political economy, and provided for Dr Johnson's remark that a man is never so harmlessly engaged as when making money, a philosophical support that fitted it for the optimistic and progressive spirit of the trading years.

Bentham translated this optimism into the language of moral philosophy, losing, in the process, most of the moral and philosophical insights for which British empiricism is remembered. Adam Smith had shared those insights, and wrote with delicacy and tact on moral and political issues. He therefore produced no new system, expressing his cheerfulness of outlook in reflections about matters which, because they were so new, lay outside the accepted purview of philosophy. These matters awaited the work of later philosophers – and in particular of Marx – to become the subject of philosophical examination.

It was therefore through Bentham that the optimistic spirit found its philosophical expression. Bentham's outlook in all matters was one of 'radical reform'. The resistance to the ethos of reform had expressed itself in the work of Edmund Burke (1729–1797), another philosopher whose roots were in eighteenth-century moral psychology. But Burke's high-minded literary allusions to the complexity of human things proved unsatisfying in the age of the political amateur and the merchant moralist. A system was needed, and Bentham provided that system, giving expected answers to predictable questions, in terms of intelligible profit and loss. Trained as a lawyer, he had an acute eye for the law, together with a vision both narrow enough to focus his imagination on its details and simple enough to cast the same light on each of them. His *Introduction to the Principles of Morals and Legislation* (1789) has the singular merit of deriving a philosophy of radical legal reform from a theory which also seemed applicable to morals. Thus he resolved the difficult question of the relation between law and morality to the satisfaction of many at a time when the law, and the institutions which it upheld, were the subject of repeated moral critique.

Bentham's premise was simple, namely psychological hedonism. Men seek pleasure and avoid pain, and that is the single moral fact.

> Nature has placed mankind under the governance of two sovereign masters, *pain* and *pleasure*. . . . They govern us in all we do, in all we say, in all we think: every effort we can make to throw off our subjection will serve but to demonstrate and confirm it. In words a man may pretend to abjure their empire, but in reality he will remain subject to it all the while.

This observation Bentham at once transformed into a principle, saying that it is for pleasure and pain alone 'to point out what we ought to do, as well as to determine what we shall do'. From this it is but a small step to the famous 'principle of utility', which states that 'the greatest happiness of all those whose interest is in question', is 'the only right and proper and universally desirable end of human conduct'. Bentham makes no distinction between happiness and pleasure, expressly dismissing, as metaphysical obfuscation, those philosophies, such as Aristotle's, in terms of which such a distinction had been made.

The principle of utility had of course been stated before – for example by Hutcheson. Bentham's novelty consists in his faith in the *ultimate* nature of the principle. There is no further fact – such as conscience, or moral sentiment or the moral law – which justifies or requires the principle. On the contrary, anyone who appeals to such a further fact must answer the question 'Why does that settle the issue?' And nothing can provide the answer, save the principle of utility itself.

The great apparent advantage of the principle is that it enables ethics to be conceived in quantitative terms. We can envisage units of pleasure and pain (to be evaluated in terms of intensity, duration, certainty, propinquity and so on) whereby to measure one course of action against another. Bentham (following the earlier, less devoted, example of Hutcheson) conceived of a 'felicific' calculus, which would settle all statable questions of right and wrong. Provided pleasures and pains are thought of as bearing only a quantitative, but not a qualitative, relation to each other (that is, provided the principal aim and subject matter of ethics is forgotten), then it is possible to envisage a solution to all moral problems.

The method extends automatically into politics. In fact there are reasons for thinking that politics is its natural home. But it at once gives rise to the philosophical problem for the discussion of which the nineteenth-century utilitarians acquired that part of their reputation which is genuinely deserved: the problem of political freedom. For if the right thing to do is that which maximises human pleasure, we must know how to summate the pleasures of individuals. And there is no *a priori* reason for thinking that the entire pleasure of one individual might not be usefully sacrificed for the greater benefit of the whole.

It is the problem raised by this last thought which occupied John Stuart Mill (1806–1873) in his most significant works of moral theory: *Utilitarianism* (1861), *On Liberty* (1859), and those parts of the earlier *System of Logic* (1843) (a work of considerable ingenuity and power) which deal with ethics and politics. J. S. Mill's father, James, was an ardent disciple of Bentham and particularly anxious to incorporate the new-found utilitarian principles into a satisfactory theory of political economy. The interest in these matters was bequeathed to his son (along with certain emotional disabilities vividly recorded in the latter's *Autobiography* (1873)). But Mill reacted against the influence of Bentham, and attempted to remedy the evident defect of the principle of utility, which is that it is founded in no theory of human nature that could distinguish people from pigs. This seems absurd, since it is only *some* creatures who are moral agents or who are treated as such. We ought therefore to present a moral theory that will be answerable to the distinguishing characteristics of the moral agent. To put it bluntly, the concept upon which all the great moral theories from Plato to Kant had been founded, the concept of the rational agent or person, had dropped out of utilitarian philosophy altogether, not because it had been examined and found wanting, but because it had not been examined.

Mill, like his predecessors, came to philosophy from an interest in political economy, in which subject he had been profoundly influenced by Adam Smith. His encounter with the writings of the French socialist Saint-Simon (1760–1825), caused him, however, to introduce qualifications into the ideology of laissez-faire, and indeed to end life (as he had begun it) on a square of self-contradiction in political matters which his vehement style barely served to conceal. In ethics, too, his outlook was contradictory. He had absorbed something of the romantic anti-utilitarianism of Coleridge and Carlyle, but showed little understanding of the German philosophy which had created it. He felt strong upsurges of rebellion against the flatness and philistinism of the Benthamites, but he did little to undermine its philosophical basis. In the end *Utilitarianism* and *On Liberty* – which, like all his moral works, hide intense intellectual conflict behind a mask of superficial clarity – are expressions of an inauthenticity of outlook, which is worth our attention now partly because of the vast numbers of people who have been tempted to share in it.

Like Bentham, Mill did not clearly distinguish pleasure from happiness, and he affirmed the 'greatest happiness' principle in terms which would have been largely acceptable to his predecessor. He attempted, however, to provide an independent argument for it, based on the concept of desirability. Happiness, he said, is not just desired, but desirable, and what could be greater proof of this than the fact that men desire it? Not much of an advance, you might think; but at least the argument has the merit of introducing into the discussion a concept which is peculiar to the mental life of rational beings – the concept of the desirable.

Again, in his discussion of happiness or pleasure, Mill introduces a covert reference to a distinguishing feature of rationality. He argues that there are qualitative differences between pleasures. Thus Mill is led to reject the purely quantitative approach of the 'felicific calculus'. He fails to notice however that this amendment removes all authority from the philosophy which he uses it to endorse. For what is the standard of 'quality' in pleasure? What tells us that the pleasure of love is more valuable than the pleasure of carnal desire? We seem to have invoked another criterion of value which, because it makes the principle of utility applicable, is presupposed in that principle, and so not provable from it.

The argument continues in this vein, introducing all the objections to utilitarianism through spurious refutations. One objection in particular springs out at the reader. The principle of the greatest happiness, fine though it may be as an ideal, does not identify a motive. Why, we may ask, should a rational being be led to obey it? Mill, like Bentham, was driven to believe that there is a principle in human nature – the old empiricist principle of benevolence or sympathy – which automatically provides the missing motive. (Bentham was sufficiently impressed by the associationist psychology of the eighteenth century to try to develop a theory of this benevolent motive.) But consider the following case. A tribe observes strict laws of religious devotion, and imposes strict penalties for sacrilege. This practice has a utilitarian justification: it sustains the cohesion of the tribe and so protects it from its foes and predators. But the utilitarian justification, which may be furnished with the most elaborate theories by some observing anthropologist, is not, and could not be, the motive for the religious act. A member of the tribe who engages in religious ceremony in order to sustain social cohesion has lost the sense of religion. In his heart, he is already alienated from the social organism which he seeks to uphold. A wise anthropologist might, in such circumstances, refrain from revealing the utilitarian reasons that underlie the natives' practice, for fear of doing irreparable harm.

Here we see that the utilitarian justification of an action may be *insepa-rable* from a third-person viewpoint. It cannot be made part of the 'first-person' outlook which generates action. It will not, then, be a reason for the agent to do what he does, but only an endorsement of his action in the eyes of an observer. Mill had some inkling of this when he argued that happiness is most rarely arrived at when it is most directly pursued, but he did not see its consequence, which is that, by the principle of utility, the principle of utility must often be concealed from the agent. In which case the agent requires some other source of his values. The fault here lies in the loss of that first-person standpoint which, as the Kantian philosophy makes clear, is the premise of moral thinking.

It is in addressing himself to the problem of political freedom that Mill wrote his most influential and in some ways most impressive work – the little tract *On Liberty*. Elaborating the issue already discussed by Bentham, he argued that the problem of political freedom could be resolved once the matter is seen negatively, in terms of the restraints that can legitimately be placed on the individual. Since happiness lies in the satisfaction of desire, then political liberty, if it is to be a value in accordance with the principle of utility, must consist in the liberty to satisfy desires. However, one person may desire to do something which impedes the satisfaction of the desires of another. What principle should be invoked in legislating between them? Or should there be no principle; only the struggle of nature for dominion?

It seemed to Mill that there ought to be constraint, but that it could not be founded merely on the principle of utility: for that would lead to no settled law, and no civil allegiance to the established order. Each person might differ in his opinion as to which satisfaction would be the greater or most beneficial in the long run. Hence, Mill argued, we need a more straightforward criterion. He therefore proposed the criterion of harm. According to this, a person is at liberty to pursue whichever of his desires causes no harm to his fellow human beings. Mill recognised that there are difficulties in defining what is meant by harm, and in his exposition of the concept he exercised his usual talent for dogmatic self-contradiction. But in some ways this self-contradiction is generic to the 'negative' concept of political freedom, as it has come to be known. Many of the things that we wish the law to forbid harm us, not physically, but morally. And in these cases our being harmed and our wishing for legal constraint are not two phenomena but one. We are 'harmed' in this sense by the spectacle of offensive pornography, by indecent exposure, by insulting gestures. The concept of harm begins to bring with it precisely that reference to shared moral intuitions which the idea of utility and the negative concept of freedom were designed to replace.

Despite such difficulties, Mill's theory of liberty has survived in essence to our own day. His influence passed through Sidgwick and Herbert Spencer to provide what has become liberal orthodoxy in jurisprudence. Mill himself was attached to it because of an ideal of self-development. This ideal was suited to the progressive and individualistic spirit of the age, but not obviously compatible with the classical principles of utilitarianism. However liberty is to be curtailed, it also has, for Mill, a positive content. This positive freedom consists in the ability to exercise and extend one's desires, to conduct those 'experiments in living' without which human progress will be abridged or impeded, to fulfil one's nature through gestures which reflect fundamental choices that are the responsibility of the individual alone. It should be noted that, neither in describing its containment, nor in gesturing towards its positive reward, is Mill referring to 'freedom' in any sense other than the political. His discussion proceeds, as it should proceed, independently of that metaphysical issue of free-will, which asks not about the nature of individual fulfilment and social constraint, but about the metaphysical status of those actions and omissions which we recognise as free.

It is in this theory of positive freedom that Mill's naivety about human nature is most apparent. Although at one point he makes a hesitant reference to the desires that a person 'makes his own', in distinction from those towards which his attitude is reserved, he has no theory which will distinguish the two, or justify our common belief that the one, but not the other, is worthy of satisfaction. When Hegelians and Marxists distinguished the true from the alienated desire, they meant to separate those desires in which a person's self or personhood finds expression, from those which overwhelm him and constitute themselves as independent forces. Some desires force the self from its sovereign place as subject, and reduce it to the status of an object, victim of a passivity which could in certain circumstances destroy its fulfilment altogether. Mill lost sight of such ideas, having no philosophy of mind that would enable him to describe the human person as a mediator or arbitrator among his own desires. As a result his 'free development of the individual' sometimes seems little different from individual anarchy – that is, from the submergence of the personality in whatever impulse might be ready to assume command of it. Such an ideal is not merely repellent. It is not an ideal of *freedom* at all. Ibsen wrote to Mill's Norwegian translator of the 'sagelike philistinism' of the utilitarian gospel, adding that 'when I remember that there are authors who write philosophy without knowing Hegel ... many things seem permissible'. Certainly, a sympathy for Hegel might have provided some corrective to Mill's underlying conception of the human spirit.

Those difficulties were apparent to the literati among Mill's contemporaries, and Matthew Arnold's *Culture and Anarchy* (1869) had already alerted Victorian readers to the preposterousness of utilitarianism and the theories of freedom which it had engendered. But the anti-utilitarians lacked the rival philosophy with which to undermine the empiricist presuppositions of Mill's thought. Mill possessed an atomistic picture of the human agent, according to which the mind is in some way constituted from individual desires, beliefs and sensations. As long as this picture was the received philosophy, the task of providing an anti-utilitarian account of the moral life seemed impossible. It was not until the late nineteenth century that there began to emerge in Britain the school of philosophical idealists who sought to undermine the outlook of utilitarianism, by replacing its wholly inadequate philosophy of mind.

British idealism began, like the empiricist philosophy it sought to replace, from intuitions concerning the nature of mind, morality, and the political realm. The first advocate of this idealism was the Oxford philosopher T. H. Green (1836–1882), who reacted strongly against the failure of his contemporaries to take account of Kant's attack on the metaphysical foundations of empiricism. There could, Green thought, be no serious moral or political philosophy that expressed itself in empiricist terms. He himself attempted to revive the Hegelian conception of the state. For Green the state was not means but end, the citizen's allegiance being irreducible either to utility or to any fulfilment that could be described in individual terms. (It is interesting to note that Kant's own ideas on politics read now much more like a premonition of Mill's than of those views which were ostensibly Kantian in inspiration. Mill would certainly have found little to disagree with in this: 'a constitution allowing the *greatest possible human freedom* in accordance with laws by which *the freedom of each is made to be consistent with that of all others* – I do not speak of the greatest happiness, for this will follow of itself – is ... a necessary idea, which must be taken as fundamental not only in first projecting a constitution but in all its laws' (Kant, *Critique of Pure Reason*, B.373).)

In retrospect it is perhaps not unjust to treat T. H. Green as a gifted but wayward harbinger of his far greater successor among the Oxford idealists, F. H. Bradley (1846–1924). Bradley developed to the full a polemical scepticism and a metaphysical daring which he first exercised against the philosophy of man underlying the utilitarianism of Mill. He embodied his criticisms in a series of related essays published in 1876 as *Ethical Studies*. Written with vigour and passion, and in a style that T. S. Eliot later praised as a model of English prose, this short work was directed against the theories, the methods and, above all, the self-image of utilitarianism. Behind all utilitarian theory, and all the conceptions of liberty and 'free development' with which it had embellished itself, Bradley discerned the same, in his view pernicious, myth. According to this myth, the individual springs into existence fully armed with needs, desires and appetites; he encounters the world as though it were a neutral independent object from which to wrest the satisfactions which he already craves. The satisfaction of the community is simply the sum of the satisfactions of the individuals, while the satisfaction of the individual consists in the satisfaction of the sum of his desires. The whole philosophy, however, is founded on a mistake. This is the mistake of supposing that the individual exists antecedently to the social arrangements and social constraints which make his activity possible.

For metaphysical reasons, Bradley was later to cast the whole concept of the 'self' in serious doubt. At this stage, he was content to point to the fact that, as he saw it, the self, and the moral choice through which it finds expression, is an artifact. Its freedom is not some absolute given, in terms of which the limits of social interference can be drawn; nor is its happiness to be understood atomistically, in terms of the satisfaction of this, that, or however many desires. The individual is as much created by the social arrangement as constrained by it, and the freedom of choice which is the condition of his values is the outcome of a process of elaborate social education. Moreover, the happiness of the individual is not to be understood in terms of his desires and needs, but rather in terms of his values – which is to say, in terms of those of his desires which he incorporates into his self, as representing what he *really* wants. Such desires are informed by a conception of what is desirable; they are the locus of rational choice, and the instrument of self-identification. All other desires are seen as alien to the self, extorted by external forces, or forced by the lingering influence of the undifferentiated consciousness that the true moral agent attempts to leave behind.

The vision of self-realisation is given the structure, if not the phraseology, of the Hegelian 'moment'. In the successive chapters of *Ethical Studies* Bradley describes, in terms which have all the ambiguity between history and logic, between time and the timeless, that Hegel manipulated so adeptly, the development of the soul towards its ideal of autonomy. One of the stages in this progress, and that which marks the emergence of the true moral consciousness from the anarchy which Mill calls freedom and which Bradley dismisses as a kind of tyranny of appetite, is described, in a famous phrase, as 'my station and its duties'. This is the point of rest from which true individuality can be attempted, but without which there is neither freedom nor the lack of it.

Bradley saw the concepts of obligation and duty as inseparable from a sense of social station (by which he did not mean social class). He argued vehemently against the democratic, reformist view that the sense of obligation could be detached from allegiance to a given social order, or set up as an independent standard in the light of which all order and allegiance could be called in question. On the contrary, this detaching of the sense of obligation merely transplants it into the desert of relativism, where it withers and dies. What results is not the freedom which the reformer craved, but a kind of apathetic anarchy with no clear conception of the goals of life, or the value of attaining them.

Bradley's detailed criticisms of utilitarian individualism are persuasive and finely phrased. But it is fair to say that the positive philosophy of

Ethical Studies is less clear than it ought to be, and becomes clear only when read in the light of the *Phenomenology of Spirit*. Bradley, however, often denied that he was a Hegelian, and in his later work attempted to derive an idealist metaphysics more compatible with his sceptical temperament than was the grandiose world-system of Hegel. This he attempted in two books, *The Principles of Logic* (1883) and *Appearance and Reality* (1893) and it is fitting to close with a brief discussion of these, since they will serve to introduce the topic of the chapter which follows.

The *Logic* was written at a time when its subject matter was being transformed by the work of Frege. While it shares some of its theses with the new logic, its metaphysical intention allies it more with the logic of Hegel than with the scrupulous work that was soon to cast it into shadow. Bradley, arguing for what is known as the coherence theory of truth, wished to assert that no single judgement can express a complete fact. His reasons were not logical but metaphysical. He thought that everything exists in complete interdependence, and that no single fact exists that is not 'internally related' to some other fact. An internal relation is one that enters into the understanding of the very terms related. Thus when I say that 'John is thinking about Rome', I assert an internal relation between John's thought and the idea of Rome. I cannot understand the nature of the thought without reference to this idea, which represents its content. Here the word 'about' denotes an internal relation. Bradley thought that all relations are internal. To isolate any fact from the whole which is the single true object of our understanding is to set it in an isolation which negates all that constitutes its reality. (This 'logical' thesis is the or metaphysical restatement of the social theory of *Ethical Studies*.)

In his metaphysical treatise, *Appearance and Reality*, Bradley set out to demolish all received metaphysical ideas – what he called the metaphysics of common sense. Among these received ideas he singled out the following: that there is a distinction between primary qualities inherent in things, and secondary qualities which merely reflect our ways of knowing things; that there is a distinction in reality between thing, quality and relation; that objects exist in space and time; that there is a subject of experience – the self – who perceives and knows these things. His attack on those conceptions owed much to Hume, and yet was used to support a conclusion that is rightly seen as Hegelian (however much Bradley resented the label).

Bradley argued that if a thing is to be distinct from its qualities, it cannot be defined in terms of any set of them. It must therefore constitute some peculiar kind of relatedness among qualities. But what is this relatedness that gives *unity* to the qualities of a thing? Surely it can only be a further quality – a quality of qualities. In our search for the bearer of qualities we find only another quality which they themselves are supposed to bear. Does this not suggest a contradiction at the very heart of the common sense distinction between thing and quality? Bradley went on to expose what he thought to be contradictions intrinsic to all the concepts of our unthinking metaphysics: thing, quality, space, time and self.

What, then, is real? Not surprisingly, Bradley begins his answer to this question from the thought that 'ultimate reality is such that it does not contradict itself'. Moreover, it must be 'harmonious', which means individuated, but undivided, in the manner of an organism. In order to establish this second point Bradley relies on the datum of the moral life, as he had described it. 'Feeling' – which provides our fundamental intuition of the nature of reality – has a content which is at once manifold and unitary. But in itself it is innocent: it does not divide and mutilate the world of knowledge but finds itself in undifferentiated harmony with it. Thought, by making judgements and seeking knowledge, must inevitably fragment what is innocently known. In order to overcome this destructive tendency, thought must be provided with system. It is only system that enables us to grasp the whole of things and so rediscover at the level of consciousness what we lost in becoming conscious, but knew intuitively before.

System gives us knowledge of the absolute, which is 'everything that is the case seen as constituting a single self-differentiating system'. Bradley is careful to argue that the absolute is not something transcendent: it names a way of seeing, and not a particular thing that is seen. Hence appearance is not unreal, it is only partial. What is needed to complete our partial knowledge is not the transcendence of appearance towards some Kantian thing-in-itself, but rather the summarising of experience within a systematic mode of knowledge which restores its totality.

These ideas of Bradley's – in particular those concerning the unreality of space and time – were soon to be attacked in the name of common sense by Russell and Moore. But what gave Russell and Moore their critical power was not some persuasive rival vision of metaphysical truth, but rather the new mode of philosophical analysis which rested, not so much on empiricist theory, as on logic, conceived as a formal science. In order to understand the consequent revolution in philosophy we must, therefore, first turn our attention to the new logic, and to its principal discoverer, Gottlob Frege.

Part Five

Recent philosophy

17

FREGE

There is no greater proof of the fact that the history of philosophy needs constantly to be rewritten than the change in perspective that has followed the recent discovery of the importance of Gottlob Frege. Born in 1848 but bearing no marks of the political upheavals of that year, Frege lived and taught in Jena from 1874 to 1914, leading a secluded scholarly life, detached from worldly affairs. When he died in 1925 one modern logician wrote,* 'I was an undergraduate, already interested in logic, and I think that I should have taken notice if there had been any speeches or articles published that year in his honour. But I can recollect nothing of the kind.'

Despite this neglect (he lived in the shadow of the new phenomenology) Frege secured the admiration of Russell, and of Wittgenstein, each of whose thought was formed and transformed by wrestling with problems and conceptions which he had bequeathed to them. In his own country his work went unnoticed, and only during the last twenty years has it become apparent that Frege was not merely the true founder of modern logic, but also one of the greatest philosophers of the late nineteenth century. He had not the range of Mill, Brentano or Husserl; but what he lacked in extensiveness he made up for in depth, and his occurrence at a time when philosophy stood in sore need of a mind that could focus on

* W. M. Kneale, in A. J. Ayer et al., *The Revolution in Philosophy*, New York, 1956, p. 26.

fundamental questions guaranteed both his eventual reputation and his contemporary neglect.

Frege's achievements were, first, to overthrow the Aristotelian logic that, in one form or another, had dominated Western philosophy since ancient times; secondly, to lay the foundations for the modern philosophy of language; thirdly, to show the deep continuity between logic and mathematics. Together these achievements provided the basis for modern analytical philosophy, and also for the philosophy of Wittgenstein, both in its earlier and in its later versions. In the hands of Russell and Wittgenstein, the Fregean conception of logic and mathematics was to provide a new epistemology, a new metaphysics and a new vision of the nature of philosophical argument. I shall perforce refer to Russell only rarely: as a character he is well enough known, and his copious powers of self-advertisement might perhaps suffice to justify my perfunctory treatment of his philosophy. However, much of what I attribute to Frege might equally be attributed to Russell. They laid the foundations of modern logic together (though largely independently), and each used those foundations to explore the principles of mathematical thought. I choose to concentrate on Frege because while, in the long run, his influence has not proved more decisive, his thought was deeper and more exact.

The ground was prepared for Frege's logic by certain discoveries in the foundations of mathematics, and in the techniques of formalisation. But the new logic arose also from Frege's sense of the deep connection between logic and metaphysics, and of the philosophical errors that had been perpetuated in the name of logic. In particular Frege believed that the Kantian theory of mathematics – that all mathematical truth is synthetic *a priori* – was mistaken, and could be shown to be mistaken by the adoption of a logic free from the Aristotelian preconceptions that had mesmerised Kant. Frege offered to demonstrate that arithmetical truth is not synthetic but analytic, in the sense of following from laws of logic so basic that they cannot be denied without self-contradiction. Frege was a kind of 'Platonist'; he believed in a realm of mathematical truth independent of the human capacity to gain knowledge of it. Nevertheless, as a result of his ideas, the science of mathematics was soon to be construed, not as the exploration of a realm of timeless entities, nor as a prime example of synthetic *a priori* knowledge, but as the projection into logical space of our own propensities towards coherent argument. What appears as an independent realm of mathematical entities or mathematical truth, is simply a shadowy representation of our own intellectual powers. The number one is no more an entity than is the average man, and the laws of mathematics no more truths about an independent world than the assertion that 'all bachelors are unmarried'.

On this account (which Frege made possible but only partly accepted), if we have *a priori* knowledge of mathematical truth it is because we ourselves have *constructed* that truth. (This explanation of *a priori* knowledge is an old one, and was given by the mediaeval nominalists, who lacked the means to determine whether it could be applied to mathematics.) Clearly such an interpretation of mathematics has enormous philosophical consequences. Not only Platonism, but also the entire rationalist tradition, had relied in one way or another on mathematics as giving an immediately intelligible example of the 'truths of reason', and so demonstrating the superiority of reason over empirical investigation, in point of certainty, completeness and ultimate veracity. Since Kant had identified metaphysics with the realm of synthetic *a priori* knowledge, and given mathematics as the most persuasive example of this knowledge, the demonstration that mathematics is analytic would open the way to a wholly new and characteristically modern rejection of metaphysical argument.

Empiricists had attempted to reject the Kantian theory of mathematical truth, and these attempts were renewed by J. S. Mill, in his *System of Logic*. This work, as the most systematic nineteenth-century exposition of the tenets of British empiricism, deserves lengthier treatment than I can here accord to it. Not only did Mill present a sustained and, in many ways, convincing theory of the distinction between logic and science (between the logic of deduction and the logic of induction), thus laying the foundations for the modern philosophy of science; he also addressed himself to many of the patterns of thought that had given rise to prevailing metaphysical illusions. The fact that his own illusions escaped him in the course of this examination is more a cause for satisfaction than surprise, for it was the absurdity of Mill's theory of mathematics that made clear to Frege the strange fact that mathematics can be completely known to someone who wholly misunderstands it.

For Mill our ideas of numbers are abstractions from experience. The number three is made familiar to us in the perception of threesomes, four in the perception of foursomes and so on. Moreover, mathematical truths themselves, such as $2 + 3 = 5$, can be seen as reflecting very basic laws of nature, which have been observed to govern the aggregates to which they refer. Frege argued, in his *Foundations of Arithmetic* (1884), that neither this, nor any other empiricist account of the nature of numbers, could be accepted. Not only does Mill give us no clue as to how we understand the number zero; he also fixes the limit of our mathematical knowledge at the limit of our experience. But 'who is actually prepared to assert the fact which, according to Mill, is contained in the definition of an eighteen-figure number has ever been observed, and who is prepared to deny that the symbol for such a number has, none the less, a sense?' In asserting that the laws of arithmetic are inductive generalisations, Mill confuses the application of mathematics with mathematics itself. Mathematics is intelligible independently of its applications. Finally, Frege points out, ' induction must base itself in the theory of probability, since it can never render a proposition more than probable. But how probability theory could possibly be developed without presupposing arithmetical laws is beyond comprehension.'

Frege was not the first philosopher to believe that the truths of arithmetic are analytic. Leibniz had attempted to prove the same. However, since Leibniz believed that all subject–predicate propositions are, at least from God's point of view, analytic, this can hardly be called a distinctive theory of arithmetic. Moreover Frege was the first to develop a logic in which this theory could be stated and proved. The details of the theory lie beyond the scope of the present work, but one or two important steps in the argument need to be grasped as a prelude to understanding Frege's philosophy as a whole.

If we ask the question 'What are numbers?' we find ourselves, Frege argues, at a loss for an answer. Are they objects? Are they properties? Are they abstractions? None of these suggestions seems satisfactory. When I say, 'Socrates is one', I do not attribute a property to Socrates, as I attribute a property in calling him wise. If Socrates is wise and Thales is wise then I conclude that Socrates and Thales are wise: they each possess the property singly, and so continue to possess it when described as a pair. But from 'Socrates is one' and 'Thales is one' we cannot conclude that 'Socrates and Thales are one'.

If, on the other hand, numbers are objects, how do we identify them? We ought to be able to indicate which objects they are. This is where we fall into a philosophical vertigo – we seem unable to give a definition, ostensive or descriptive, of any actual number. Numbers are like objects in this:

that they are the subject of identities. When we say that the number of planets is nine we are asserting that two names, 'the number of the planets' and 'nine', refer to one thing. But numbers are unlike objects in that reference to them is entirely dependent upon the identification of a concept to which they are attached. If I point to an army in the field and ask the question 'How many?', then the only sensible answer is: 'How many of *what*?' I may say 12,000, 50 or 2 depending on whether I am counting men, companies, or divisions. In other words, the answer is indeterminate until I have specified a concept according to which counting is to be carried out. Is a number then a property of a concept, a second-order property, as it were? This was the suggestion from which Frege began, and he took his inspiration from an area of logic the discovery of which was largely his – the logic of existence (or quantification, as it is now called).

Kant had argued, against the ontological argument, that existence is not a true predicate (or property), but he had failed to develop a logic that would accommodate this fact. Leibniz, who made certain advances in formal logic, recognised the differences between existential propositions (propositions of the form '*x* exists') and subject-predicate propositions, but again was unable to represent these differences in a systematic way. This deficiency in the traditional logic was far-reaching. It was what had erected the artificial barrier (as Frege considered it) between arithmetic (the logic of quantity) and logic (the logic of quality).

We know, independently of theory, that there is a coherent logic governing terms like 'exists'. We know that the statement 'Something exists which is not red' entails the falsehood of the generalisation 'Everything is red'. The traditional Aristotelian logic had no way of representing this relation. It can be represented, Frege argued, only when we realise that 'exists' and 'all' have a special logical character. They denote not properties of objects but, as it were, second-order properties of properties. To say that a red thing exists is to say of redness that it has an instance. And to say that all things are not red is to say that redness has no instances.

It proved possible on this basis to give a formal logic of existence and universality, and to vindicate Kant's insight that existence is not a predicate and leads to fallacies when treated as one. New analytic truths now have to be recognised, which are not of subject-predicate form, and the laws of logic must be extended to cover them. It seems natural to suggest that this logic of existence and universal quantification should provide the basis for a general 'logic of quantity'.

But what now of numbers? We speak of them as objects (which are the subjects of identity), and yet we do not allow them to be determinate independently of a concept to which they are attached. To resolve this seeming paradox, Frege proposed a general 'criterion of identity' for numbers. This criterion had to be provided contextually, he argued, since numerical expressions can be used to say true things only when attached to a concept which determines what is being counted. In other words, it is only in a given context that a number-term denotes anything specific. Suppose one could specify what makes an arithmetical statement of the form '$a = b$' true without invoking the concept of number. One will then have explained the use of the arithmetical concept of identity. One will also have provided what was later to be called an 'implicit' definition of number. An analogy might make this clear. Suppose you wish to know what is meant by the direction of a line. I can give a general definition of 'same direction' which does not invoke the idea of direction. (Lines have the same direction if and only if they are parallel.) I have then, in effect, defined direction. The direction of a line ab is given by the concept: lines which have the same direction as ab.

In like manner, Frege derives his famous definition of number in terms of the concept 'equinumerosity', a concept which had been introduced into the discussion of the foundations of mathematics by Georg Cantor (1845–1918). The word 'equinumerosity' can be defined in purely logical terms, and denotes a property of a concept. Two concepts are equinumerous if the items falling under one of them can be placed in one-to-one correspondence with the items falling under the other. Frege shows that this idea of one-to-one correspondence can be explained without invoking that of number. He then defines the number of a concept F as the extension of the concept 'equinumerous to F'. I have used the term 'extension' here, as Frege does – the usage goes back to the 'Port-Royal' logic discussed in chapter 4. The extension of a term or concept is the class of things to which the term applies. Hence the definition of number incorporates the generalisation of the idea, already invoked in the logic of existence, of the 'instance' of a concept. The definitions of the individual numbers can be derived from the general definition, Frege thought, by the use of the basic laws of logic. It suffices to define the first of the natural numbers – zero – and the relation of succession whereby the remaining numbers are determined.

Zero is the number which belongs to the concept 'not identical with itself'. Frege chose this definition because, he argued, it follows from the laws of logic alone that the concept 'not identical with itself' has no extension. At every point in the argument Frege wished to proceed in that way, introducing no conceptions which could not be explained in logical terms. Following this method he was able to derive the definitions and laws of arithmetic so as to show, he thought, that all mathematical proofs were complex applications of logic, and all arithmetical statements were, if true, true by virtue of the meaning of the terms used to express them.

Frege's achievement was astonishing. But it was marred by Russell's discovery of a paradox, and the resolution of this paradox seemed to require a departure from purely logical ideas in a direction of the kinds of metaphysical assumption that Frege had wished to eliminate from the foundations of mathematics. Moreover, Kurt Gödel in a famous theorem (1931) demonstrated that there are arithmetical truths which are unprovable in any logical system which can be proved to be self-consistent. Hence logic cannot, in principle, embrace the content of mathematics. In the light of these results it might seem that we should reject Frege's 'hypothesis' (as he put it) of the analyticity of arithmetic, and reinstate some version of Kant's theory, that mathematics is synthetic *a priori* and *sui generis*. However, Frege came so *near* to reducing arithmetic to logic, and Gödel's result is so puzzling, that the issue of the status of mathematical truth has in consequence become one of the most important modern philosophical problems. It seems impossible to abandon the direction in which Frege pointed us, and yet also impossible to proceed further along it. It is no mean achievement to have created an irresolvable philosophical problem from something which every child can understand.

Frege's researches into the foundations of mathematics were to have profound philosophical consequences, not the least of which was the recognition that mathematical conceptions could be and should be used to give form to otherwise nebulous problems in the philosophy of logic and language. In the *Begriffsschrift* (1879) Frege set forward the first truly comprehensive system of formal logic. His purpose was to give clear philosophical background to the arguments of his earlier work on the foundations of arithmetic, and also to represent logic in a manner that freed it from the confusions imported into it by its use of ordinary language terms. He thereby invented the modern science of formal logic; and in the course of doing so he overthrew the theories of Aristotelian and post-Aristotelian logic that had impeded advance in the subject for two thousand years.

There was a particular consequence of this overthrow which Frege did not at first foresee. The old logic had taken its cue from the grammar of ordinary language. It was this that made it so difficult to represent the difference between 'Socrates exists' and 'Socrates is alive'. The difference is in fact so radical that we are forced to conclude that grammatical form in ordinary language is no guide to logical behaviour. To put it in Russell's way, the true logical form of the sentence 'Socrates exists' is not reflected in its grammar. How then should we represent this sentence? The natural answer is to seek for a system of symbols that would allow expression only to the true 'logical form' of any sentence. This intrusion of mathematical method into the foundations of logic was the first of many. Since logic itself governs much of philosophical argument, the process can be continued further; eventually it resulted in the almost entirely mathematised philosophies of atomism and positivism which I shall mention in the final chapter.

There are more specific ways in which Frege's adoption and extension of mathematical ideas changed the nature of philosophy. This can be seen in Frege's theory of the nature of language. It was clear to Frege, as it had been to Leibniz, that statements of identity are different in form from statements which predicate a property of an object. The 'is' of identity and the 'is' of predication are logically distinct. If I say 'Venus is the Morning Star' then I make a statement of identity. The statement remains true (or, if false, false), when the names are reversed: the Morning Star is as much Venus as Venus is the Morning Star. In the sentence 'Socrates is wise' the terms cannot be reversed in the same way. The whole sense of the sentence depends upon my ascribing a different role to the subject term 'Socrates' and the predicate term 'wise'.

Now the distinction between subject and predicate is basic to thought. A creature who could not understand it, who spoke only of identities, would know nothing of his world; he would know only the arbitrary determinations of his own usage, whereby he is able to substitute one name for another. But he would know nothing about the things that he thereby names. It behoves us, therefore, to try to understand the relation between subject and predicate – in so far as anything so basic will yield itself to logical investigation.

Frege's analysis of this relation is contained in a series of articles among which the most important is 'On Sense and Reference'. Frege there advances various theses, some of which had already proved important in describing the nature of arithmetic. Two theses of particular interest are these: first, that it is only in the context of a whole sentence that a word has a definite meaning; secondly, that the meaning of any sentence must be derivable from the meanings of its parts. These seem to be, but are not, contradictory. The first (an application of which is found in Frege's contextual definition of number) says that the meaning of a word does not belong to it in isolation, but consists in its potentiality to contribute to a completed 'thought'. It is because sentences can express thoughts that the words which compose them have a meaning. The second thesis states that the meaning of the whole sentence (or of any other composite linguistic entity) must be wholly determined by the various 'potentialities' belonging to its parts. Thus the word 'man' has the meaning it has because we use it to talk about men. Equally, the sentences with which we talk about men derive their meaning in part from that of 'man'. This mutual dependence of part on whole and whole on part is characteristic of language. As linguists have begun to realise, it is what makes language learnable. If the meaning of the sentence is determined by the meaning of its parts, then, knowing only a finite vocabulary, I may yet understand indefinitely many sentences. My language-use is automatically 'creative', and gives me the capacity for unlimited thought.

How then do we proceed to describe the component parts of a subject-predicate sentence? Consider the sentence 'Socrates is wise'. Frege argues that, for the purpose of clearer representation, we can assume this to be composed of two parts, a name and a predicate. Names may seem to be more intelligible than predicates: we understand them because they stand for objects, and if we know which objects they stand for we seem already to know what they mean. But, Frege argues, matters are more complicated than that. Consider the sentence 'Hesperus is Phosphorus'. This uses two names, only one in fact the name of the Evening Star. Surely I could understand it without knowing it to be true? But if to understand 'Hesperus' is to know to which object it refers, then I ought to know that the sentence is true just as soon as I understand it. But I do not. Frege took this example as proving that there is a general distinction in language between that which we understand (the sense of a term) and that which a term refers to or 'picks out' (the reference of the term). The sense of a term directs us towards the reference: but it is not identical with it.

In the case of a name the sense is something like a complex description – 'the planet which . . . ' or 'the man who . . . '. The reference, on the other hand, is an object. This may seem intuitively acceptable – although in fact it is now widely devoted. But what about predicates? And what about the sentence taken as a whole?

In discussing Frege's theory of arithmetic I wrote loosely of concepts, properties and predicates, wishing to postpone the question of the interpretation of these terms. But now it is necessary to be more precise. A predicate has as its reference a particular concept: in understanding the predicate 'is wise' I am 'led to' the concept of wisdom, by its sense or meaning. What then can we say, from the philosophical point of view, about the nature of concepts? Frege was clear about one thing: concepts are public, and belong as much to the publicly recognisable aspect of language as do the words which express them. The 'senses' of predicates are therefore equally public. Otherwise the meaning of words could not be taught, and language would cease to be a form of communication. Senses are to be distinguished from private associations, from images and from every other merely 'inner' episode. They are determined by rules of usage which are available to every speaker.

Embodied in the idea of the publicity of 'sense', is a rejection of the traditional empiricist theories of meaning. All these theories confuse meaning and association, since they identify the meaning of a term with some subjective idea aroused in the mind of a person who either uses or hears it. Frege also, through his theory of reference, develops the basis for a novel metaphysical rejection of idealism.

How do predicates refer? How is their reference distinct from their sense? Frege argued that, unlike names, predicates are 'unsaturated'. Their reference can be understood not as a complete object, but only as an operation which needs to be completed before any object is determined by it. Borrowing a mathematical idea, he called this operation a function. Consider, for example, the mathematical function $(\ )^2 + 2$ (or, using the symbol for a variable, $x^2 + 2$). This yields a value for any particular number: the value 3 for $x = 1$, 6 for $x = 2$, and so on. And its significance lies wholly in that. The mathematical function transforms one number into another.

Likewise the predicate, 'x is wise' should be conceived as determining a function which yields a value for each individual object that is referred to by the name substituted for 'x'. What is this 'value' to which the sentence refers? Frege argued that it can be nothing more nor less than the reference of the sentence as a whole. For having combined the reference of the subject with that of the predicate, we must obtain the reference of their combination.

To what then do sentences refer? Frege's answer to this question constitutes what is perhaps the most original part of his philosophy. It is tempting to think that if a sentence refers to anything it is to a fact, or to a state of affairs, or to some such thing. 'Socrates is wise' refers to the fact that Socrates is wise. But then to what do false sentences refer? And how many states of affairs are there? If you try to answer the second question, you soon realise that the *only* way to count states of affairs is by counting either sentences, or their meanings. In which case your idea of the *reference* of a sentence has been confused with your idea either of the sentence itself, or of its sense. By a series of extremely subtle and persuasive arguments Frege was able to conclude that in fact the only possible answer to the question, 'To what does a sentence refer?' is: 'To its truth value'. That is, to truth, or to falsehood. Truth and falsehood stand to sentences as objects do to names. And predicates refer to concepts which determine functions yielding truth or falsehood according to the objects to which they are applied.

The analysis of the subject–predicate sentence is completed by answering the question: what is the *sense* of a completed sentence? Frege argued that the sense is a thought: the thought, in our example, that Socrates is wise. A thought, like a concept, is a public thing, not to be confused with any private penumbra or 'tone'. It is to be identified in terms of the conditions which make a sentence true. Anyone who supposes that Socrates is wise, supposes that certain conditions are fulfilled, in virtue of which the sentence 'Socrates is wise' is true (or, to put it more formally, in virtue of which the sentence refers to the truth value: true). The final analysis of the subject–predicate sentence thus attributes to it two complete levels of meaning, in the following way:

	Subject	*Predicate*	*Sentence*
syntax:	Socrates	is wise	Socrates is wise
sense:	description	sense of predicate	thought (= truth-conditions)
reference:	object	concept/function	truth-value

Just as the sense of the whole sentence is determined by the sense of its parts, so too is the truth-value determined by the reference of the individual words.

The significance for philosophy of this quasi-mathematical analysis of linguistic structure is enormous. If Frege is right, then the old distinction between extension and intension can be applied to sentences. The extension of a sentence is its truth-value, and the intension its truth-conditions. The extension of a term is detachable from it, and identifiable in other ways. It can therefore be accorded an independent existence. We can think of a sentence as *standing for* the true or the false. The notion of a logical relation between sentences now becomes completely clear. The complex sentence '*p* and *q*' for example, is true if and only if *p* is true and *q* is true. Hence the inference from '*p* and *q*' to '*q*' is valid: it takes us from truth to truth. Other 'logical connectives' such as 'if' and 'or' can be clarified in the same way and their logic explained. The principle of extensionality – that every term stands for its extension – can now be used to construct a complete logic of the relations between sentences. It was this idea which revolutionised philosophy, leading first to the 'logical atomism' of Russell and Wittgenstein, and then to the new forms of analytical metaphysics which gradually came to replace it.

Moreover, if Frege's theory of language is right, the fundamental notion involved in understanding words is that of truth. Some have wished to argue thus: a sentence has meaning because people use it to make assertions. It is therefore the peculiar function performed in assertion that we ought to analyse. It is this 'assertion' that provides the essence of linguistic communication, and hence must be isolated as the basic subject matter of any philosophy of language. But consider the following argument: (1) *p* implies *q*; (2) *p*; therefore (3) *q*. In (1) the sentence '*q*' is not asserted; in (3) it is: yet the argument is valid. Hence '*q*' must mean the same in each occurrence, otherwise there would be a fallacy through equivocation. It follows, Frege argues, that 'assertedness' cannot be part of the meaning of a sentence. If we ask ourselves what we understand in understanding a sentence, or an argument, then the answer always leads back, not to assertion, but to truth. What we understand is either a relation among truth-values, or the conditions which make a sentence true. Frege also believed that the relation of a sentence to its truth-conditions must be objectively determined. Hidden within the very logic of discourse we discover a metaphysical assumption. This is the assumption of an objective truth, at which all our utterances are aimed, and from which they take their sense.

These thoughts of Frege's have been slowly, and somewhat erratically, incorporated into the framework of modern analytical philosophy. Some thinkers object to Frege's idea that truth-conditions determine meaning. Others object to the specifically 'realistic' or 'anti-idealistic' interpretation which Frege gave to this idea. In this way, discussion of Frege has reactivated the fundamental question posed by Kant's metaphysics. How do we steer the middle course between 'transcendental realism' and 'empirical idealism'? This question has now become: 'What is fundamental to understanding language; truth considered independently of our ability to assess it, or assertion considered as an act circumscribed by our own epistemological powers?'

Other philosophers object to Frege's description of the nature of predicates, and his characterisation of the logic of ordinary language in quasi-mathematical terms. Whatever position is adopted, however, whether in the theory of meaning, or in metaphysics, we can be sure that, if the position belongs to the tradition of 'analytic' philosophy, it will have tacitly relied on Frege's ideas, if not to provide its arguments, at least to provide the terminology in which they are expressed.

18

PHENOMENOLOGY AND EXISTENTIALISM

The movement to be discussed in this chapter has a history as long as that of modern logic, and indeed, at the beginning, was hardly separable from the new post-idealism represented at its best in the work of Frege. The term 'phenomenology', invented by the German eighteenth-century mathematician J. H. Lambert to describe the science of appearances, had been used by Hegel in his work on the nature of the 'subjective spirit' – spirit as it appears to itself. However, despite the shared language and shared pretensions, it is clear that Hegel and Husserl are engaged in different forms of enquiry; we must therefore look for the latter's intellectual origins elsewhere. In fact the thinker with the strongest claim to be the founder of the phenomenological movement was, in his own eyes, more a psychologist than a philosopher, and a psychologist who professed allegiance to methods which he called empirical. In *Psychology from an Empirical Standpoint* (1874), Franz Brentano (1838–1917) embarked on an investigation of the human mind which expressly rejected the premises of idealism, and in particular the notion that the true subject matter of psychology is some universal, abstract '*Geist*', which pursues its courses through the world as though related to individual humans only occasionally and by accident. Psychology cannot take such abstractions as its point of departure. Like any other science, it must start from the individual case, and that means from the first-person case, which is known to the investigator directly. Brentano, partly because of his emphasis on the first person, did not venture very far into the realm of what we would now call empirical psychology. Instead, he became intrigued by an old philosophical problem, that of the nature of first-person knowledge. What is it that I *know* when I am presented with the contents of consciousness? And how is the knower distinguished from the known?

In attempting to answer those questions Brentano reintroduced into philosophy a technicality common in the mediaeval schools: the concept of intentionality. Every mental state or event is, he argued, characterised by the 'reference to a content', or the 'direction upon an object' (hence by an internal 'aim' or 'intention'). If I believe, then there is something that I believe; if I hate, then there is something that I hate; if I see, then there is something that I see. In every such case, the 'content' or 'object' is characterised by certain peculiar features. It might be indefinite; it might not exist in actuality; or it might be other than I think it to be. For example, I may be afraid of a lion, but of no particular lion; I may hate the man who tore up my daffodils, although there is no such man; I may admire the man who endowed the hospital but despise the man who killed the Mayor, even though they are one and the same.

The best way to describe this phenomenon of intentionality is to make a distinction, again relying on scholastic terminology, between the 'material' and the 'intentional' object of a mental state. When I see as a ghost what is in fact a piece of fluttering cloth, then the intentional object of my seeing is a ghost, while the material object is a piece of cloth. The intentional object is that which is 'present to consciousness', and it may not correspond to any material reality. This possibility of non-correspondence explains the peculiarity of the intentional object. Intentional objects are of many logical types: they can be propositions (the objects of belief), ideas (the objects of thought), individuals (the objects of love and hate). They can be indeterminate (a lion), or determinate (the lion before me). In every case they have no existence independent of the mental state that 'refers to' or is 'directed onto' them. There is no 'real relation' between fear, say, and its intentional object, since the two cannot be thought of as existing separately. This is one of the few genuine cases where one might wish to speak, in Bradleyan terms, of an 'internal' relation. (See p. 232.)

Brentano believed that this property of intentionality is peculiar to mental phenomena and common to all of them. It therefore formed, for him, a distinguishing mark of the mental. The property has, however, an intricate logic, and presents rather more difficulties in the description than my brief summary conveys. It has therefore proved difficult to substantiate this particular aspect of Brentano's thought, or fully to understand its implications. In particular a confusion, sometimes accidental, sometimes deliberate, between intentionality and a lack of what logicians call extensionality (see the last chapter) has made discussions of this topic in recent years peculiarly vertiginous. It must be said of the phenomenologists, however, that their knowledge of modern logic has not, in general, been sufficient to permit these confusions. It is the *phenomenon* of intentionality that has been of interest to them, and not the search for some general differentiating characteristic of the mental.

The first important phenomenologist was Brentano's pupil Edmund Husserl (1859–1938), who began his philosophical career with a book on the foundations of arithmetic that is now chiefly remembered for Frege's devastating critique of it. Among Husserl's many writings, those that have attracted the most attention are the *Logical Investigations* (1900–1), *Ideas for a Pure Phenomenology* (1913) and *Cartesian Meditations* (1929, first published 1950). The first of these is of great interest, announcing the theme for which Husserl is known, that of a 'pure phenomenology'. This theme is further elaborated in the second of his major works. In these works he begins the description of what he was to call the 'method' of phenomenological reduction. Husserl's thought rests on two master-premises. First, he reaffirms the essence of the Cartesian position, that the immediate knowledge that I have of my own conscious mental states is the one sure foundation for an understanding of their nature, provided only that I can isolate what is *intrinsic* to the mental state, and separate it from all that is extraneous. Secondly, the intentionality of the mental makes 'meaning' or 'reference' essential to every mental act. To focus on the revealed nature of mentality is therefore also to understand the fundamental operation of 'meaning', whereby the world is made intelligible. In virtue of these two premises Husserl was able to construct a philosophy which, like that of Descartes, aimed to produce a complete metaphysical vision from reflection on the peculiarities of consciousness.

But study of the first-person case is blind if it is impossible to isolate what is contained in it. Just as Descartes sought to separate the 'clear and distinct' idea from the mental states with which it is mingled, so did Husserl propose a method whereby to isolate the pure deliverances of consciousness from the encumbrances which impede our understanding of them. This method is that of 'phenomenological reduction', or 'bracketing' (*epoché*, from the Greek). All reference to what is susceptible to doubt or mediated by reflection must be excluded from the description of every mental state, leaving the remnant of pure immediacy alone. Let us consider the case of fear. I must not suppose that the object of fear exists independently of my fear. Fear does not guarantee the existence of its object, but only of its own 'direction' towards an object. We should therefore 'bracket' the material object in examining the nature of fear. But the intentional object remains: we cannot eliminate from fear the *idea* of an object, since this is contained in the mental state and immediately present to the consciousness of the one who fears.

What else remains, after the process of bracketing? Husserl spoke of a 'mental act', the process of direction itself, which in some way constitutes the essence of fear. The peculiar method of phenomenology is that it takes this mental act as its datum. Nothing else can be described which is either more fundamental to knowledge, or more able to reveal the essence of what is known. Is not the phenomenologist burdened, then, with the old Cartesian question, of how to advance beyond the first-person case to knowledge of an independent world? The title of Husserl's later, impenetrable work – *Cartesian Meditations* – suggests, as does its content, that his 'method' has indeed cast him into the pit of scepticism. But the major object of this scepticism is, historically speaking, somewhat surprising. It is not the objective world but the observing subject himself. The person (or self) exists for Husserl only in the performance of intentional acts. But he is not identical with any of these intentional acts. Nor can he be the object of such an act since, if he were, then there would have to be some other subject performing the act of which 'he' is the object. But who is this subject if not himself? The 'I', as Ryle expressed it in another context, is systematically elusive. In what sense, then, can we know that it exists? The 'I' exists, Husserl thought, only as the subject and never as the object of consciousness. It must therefore be 'transcendental' in something like the sense of Kant's 'transcendental self'. Many of Husserl's voluminous writings are spent in the pursuit of this creature which he declared to be unknowable, and it is not surprising that they have seemed to many, in consequence, to be unreadable.

It is unclear from what I have said that there is any special 'method' of phenomenology. How, for example, is it distinguished from the psychology of introspection? In the *Logical Investigations* Husserl expressly rejects 'psychologism' – the view that logic is a very general science of the mind. In setting up phenomenology in its place, he claimed to be enunciating a method that is free from, and indeed presupposed by, every empirical enquiry. (His view about the status of his theory was therefore the opposite of Brentano's; which of them was right is not a matter that I feel able to decide.) Phenomenology is the necessary preliminary to any science of the mind, since it locates – prior to any description, classification or explanation – the individual mental acts which psychology must investigate. Moreover, it is the sole access to meaning. Meaning is created by mental acts, and the world becomes present to consciousness only through those acts. Hence our understanding determines the essences of things, by fixing the manner in which they are known. Phenomenology therefore yields a knowledge not of facts, but of essences. It is consequently (so it is argued) an *a priori* science.

Husserl was aware of the impasse into which he had been driven by his Cartesian method, and in his last unfinished work – *Transcendental Phenomenology and the Crisis of the European Sciences*, published posthumously in 1954 – he attempted to overcome the subjective emphasis of phenomenology by means of a theory of the social world. The focus shifts from 'I' to 'we', albeit a 'transcendental "we"'. This plural subject is something like the implied community of language users, who together construct the common-sense world in which they are situated. Husserl calls this common-sense world the *Lebenswelt*, or 'life-world': it is a world constituted by our social interaction, and endowed with the 'meanings' that inhabit our communicative acts. We reach the transcendental 'we' by an imaginative self-projection, from the 'here' of first-person awareness to the 'there' of the generalised other. What is given in this process is not the elusive residue of some phenomenological reduction, but the *Lebenswelt* itself.

The concept of the *Lebenswelt* enabled Husserl to revive a project of post-Kantian idealism: the project of distinguishing the human realm (the realm of meaning) from the realm of nature (the realm of science and explanation). Inspired by Kant's division between understanding and practical reason, the romantic theologian F. D. E. Schleiermacher (1768–1834) had argued that the interpretation of human actions can never be accomplished by the methods employed in the natural sciences. The human act must be understood as the act of a free being, motivated by reason, and understood through dialogue. The same is true of texts, which can be interpreted only through an imaginative dialogue with their author. 'Hermeneutics' – the art of interpretation – involves the search for reasons rather than causes, and the attempt to understand a text as an expression of rational activity – the very activity that is manifest in me.

A later Kantian philosopher, Wilhelm Dilthey (1833–1911), extended Schleiermacher's hermeneutical method to the entire human world. Our attitude to other people, he argued, is fundamentally distinct from and even opposed to the scientific attitude. We seek to understand their actions not by explaining them in terms of external causes, but 'from within', by an act of rational self-projection that Dilthey calls *Verstehen*. In understanding human life and action I must find the agent's reasons for what he does. This means conceptualising the world as he does, seeing the connections and unities that he sees. For example, I understand your fear of speaking in a certain place, once I conceptualise it as you do, as somewhere 'sacred'.

Our every-day ways of conceptualising the world do not, as a rule, follow the direction required by scientific explanation. Rather, Dilthey suggests, they represent the world as 'ready for action'. I see the world under the aspect of my own freedom, and describe and respond to it accordingly. This before me is not a member of the species *Homo sapiens* but a *person*, who looks at me and smiles; that beside her is not a piece of bent organic tissue but a *chair* on which I may sit; this on the wall is not a collection of tinted chemicals but a *picture*, in which the face of a saint appears; and so on. In short, we are not merely in dialogue with each other; we are in dialogue with the world itself, moulding the natural order through concepts, so as to align it with our aims. Our categories do not *explain* the world, so much as endow it with *meaning*.

Husserl took this idea a stage further, by suggesting that the pre-scientific vision of the world expresses not merely our identity as rational beings, but our *life*. The world appears to us in the guise of a 'lived environment': a place in which we situate ourselves as acting and suffering organisms. We understand objects as 'friendly' or 'hostile', 'comfortable' or 'uncomfortable', 'useful' or 'useless', and in a thousand ways divide the world according to our interests. Our classifications form no part of the enterprise of scientific explanation, and have an authority that no science could remove. The new task of phenomenology is to awaken us to the *Lebenswelt*, and to vindicate those 'we'-thoughts in which the meaning of objects is created and made public.

Dilthey was the first to attempt a systematic distinction between the *Geisteswissenschaften* (humanities) and the natural sciences, suggesting that the first are really extended and transhistorical exercises in *Verstehen*. Husserl recognised, however, that these 'human sciences' had entered a condition of crisis during our century, precisely because natural science had presumptiously invaded their territory, and so prompted people to throw away, as useless remnants of a vanished world-view, the concepts through which the *Lebenswelt* is understood and organised. The crisis is not only intellectual; it is also moral, indeed, a crisis of civilisation itself. For the *Lebenswelt* falls apart when not sustained by reflection. The result is a loss of meaning, a moral vacuum, into which we are led whenever we surrender to the false gods of science.

No philosopher in our time has been more acutely aware of this moral vacuum than Martin Heidegger (1889–1976), a pupil of Husserl's, who can fairly claim to be the most important thinker, and the darkest, of the existentialist school. Husserl had delivered, during his middle years, two series of lectures, later published as *The Phenomenology of Internal Time Consciousness*, in which he claimed to rediscover, on the level of phenomenological analysis, the age-old metaphysical problem of time. Inspired by this and other later Husserlian writings, Heidegger composed his *Being and Time* (1927), which is the most complex of the many works inspired, directly or indirectly, by Kant's theory of time as the 'form of inner sense'.

It is impossible to summarise Heidegger's work, which no one has claimed to understand completely. In the next chapter I shall give reasons for thinking that it may be unintelligible, from the very nature of the phenomenological 'method' which it employs. Its language, like that of the later Husserl, is metaphorical and contorted to the point almost of incomprehensibility; the reader has the impression that never before have so many words been invented and tormented in the attempt to express the inexpressible.

Heidegger claims that his method is phenomenological, and that its essence is captured in the slogan, 'To the things themselves!' Philosophy is the study of phenomena, where 'phenomena' is taken in its original Greek sense as referring to whatever 'shows itself'. Phenomena are not mere appearances, but those things which *show themselves* to consciousness. Hence the priority of phenomenology over any physical or psychological science. Phenomenology is also the fundamental form of 'ontology' – the study of what is. Despite its Cartesian beginnings, phenomenology in the work of Heidegger breaks loose from epistemology and launches itself, with a daring unprecedented since Hegel, onto the sea of speculation, with only one question as its guide. This question is that of 'the meaning of being', a question which, we are invited to suppose, was the subject-matter of all those ancient philosophies, Socratic and pre-Socratic, which the Cartesian method submerged.

Being (*Sein*) must be distinguished from *Dasein. Dasein* is the kind of being that characterises human self-consciousness. It is the 'thing which understands being'. It would be convenient if we could give the term '*Dasein*' its normal translation of 'existence'. Unfortunately, Heidegger, who can certainly be thought to multiply terms to the limit of possibility, whether or not beyond necessity, has forestalled us. He introduces a third term, *Existenz*, which denotes 'that kind of Being towards which *Dasein* can comport itself in one way or another, and always does comport itself somehow'. *Dasein*, by contrast, has its being '*for its own*'. *Dasein* is what Sartre later described as *être pour-soi*, and what Hegel had already described as being-for-self (*Fürsichsein*).

As we shall see, both Heidegger and Sartre owe far more to Hegel than their vocabulary. All these are more or less pompous ways of distinguishing things from persons. What then is the argument, or, failing that, the thesis, of *Being and Time*? I am not sure, but perhaps the following represents a part of it. First, while Heidegger rejects the use of such terms as 'subject' and 'object', preferring technicalities of his own, he is clearly concerned with the modern problem of self-knowledge. What is self-knowledge, what is its object and what does it yield by way of insight into the objective world? He begins, therefore, from the first-person case, saying that 'the assertion that it is I who in each case Dasein is, is ontically obvious'. But ontical obviousness is one thing, content another. We must answer the 'problem of being'. This poses itself initially as the question: 'Who (what) am I?' As Kant showed in the Paralogisms, no amount of study of the immediate knowledge characteristic of the first person will answer this question. Heidegger notices and applauds the result, but does not, as he perhaps should, feel threatened by it. Now, we can know from phenomenological analysis that the essence of *Dasein* lies in its existence: it *at least* has existence, and it has existence *essentially*. This ontological argument for the existence of the subject should not be taken too seriously. For if we know nothing else about this *Dasein* than that it exists, we have hardly advanced even so far as the first Cartesian question.

Heidegger precedes his theory of being (which is in fact a theory of self-consciousness) with a fascinating, but maddeningly abstract, description of the world of phenomena. Since all being is being in the world, then the essence of the world as phenomenon must be explored if being is to be understood. We learn that the world contains things, but that thinghood must be construed not in its modern, scientific sense, but in its ancient meaning – the meaning of the Greek term *pragmata*. Objects are 'to be used', or 'ready to hand'. Hence we can understand them as 'signs'; that is, we interpret them as bearing an immediate relation to ourselves. (Here we again encounter the influence of Dilthey.) The world first comes into consciousness as a sign, as *logos*. It is that which 'bears a meaning for us'. This explains *Dasein*'s 'fascination with the world'. Seemingly independent objects can be constantly appropriated for *Dasein*'s own uses, made into expressions, and assigned a meaning. This is the 'abolition of distance' (*Entfernen*) between objects and ourselves. We are led to understand that this abolition of distance also provides the first 'phenomenon' of space – it is this which leads to my sense of having spatial position in my world.

But this peaceful union of *Dasein* and its world is broken, as ever, by the appearance of the Other. (Or, the *Zeitgeist* having become more paranoid since Hegel's day, by the intrusion of 'them'.) In relation to this existence of others my own existence is put in question. I become aware of what Heidegger calls my 'thrown-ness' (*Geworfenheit*), which is the lack of any reason for my existence in the world, the fact that I am simply there. It is this which appears in the phenomenon of fear, and which precipitates that great turning away from the world which others have called alienation, but which Heidegger prefers to call 'the Fall'. *Dasein* 'falls', not into sin or Hell, but into 'inauthenticity'. Confronted with the absolute enigma of my own being I flee from myself. I lose myself in anxiety, and in order to escape that anxiety I try to cease to be myself and instead become one of 'them'. I become an object, part of that world which first shattered my composure by showing my arbitrariness, and which now tempts me to deny myself, by melting into the impersonal 'they' of role, form and 'idle talk'.

However, this inauthenticity brings with it a sense of the absurd. This is the sense that objects are *without* meaning. They had a meaning for *Dasein*, but have no meaning for the consciousness which identifies itself only impersonally, as a part of 'them'. This sense of absurdity translates itself into anxiety, and in anxiety the first answer to the question of being is formed. 'Who am I? – answer: myself.' Whatever else I am, I am that. Anxiety, as Heidegger puts it, ' individualises'. Precisely because it has no object, because its intentionality is universal, undifferentiated, without focus, it can only be grasped as mine. In the experience of anxiety I am cut off from them, and thrown back into my individuality, my existence, as the ultimate fact.

This sense of individuality has, as its principal manifestation (one might almost say 'moment'), the exercise of a peculiar mental capacity which Heidegger calls 'care' (*Sorge*). The attitude of the anxious self to the world is one of care: apprehension for itself and for others, and the attempt to understand the world as an object of knowledge and activity. This care brings with it the separation of subject and object, and the idea of objective truth. As Heidegger puts it, care 'uncovers the world', and so finds what is objective in relation to itself. (At this point Heidegger recognises that he is touching on the old Kantian problem of the pre-suppositions of self-knowledge, but rejects the idea that we need to prove the existence of an objective world. Apparently, what is presupposed needs no proof, only an 'uncovering'.)

The 'caring' self has a new kind of being – a wholeness which Heidegger also describes as a being-towards-death. For anxiety brings with it the apprehension of finiteness and vulnerability; and 'care' is simply understanding the world as the locus of finite and vulnerable existence. In being-towards-death I recognise my predicament as a creature conditioned by time, and see that only *in* time is my redemption possible, so that care becomes the 'call of conscience'. I have to make myself responsible for my acts and my existence: this is the single answer that I have to undifferentiated anxiety, and it is my first glimpse of authenticity. I am more fully myself in recognising the call of something that is both integral to me, and yet which also points beyond me. I have been summoned out of the lostness of 'they' and called upon to announce myself in resolution. (The archetype of this way of thinking can be found in Hegel's *Logic*, in a passage entitled 'Barrier and Ought'.)

But resolution requires what Heidegger calls an 'anticipatory resoluteness'.

I must see the future in a certain way – as at least partially closed to me – if I am to have this attitude. I can decide to do something only in so far as I do not regard the question whether or not I shall do it as already settled. The future must therefore have a special status for me. It must be the object of different attitudes from those that I direct towards the present and past. It follows that I can only become authentic if I realise that my being is in time, not just in the sense that all things are in time, but in the deeper sense that time must form and determine all my outlook on the world, separating the future, which is the object of resoluteness, from the past, which is the object of guilt and responsibility. It can do that, Heidegger says, only if I see my freedom and my temporality as one and the same thing. This is ' being free for death' . The final answer to the riddle of existence is this: I am a being who is extended in time, and whose redemption lies in that freedom which time alone provides, the freedom to make of my life what I choose it to be, and thereby to change from thrown-ness to resolution. In that change lies the realisation, and acceptance, of mortality.

There is a certain poetry in Heidegger's vision, and moments of true philosophical insight. But how much of it is really philosophy, and how much an embroidered description of a private spiritual journey? Such questions take us into the heart of philosophical method. One thing is clear, which is that Heidegger's conclusions, where intelligible, are clearly intended as universal truths, not merely about the human condition, but about the world as such. Their status is synthetic and *a priori*; they could be neither proved nor disproved by any form of science. It is tempting sometimes to interpret them in a scientific or pseudo-scientific way, as gestures towards a psychology of self-consciousness. But that interpretation can hardly account for the generality and abstractness of what is put forward, besides suggesting (what is clearly false) that these theories could be measured against empirical evidence and so refuted or confirmed. On the other hand, Heidegger does not give any arguments for the truth of what he says. Most of *Being and Time* consists of compounded assertions, with hardly a 'thus', 'therefore', 'possibly', or 'it might follow that', to indicate the relations which are supposed to hold between them. The crucial thesis that idealism does not need a refutation, since its falsehood is *given* in *Dasein*'s quest for self-knowledge, is supported, not by argument, but by etymology, and the etymology of a Greek word to boot. (This Greek word being *aletheia*, which etymologically means 'uncovering', but literally means 'truth'.) Even if the whole of Heidegger's philosophy is both meaningful and true, therefore, we have yet to be given a reason to accept it. Looked at critically, Heidegger's ideas seem like spectral visions in the realm of thought; vast, intangible shadows cast by language. Perhaps, if there were no distinction in grammar between *Sein* and *Dasein*, no abstract nouns of the kind exemplified by '*Geworfenheit*', these shadows would dissolve, and nothing come to replace them. This sort of philosophy shows, in Wittgenstein's words, ' the bewitchment of the intelligence by means of language'.

This lack of argument persists in the writings of Jean-Paul Sartre (1905–1980), the French pupil of Husserl and of Heidegger who has done the most to propagate existentialism as a moral and metaphysical doctrine peculiarly suited to the demands of the modern conscience. But it is to some extent compensated for by literary graces, and by an art of persuasion that has made Sartre into one of the most influential writers of our time. In plays, novels and essays he has repeatedly expressed, modified and resurrected the existentialist vision; transforming it from abstract theory to imaginative experience. In his philosophical works the same imaginative methods persist. Faced with the question, 'Is this philosophy or is it psychology?' he would no doubt answer, 'Neither and both'. I shall try to present a philosophy which I believe to be Sartre's. Those parts that might seem to be psychological in nature are so evidently derived from Hegel, that it will need no apology to discuss them as though they were integral to the philosophical history of our time.

Sartre's early work on *The Psychology of the Imagination* (1940) (*The Imaginary*, as its title should have been translated), shows the influence of Husserl very strongly, and, while the English title (and French subtitle) suggest a reluctance to accept that phenomenology and psychology are distinct, the content makes it clear that Sartre is able to argue persuasively for conclusions about the nature of the human mind which are by any standards philosophical. These conclusions reappear, transmuted from their phenomenological form, in Sartre's famous lecture *L'Existentialisme est un humanisme*. This was delivered in 1945, after war-time experiences which had so transformed every aspect of Sartre's intelligence that it is usual to ignore the (in my view) more original and more important work which preceded them. I shall follow the usual practice, and regard this lecture, together with the vast and rambling reflections of *Being and Nothingness* (1943) as containing the fundamentals of Sartre's existentialism.

The premise of Sartre's philosophy is expressed in surprisingly mediaeval terms, as the proposition that 'existence precedes essence'. There is no human nature, since there is no God to have a conception of it. Essences, as intellectual constructions, vanish with the mind that would conceive them. For us, therefore, our existence – which is to say, that unconceptualised individuality which was celebrated (but not described) by Kierkegaard – is the premise of all enquiry. This existence is determined by no universal idea, and has no prefigured destiny such as might be contained in a vision of human nature. Man must make his own essence, and even his existence is, in a sense, an achievement. He exists fully only when he is what he purposes to be. (Here, as elsewhere, Sartre's philosophy echoes that of Heidegger.)

The premise of philosophy is still, therefore, the premise of Descartes, the 'cogito'; but it is the cogito transformed by Husserlian phenomenology. All consciousness is intentional – it posits an object in which it sees itself as in a mirror. Object and subject arise together and are conceived in radically different ways. Because they are so familiar to us, these ways defy description in the language of common sense. Hence the need for technicalities in order to describe the fundamental difference between the knower and the known (the '*pour-soi*' and the '*en-soi*', as Sartre calls them).

In setting itself up as subject in relation to a possibly unknowable object, the self creates (or posits) a separation in its world, a kind of crevasse which no amount of experience can fill. This crevasse is called '*néant*', or nothingness, which 'lies coiled in the heart of being, like a worm'. That characteristic phrase is part of an evocative description designed to persuade us that the separation of primeval being into subject and object generates a third thing (or rather no-thing). It is this third thing that enters the world of self-consciousness in persecutory disguises.

A. J. Ayer accused Sartre of a logical mistake in introducing 'nothingness' as though it were an entity: the logical mistake of the king in *Through the Looking Glass* who takes 'Nobody' as a proper name. But perhaps such criticism, tempting though it is, misses the phenomenological point of Sartre's coinage. Sartre is attempting to describe what is *given to consciousness* in the very act of conceiving itself as related to an objective world, and he perforce must strain language in order to express an experience which is so immediate as to precede every attempt at description.

The experience of nothingness is always with us and hence is elusive, as the ego is elusive. To persuade us of its actuality, Sartre provides various vivid examples, expectation and its disappointment being prominent among them. When I enter a cafe in search of Pierre, and he is not there, he is no more not there because of my expectation than he is not there when I had not thought of him. Yet my experience is changed by my expectation. The cafe reflects back to me, in all its particulars, the absence of Pierre. Pierre's absence becomes a pervasive quality of the consciousness through which these particulars are perceived. The cafe presents a kind of narrative of Pierre's non-existence, which could not be read in any locality where I had not expected him. This idea is certainly fanciful, but it is also typical of Sartrean phenomenology, being at once observant and uncanny. Like Socrates, Sartre attempts to introduce '*aporia*', or intellectual anguish, as a prelude to the introduction of a metaphysical idea which will console the bewildered intelligence.

Only self-consciousness can bring *néant* or nothingness into the world: for the merely sentient being the fracture between subject and object has not opened. But with the sense of nothingness comes anguish. The question arises, 'How shall I fill this void – between myself and the world?', or, to put it in a way which, for Sartre, seems to be equivalent: 'How shall I make myself *part* of the world?' This is the phenomenological meaning of the question 'What shall I do?' It is the present sense of the future, and of the individual's responsibility for that future. Anguish is the proof of freedom. There can be nothing more certain to a person than that he is free, since nothing is more certain than the existential choice which compels the recognition of futurity, and of our responsibility towards it.

What is the outcome of anguish? Initially it manifests itself, Sartre says, as the sense that objects are not properly distinct from each other. They are undifferentiated, passive, awaiting agency. Our sense of the gap between subject and object translates itself into a feeling of nausea at the dissolution of things. The world becomes slime. In reaction I may run away from the future, hide myself in some predetermined role, contorting myself to fit a costume that is already made for me, so leaping across the chasm that divides me from objects only in order to become an object myself. This happens when I adopt a morality, a religion, a social role that has been devised by others and which has significance for me only in so far as I am objectified in it. The result is what Sartre calls 'bad faith', indistinguishable I think from Heidegger's inauthenticity, and once again owing what content we can ascribe to it to the 'alienation' of nineteenth-century Hegelian thought.

This false simulation of the in-itself by the for-itself (of the object by the subject) is to be contrasted with the authentic individual gesture. This, the reader will not be surprised to learn, cannot be described in its generality, but can only be seen in its individuality, in the free act whereby the individual creates both himself and his world together, by casting the one into the other. Don't ask *how* this is done. Its end point is what matters, and this Sartre describes as 'commitment'. But commitment to what?

Sartre here introduces his well-known defence of ethical subjectivism, arguing that any adoption of a system of values which is represented as 'objective' constitutes an attempt to transfer my freedom into the world of objects, and so to lose it. The desire for an objective moral order is an exhibition of bad faith, and a loss of the freedom without which no moral order of any kind would be conceivable. In what sense Sartre is able to *recommend* the authenticity which consists in the purely self-made morality is unclear. He does recommend it, but, by his own argument, his recommendation can have no objective force. He is therefore more apt to use the language of 'must' than of 'ought':

> I emerge alone and in dread in the face of the unique and first project which constitutes my being; all the barriers, all the railings, collapse, annihilated by the consciousness of my liberty; I have not, nor can I have, recourse to any value against the fact that it is I who maintain values in being; nothing can assure me against myself; cut off from the world and my essence by the nothing that I *am*, I have to realise the meaning of the world and of my essence: I decide it, alone, unjustifiable, and without excuse.

In such a way Sartre tries to preserve Kant's ethic of moral 'autonomy', while divesting it of the commitment to a moral law.

So far, as I said, there is not much to distinguish Sartre's philosophy from Heidegger's, except for a greater ease and clarity of expression, and a taste for vivid examples. But Sartre picks up another part of the Hegelian legacy. He gives his own version of the master and slave argument, this time under the guise of an examination of love. He attempts to show that all love, and indeed all human relation, is founded in contradiction. He introduces the notion of 'being-for-others' in order to describe the peculiar position in which a self-conscious being can find himself, of being at once a free subject in his own eyes, and a determined object in the eyes of others. (Compare Kant's distinction between the transcendental and the empirical self.) When another self-conscious being looks at me, I know that he searches in me not just for the object, but also for the subject. The gaze of a self-conscious creature has a peculiar capacity to penetrate, to create a demand. This is the demand that I, as free subjectivity, reveal myself in the world.

Taking his cue from 'the life and death struggle' of the *Phenomenology of Spirit* (see p. 169), Sartre now proceeds to describe all human relations in terms of struggle. If I love a woman then this is never simply a matter of lusting to gratify myself on her body: if it were just that, then any object, even a simulacrum of a human body, would do just as well. What I want is *her*: that is, the individual who is only real in her freedom, and who is falsified by every attempt to represent her as an object. As Sartre puts it: love wants the freedom of another, in order to make that freedom its own. But of course, the peculiarity of freedom is that it cannot be borrowed, shared or stolen. It is mine and mine alone. The lover, who wants to possess the body of another only as, and only in so far as, the other possesses it himself, is tied by a contradiction. His desire will fulfil itself only by frustrating itself, leaving him with the freedom of the other yet further removed. In the act of love, the other *becomes* his body, and so loses in the eyes of the lover the subjectivity which defines him. The most evident case of this, Sartre suggests, is sadomasochism, of which he gives a detailed and fascinating analysis.

Sartre's cheerless account of human affection perhaps contains some of his most lasting contributions to thought. Philosophically it is not original, owing what strength it has to the deeper discussions of Hegel. 'Love', wrote Hegel, 'is the most tremendous contradiction; the understanding cannot resolve it' (*Philosophy of Right*, addition to paragraph 158). But contradictions worried Hegel less than they worry others: they were there to be transcended, through the dialectical movement which belongs, not to understanding, but to reason, whether in its pure or in its practical form. Sartre's account stops short of any such metaphysical solution. Nevertheless, it remains in some ways more acute, and more terrifyingly persuasive, than the Hegelian arguments which it borrows. It is in this area – that of the observation of the human world – that latter-day phenomenology has been most influential. Sartre's studies of love, of 'the gaze', of hesitation, guilt and anguish, have been matched by other contributions of equal eloquence and power. Perhaps the most important among these have been those of Maurice Merleau-Ponty

(1908–1961) in *The Phenomenology of Perception* (1945) and *Signs* (1960). The result has been a mass of phenomenological lore. I call it lore, not out of disrespect, but because of the impossibility of ascertaining its intellectual status. The results of phenomenology can seem both true to experience and yet irritatingly paradoxical, both in their style and in their philosophical presuppositions. Some reasons for this air of paradox will emerge in the chapter which follows.

19

WITTGENSTEIN

Our discussion has brought us, by various routes, to that point in philosophical history from which, for a long time, many philosophers have dated its commencement. The discovery of the new logic precipitated 'analytical' philosophy, bringing about, first logical atomism, then logical positivism and finally linguistic analysis, the practitioners of which have often paid scant heed to the arguments and aims of their predecessors. A single figure contributed decisively to the formation of each of these schools, and the same figure sowed in each of them the seeds of its destruction.

The rise of 'analytical' philosophy

Much has been written in recent years about the life and philosophy of Ludwig Wittgenstein (1889–1951). It is now widely thought that he is the most important philosopher of our century. It is hard, nevertheless, to fit his thought into the history of the subject, partly because of its later iconoclasm, partly because, like Frege, he began from reflections which, in the light of that history, may seem parochial and even without philosophical relevance. As a prelude, therefore, it is necessary to say something about the state of English philosophy at the time when Wittgenstein first took an interest in it. This interest presaged the prolonged influence of Viennese ideas on Anglo-American thought. We must return a little in time, to the ideas of Russell and Moore.

Bertrand Arthur, third Earl Russell (1872–1970) has been mentioned so far in connection with the new logic, which he transformed into a powerful tool of philosophical analysis. No less important historically was his friend G. E. Moore (1873–1958), the writer of an important treatise on ethics, *Principia Ethica* (1903), and the relentless foe of all forms of metaphysical speculation that seemed to be the enemies of common sense. Together, Moore and Russell devoted themselves to the demolition of the arguments of British idealism, as these were represented by Bradley (at Oxford) and J. M. McTaggart (1866–1925) at their own university of Cambridge. Russell, in his early work on the foundations of geometry, acknowledges the influence of Bradley's *Logic*. But this did not prevent him from discerning, in Bradley's famous proof of the makeshift character of both objects and qualities (see p. 233), a confusion between the 'is' of predication and the 'is' of identity, or from accusing Bradley and McTaggart of sleight of hand in almost all their proofs for the inadequacy of our common sense conceptions of space, time and matter. Moore joined in the battle, adding not so much arguments as peculiarly dramatic assertions. How is it possible, he asked, for my belief that I have two hands to be less certain than the validity of all the philosophical arguments which have been adduced to disprove it? The combination of Russell's mercurial logic, and Moore's robust refusal to think further than his nose, or hands, proved extremely destructive, and it became fashionable to describe idealist metaphysics not as false, but as meaningless. Other philosophers – notably Hume – had said similar things. But now more than ever it seemed possible to prove the point, by developing a theory of the structure of language that would show precisely what could and what could not be said. And it was supposed that among the things that could not be said, metaphysics was the most easily recognisable.

The first such theory was logical atomism, adumbrated by Russell, and more or less completely expressed in Wittgenstein's *Tractatus Logico-Philosophicus* (1921). This work, more succinct even than Leibniz's *Monadology*, claimed to give the final answers to the questions of philosophy. It was inspired in part by Russell's famous theory of descriptions, published in 1905, in an article that F. P. Ramsey (1903–1930) described as 'a paradigm of philosophy'. This theory will therefore serve as a fitting introduction to Wittgenstein's work.

The theory of descriptions

It is strange, but nevertheless true, that one of the most important publications in modern philosophy should have had, as its ostensible purpose, the explanation of the meaning of the word 'the'. What is the difference, Russell asks, between the sentence 'a golden mountain exists' and the sentence 'the golden mountain exists'? The first expression is explained by the new logic as follows: the predicate 'golden mountain' is instantiated, or, more formally, there exists an *x* such that *x* is a golden mountain. This proposition is clearly false. But what about the second proposition? Here the word 'the' seems to change the predicate 'golden mountain' into what Russell would call a denoting phrase (and what Frege had called a name). This is a strange effect of grammar. It has a yet stranger logical consequence, namely, that the sentence seems to refer to something – the golden mountain. But how is that possible, if no golden mountain exists? Here, Russell argued, we have a paradigm case of a grammatical form which conceals the logical form of a sentence. Taking his cue from his own and Frege's implicit definition of number, he offers an implicit definition of the word 'the'. We cannot say explicitly what the term 'the' denotes, but we can show how to eliminate it from all the sentences in which it occurs.

Consider the sentence, 'the King of France is bald'. For this to be true, there must be a king of France, and he must be bald. Moreover, to capture the distinctive sense of the word 'the' we have to add that there is only *one* king of France. The conditions which make the sentence true give us its meaning; hence we can say that 'the King of France is bald' is equivalent to the conjunction of three propositions: 'there exists a king of France; everything which is a king of France is bald; and there is only one king of France.' (More formally – there exists an *x* such that: *x* is a king of France and *x* is bald, and, for all *y*, if *y* is a king of France, *y* is identical to *x*.) It follows from this analysis that, if there is no king of France, then the original sentence is false. The phrase 'the King of France', which seemed to be a denoting phrase or name, is in fact no such thing, but rather a predicate attached to a concealed existential claim. The King of France is, as Russell put it, a logical fiction. (There is a historical antecedent for this kind of philosophical theory in Bentham's theory of fictions.)

Philosophically, Russell directed his arguments against certain phenomenologists (notably Alexius Meinong (1853–1920)) who had wanted to conclude that, if we can think of something, such as the golden mountain, then that thing must, in some sense, exist. (If you don't like the word 'exist', then another – 'subsist' – is offered to allay your logical susceptibilities.) Russell did not fully grasp that Meinong and his associates were not so much engaged in exploring the logic of denotation, as in examining the 'intentional object' of thought. Be that as it may, however, Russell's argument lent itself to instant generalisation, and in this generalised form provided a basis for the philosophy of the *Tractatus*.

Logical atomism and the *Tractatus*

According to the *Tractatus*, everything that can be thought can also be said. The limits of language are, therefore, the limits of thought, so that a complete philosophy of the 'sayable' will be a complete theory of what Kant had called 'the understanding'. All metaphysical problems arise because of the attempt to say what cannot be said. A proper analysis of the structure of the terms used in that attempt will show this to be so, and thus either solve or dissolve the problems.

What then is the structure of language? Wittgenstein divided all sentences into the complex and the atomic, and asserted that the former were built up from the latter by rules of formation which could be fully interpreted in terms of Russell's logic (as this had been expounded in Russell and Whitehead's *Principia Mathematica* (1910–1913)). Atomic sentences are those which employ the *primitives* of the language: the elementary names and predicates which, being themselves indefinable, serve to pick out (or 'picture') what Wittgenstein called atomic facts. Only a completed proposition can be true or false, and so only a completed proposition can tell us anything about the world. Hence there can be no more basic constituent of the world than that which corresponds to the atomic sentence. This basic constituent is the atomic fact, and the world is therefore the totality of such facts.

Corresponding to complex propositions are complex facts, and to understand these complex facts we must understand the complexity of the language used to express them. This complexity is entirely given by the Fregean and Russellian logic. Thus 'the King of France is bald' is (although it seems not to be) a complex sentence, since its true structure (that is, its structure as represented by the new logic) shows it to consist of three incomplete sentences, combined and completed by quantification and the connective 'and'. Many sentences are like that. They seem to be basic, but are in fact complex. In general many of the things we refer to are logical constructions (or fictions). Sentences which describe them are shorthand for more complex sentences referring to the constituents of quite different, but more basic, facts, in which these 'logical constructions' do not occur. A sentence like 'the average man has 2.6 children' is really shorthand for a complex mathematical sentence relating the numbers of children of men to the numbers of men. 'The average man' features in no atomic sentence, which is to say that 'the average man' names no constituent of reality. The same is true of the English nation, and of many 'metaphysical' entities that have seemed to pose philosophical problems. Wittgenstein was less specific than Russell, and certainly less specific than the logical positivists, for whom nevertheless the *Tractatus* provided the complete apparatus of philosophical argument, as to which facts are atomic and which are not. He wished to give the clear statement of the logical *structure* of the world: its actual contents did not concern him.

The all-important feature of complex sentences is that the connectives which are used to build them must be 'truth-functional'. That is to say, they must be such that the truth-value of the complex sentence is entirely determined by the truth-values of its parts. This is the 'principle of extensionality' that we have already encountered in discussing Frege, and which, according to Wittgenstein, is a precondition of logical thought and analysis. Logic is concerned purely with the systematic transformation of truth-values, and hence a logical language must be *transparent* to truth-values. It must be possible to see every operation in terms of the transformation of truth and falsehood. (The word ' not' has the sense that it turns truth to falsehood and falsehood to truth; 'if' that it makes a complex sentence that is false if the antecedent is true and the consequent false, otherwise true; and so on.)

The notion of a truth-functional language gives exactness and cogency to Wittgenstein's claim that there is a real distinction between atomic and non-atomic sentences. He is able to say not only what the distinction is, but more importantly, how we are able to understand it. There is no difficulty, with a truth-functional language, in explaining how the understanding of atomic sentences leads to an understanding of all the infinite complexes that can be built from them. (This is another application of a principle of Frege's, discussed here on pp. 245–6.) The conditions for the truth of a complex sentence formed truth-functionally can be derived immediately from the truth-conditions of its parts. And hence if we understand the truth-conditions of the parts, we understand the whole.

Moreover, Wittgenstein is able to provide a novel and seemingly utterly clear distinction between the necessary and the contingent, the analytic and the synthetic, the *a priori* and the *a posteriori*. These distinctions become one distinction, that between logical truth and contingency. A sentence is a logical truth if it is made true by every substitution of terms for the 'primitive' parts which it contains. (A primitive part being one which admits of no further definition.) The paradigm example of the logical truth is the truth-functional 'tautology'. Consider the sentence '*p* or *q*'. The definition of 'or' reads thus: *p* or *q* is false if both *p* and *q* are false, otherwise true. The definition of 'not' is: not-*p* is true if *p* is false, false if *p* is true. From which it follows that the sentence '*p* or not-*p*' is always true, whatever the truth-value of '*p*'. So, no matter what we substitute for the primitive term '*p*', the resulting sentence will always be true. Sentences of this form are therefore necessarily true, and can be seen to be true *a priori* by anyone who understands the logical operations of the language.

This theory of necessary truth has the consequence, Wittgenstein thought, that necessary truths are empty: they say nothing because they exclude nothing. They are compatible with every state of affairs. The world is described by the totality of true atomic propositions: these are true, but, being atomic, might have been false, since there is nothing in their structure to determine their truth-value. Another way of putting this is that facts exist in 'logical space'. This logical space defines the possibilities; the true atomic sentences describe what is actual, while tautologies reflect properties of logical space itself.

There are deep metaphysical problems raised by this account of language. First there is the problem of the relation between atomic sentences and atomic facts. Wittgenstein calls this relation one of 'picturing', and this metaphor has misled many of his commentators. He also says that the relation cannot be described, but only shown: indeed it was his view that what is most basic *must* be shown; otherwise description could never begin. Precisely what is meant by 'showing' is not clear. Perhaps the best way to understand this theory – sometimes called the 'picture theory of meaning' – is as a denial, to use a later phrase of Wittgenstein's, that we can use language 'to get between language and the world'. We cannot give an account in words of the relation between an atomic fact and an atomic proposition except by using the proposition whose truth we are trying to explain. We cannot 'think' the atomic fact without thinking the sentence which 'pictures' it. The limits of thought are the limits of language. Wittgenstein concludes his book with the laconic statement: 'that whereof we cannot speak we must consign to silence.'

One of the problems for the philosophy of the *Tractatus* is indicated in that very utterance. Only atomic sentences, truth-functional complexes, and tautologies are meaningful. But what of the theory which says so? It is not an atomic sentence, nor any complex of such: it purports to say, not how things are but how they must be. But it is not a tautology. Is it then meaningless? Wittgenstein actually says 'yes', and with that bold gesture moves on to the conclusion of his philosophy, adding that his propositions must serve as a ladder to be thrown away by those who have managed to ascend it.

Wittgenstein and linguistic analysis

There is about the *Tractatus* something of the fascination of Kant's first *Critique*: the fascination of a doctrine that struggles as hard as possible to describe the limits of the intelligible only to be compelled, in the course of doing so, to transcend them. Wittgenstein nowhere acknowledges the likeness of his thought to Kant's, or indeed to anyone's except Russell's, but the parallel between the two philosophers becomes more and more striking, so striking, indeed, that some have seen the argument of the posthumous *Philosophical Investigations* as completing at last the work of Kant's Transcendental Deduction.

Wittgenstein's later philosophy evolved out of a reaction to the earlier, or rather to a certain extremely influential interpretation of it. In the *Tractatus* the metaphysics of logical atomism is presented with almost no reference to any specific theory of knowledge. Russell's own version of the theory was decidedly empiricist, identifying the 'atomic facts' as facts about the immediate contents of experience (or 'sense-data' as Russell called them). Using the apparatus of Wittgenstein's theory, Russell was then able to restate a version of empiricism in the sceptical spirit of Hume, proposing to construe every entity in the world other than sense-data as a 'logical construction'. Whether or not we do mean, when referring to tables, to refer to logical constructions out of sense-data, it is, Russell thought, all that we ought to mean. As he put it, 'wherever possible, logical constructions are to be substituted for inferred entities'. Philosophy thus took a step in the direction of logical positivism, according to which all metaphysical, ethical and theological doctrines are meaningless, not because of any defect of logical thought, but because they are unverifiable. The slogan of positivism – that the meaning of a sentence is its method of verification – is taken from the *Tractatus*, as was much of the apparatus whereby it sought to rid the world of metaphysical entities. But its spirit was that of Hume, and its principal theories were restatements of Hume's ideas concerning causality, the physical world and morality, in terms of an 'analytic' rather than a 'genetic' theory of meaning. By the time this programme was under way, in the work of Rudolf Carnap (1891–1970) and others of the so-called 'Vienna Circle' (see especially Carnap's *Logical Structure of the World*, 1928), Wittgenstein had renounced all allegiance to atomism and its progeny, had ceased publication and begun a hermetic, and often nomadic, existence which ensured that, until his death, what influence he had was confined to those privileged to know him personally, or to catch sight of the manuscripts which he occasionally allowed to pass from his hands. Among these manuscripts the most famous – *The Blue and Brown Books* – reached Oxford in the 1940s, and there precipitated the school of 'linguistic analysis' for which J. L. Austin (1911–1960) and Gilbert Ryle (1900–1977) were already preparing the way. But that school, consisting as it does of figures too many and too minor to warrant our attention, and being characterised less by any theory than by the refusal to subscribe to one, is not one that I shall discuss. Nor shall I consider the later development of logical positivism in America, where it entered into a fruitful marriage – through Carnap's pupils Nelson Goodman and Willard van Orman Quine with the local 'pragmatism' of C. S. Peirce, (1839–1914), William James (1842–1910) and C. I. Lewis (1883–1964). Instead I shall conclude this work with an outline of certain arguments expressed in the *Philosophical Investigations* (1953), *The Remarks on the Foundations of Mathematics* (1956) and elsewhere. Because they relate directly to the history of the subject as I have so far described it, these arguments will give some indication, however slight, of the extent to which Wittgenstein's later philosophy has transformed and even brought to an end the tradition of intellectual enquiry which began with Descartes.

The later Wittgenstein

The emphasis of Wittgenstein's later philosophy is decidedly anthropocentric. While still interested in questions concerning meaning and the limits of significant utterance, the starting-point has become, not the immutable abstractions of an ideal logic, but the fallible efforts of human communication. At the same time, the human element has not entered through the usual channel of epistemology, but in a wholly surprising way. Wittgenstein introduces it through *a priori* reflections on the nature of the human mind, and on the social behaviour which endows that mind with its characteristic structure. What is 'given' is not the 'sense-data' of the positivists, but the 'forms of life' of Kantian philosophical anthropology. To put it in another way: the subject of any theory of meaning and understanding is the public practice of utterance, and all that makes this practice possible. Thus Wittgenstein begins his later investigations into the nature of language at the point where Frege broke off. He develops the thesis of the 'publicity' of sense, which had already led Frege to reject traditional empiricist theories of meaning. The result is not only a new account of the nature of language, but also a revolutionary philosophy of mind. The metaphysical problems that had occupied Kant, Hegel and Schopenhauer are rephrased as difficulties in the interpretation of consciousness. Construed thus they suddenly seem capable of resolution.

The social perspective caused Wittgenstein to move away from Frege's emphasis on the concept of truth, or rather, to see this emphasis as reflecting a more fundamental demand that human utterance be answerable to a standard of correctness. This standard is not God-given, nor does it lie dormant in the order of nature. It is a human artifact, as much the product as the producer of the linguistic practices which it governs. This does not mean that an individual can decide for himself what is right and wrong in the art of communication. On the contrary, the constraint of publicity binds each and all of us; moreover that constraint is intimately bound up with our conception of ourselves as beings who observe and act upon an independent world. Nevertheless, it is true that there is no constraint involved in common usage other than usage itself. If we come up against truths which seem to us to be necessary, this can only be because we have created the rules that make them so, and what we create we can also forgo. The compulsion that we experience in logical inference, for example, is no compulsion, independently of our disposition so to experience it.

This kind of reflection led Wittgenstein towards a highly sophisticated form of nominalism: a denial that we can look outside linguistic practice for the thing which governs it. The ultimate facts are language, and the forms of life which grow from language and make language possible. Nominalism is not new, nor has it lacked exponents in our day. Nelson Goodman (b. 1906), for example, has advocated, using arguments that often resemble Wittgenstein's, a kind of nominalism that incorporates a whole philosophy of science together with a theory of knowledge. What is peculiar to Wittgenstein is the transition that he makes at this juncture from the philosophy of language to the philosophy of mind. During the course of this transition, he attempts to overthrow the major premise of almost all Western philosophy since Descartes – the premise of the 'priority of the first-person case'.

Wittgenstein uses a variety of arguments, designed to show what this premise really means, and in the course of doing so to demonstrate its untenability. Together these arguments provide what can best be described as a 'picture' of human consciousness. This picture has many aspects, some metaphysical, some epistemological: it involves the rejection of the Cartesian quest for certainty, the demolition of the view that mental events are private episodes observable to one person alone, the rejection of all attempts to understand the human mind in isolation from the social practices through which it finds expression. It is impossible here to give all the considerations whereby Wittgenstein upholds 'the priority of the third-person case'. I shall therefore mention one or two central strands of argument and draw some conclusions as to the historical and philosophical significance of the thesis.

The private language argument

The most famous argument advanced for the Wittgensteinian position is that which has come to be known as 'the private language argument'. This occurs in many versions in the *Philosophical Investigations* and has been the subject of much commentary. In outline, it seems to me the argument is as follows: there is a peculiar 'privilege' or 'immediacy' involved in the knowledge of our own present experiences. In some sense it is nonsense to suggest that I have to find out about them, or that I could, in the normal run of things, be mistaken. (This is the thought which also underlies Kant's thesis of the 'Transcendental Unity of Apperception', see pp. 137–8.) As a result there has arisen what we might call the 'first-person illusion'. I can be more certain about my mental states than about yours. This can only be because I observe my mental states directly, yours indirectly. When I see you in pain, I see physical behaviour, its causes, a certain complex state of an organism. But this is not the pain that you have, only some contingent accompaniment of it. The pain itself lies hidden behind its expression, directly observable to its sufferer alone.

That is, in brief, the Cartesian theory of mind, presented as an explanation of the first-person case. Both the theory, Wittgenstein argues, and the thing that it is put forward to explain, are illusions. Suppose the theory were true. Then, Wittgenstein argues, we could not refer to our sensations by means of words intelligible in a public language. For words in a public language get their sense publicly, by being attached to publicly accessible conditions that warrant their application. These conditions will determine not only their sense, but also their reference. The assumption that this reference is private (in the sense of being observable, in principle, to one person alone) is, Wittgenstein argues, incompatible with the hypothesis that the sense is public. Hence, if mental events are as the Cartesian describes them to be, no word in our public language could actually refer to them.

In effect, however, Cartesians and their empiricist progeny have always, wittingly or unwittingly, accepted that conclusion, and written as though we each describe our sensations and other present mental episodes in a language which, because its field of reference is inaccessible in principle to others, is intelligible to the speaker alone. Wittgenstein argues against the possibility of such a private language. He attempts to prove that there can be no difference made, by the speaker of that language, between how things seem to him and how things are. He would lose the distinction between being and seeming. But this means losing the idea of objective reference. The language is not aimed at reality at all; it becomes instead an arbitrary game. What seems right is what is right; hence one can no longer speak of right.

The conclusion is this: we cannot refer to Cartesian mental events (private objects) in a public language; nor can we refer to them in a private language. Hence we cannot refer to them. But, someone might say, they may nevertheless *exist*! To which Wittgenstein replies, in a manner reminiscent of Kant's attack on the noumenon, that a nothing will do as well as a something about which nothing can be said. Moreover, we *can* refer to sensations; so whatever they are, sensations are not Cartesian mental events.

Wittgenstein accompanies this argument with an acute description, from the third-person point of view, of many complex mental phenomena – in particular those of perception, intention, expectation and desire. His arguments, as he acknowledges, refute, if successful, the possibility of a 'pure phenomenology', since they have the implication that nothing about the essence of the mental (or about the essence of anything) can be learned from the study (in Cartesian isolation) of the first person alone. The 'immediacy' of the first-person case is an index only of its shallowness. It is true that I know my own mental states without observing my behaviour; but this is not because I am observing something *else*. It is simply an illusion, thrown up by self-consciousness, that the necessary authority that accompanies the public usage of 'I', is an authority about some matter of which only the 'I' has knowledge.

The priority of the third person

Despite this rejection of the 'method' of phenomenology, however, Wittgenstein showed himself sympathetic to an ambition which had become – through a series of historical accidents – allied to it. Thinkers like the Kantian Dilthey (see p. 255) had sought for the foundations of a peculiarly 'human' understanding, according to which the world would be seen, not scientifically, but under the aspect of 'meaning'. Wittgenstein, in common with some phenomenologists, such as Merleau-Ponty and Sartre, argued that we perceive and understand human behaviour in a manner different from that in which we perceive and understand the natural world. We explain human behaviour by giving reasons, not causes. We address ourselves to our future by making decisions, not predictions. We understand the past and present of mankind through our aims, emotions and activity, and not through predictive theories. All these distinctions seem to create the idea, if not of a specifically human world, at least of a specifically human way of seeing things. Much of Wittgenstein's later philosophy is devoted to describing and analysing the characteristics of human understanding, and demolishing what he thought to be the vulgar illusion that science could generate a description of all those things with which our humanity (or to put it more philosophically, our existence as rational agents) is mingled. He defends the positions not only that our knowledge of our own minds presupposes the knowledge of the minds of others, but also that as the phenomenologist Max Scheler (1874–1928) put it – 'our conviction of the existence of other minds is earlier and deeper than our belief in the existence of nature'. In other words, despite the attack on the method and metaphysics of phenomenology, Wittgenstein shares with the phenomenologists the sense that there is a mystery in human things that will not yield to scientific investigation. This mystery is dispelled not by explanation, but only by careful philosophical description of the 'given'. The difference is that, for Wittgenstein, what is 'given' is not the contents of immediate experience, but the forms of life which make experience possible.

The demolition of the first-person illusion has two consequences. First, we cannot begin our enquiries from the first-person case and think that it gives us a paradigm of certainty. For, taken in isolation, it gives us nothing at all. Secondly, while the distinction between being and seeming does not exist for me when I contemplate my own sensations, this is only because I speak a public language which determines this peculiar property of first-person knowledge. The collapse of being and seeming into each other, as in first-person awareness, is a 'degenerate' case. I can know, therefore, that if this collapse is possible, it is because there are people in the world besides myself, and because I have a nature and form of life in common with them. I do indeed inhabit an objective world, a world where things are or can be other than they seem. So, in a startling way, the argument of Kant's Transcendental Deduction is found. The precondition of self-knowledge (of the Transcendental Unity of Apperception) is, after all, the knowledge of others, and of the objective world which contains them.

Much has changed in philosophy since Wittgenstein produced his arguments. One thing is certain, however. The assumption that there is first-person certainty, which provides a starting-point for philosophical enquiry, this assumption which led to the rationalism of Descartes and to the empiricism of Hume, to so much of modern epistemology and so much of modern metaphysics, has been finally removed from the centre of philosophy. The ambition of Kant and Hegel, to achieve a philosophy which removes the 'self' from the beginning of knowledge so as to return it in an enriched and completed form at the end, has perhaps now been fulfilled.

BIBLIOGRAPHY

The purpose of this bibliography is to direct the reader towards reliable English-language versions of the more important texts of the philosophers discussed, and to provide a brief review of the available commentaries.

The study of the history of philosophy has only recently acquired a firm place on the curriculum of universities in the English-speaking world. Nevertheless, the long-delayed discovery of this fertile territory has in recent years led to an explosion of publications, which it would be a life's work to summarise. Particularly influential at the scholarly level have been the volumes published by Routledge, in the series edited by Ted Honderich entitled 'The Arguments of the Philosophers'. Oxford University Press's 'Past Masters' series contains many useful guides for the less specialised reader. It remains true, nevertheless, that the original texts, properly translated, are the surest guides to the thought of those who wrote them.

General

The most comprehensive history of philosophy in English remains Frederick Copleston's *History of Philosophy*, 12 vols, London, 1950 onwards.

Bertrand Russell's *History of Western Philosophy* (London, 1944) is amusing, but suffers from defects that make it inadequate as a supplement to the present volume. First, it deals largely with ancient philosophy, and is curt and selective in its treatment of the post-Cartesian tradition. Secondly, it is dismissive towards all those philosophers with whom Russell felt no personal affinity. Thirdly, it shows no understanding of Kant and post-Kantian idealism. It is, for all that, a classic of wit, elegance and resolute idiosyncrasy. Readers seeking a reliable, lengthy exposition of the subject might be better advised to try D. J. O'Connor (ed.), *A Critical History of Western Philosophy*, London, 1964, a book which suffers, however, from being written by many different hands.

J. Passmore's *100 Years of Philosophy*, London, 1957, concerning the period from the mid-nineteenth to the mid-twentieth centuries, is comprehensive and interesting.

1 History of philosophy and history of ideas

The literature on modern philosophy is vast. In *Modern Philosophy: An Introduction and Survey*, London, 1994, I have tried to review the entire subject as it is now conceived in the Anglo-American tradition, and to provide an effective guide to the literature. Those who prefer a shorter introduction (and who can blame them?) should read Bertrand Russell's enduring classic, *The Problems of Philosophy*, London, 1912. A sense of the subject can also be gained from reading Plato's shorter dialogues, in particular the *Gorgias* and *Theaetetus*.

Anthony Flew (ed.), *A Dictionary of Philosophy*, London, 1979, is one of the best of the many available short guides to the language of modern philosophy, while the much longer *Encyclopedia of Philosophy*, ed. Paul S. Edwards, London and New York, 1967, has retained its authoritative lead over all rival compendia. Simon Blackburn's *Dictionary of Philosophy*, Oxford, 1995, seems, on first reading, exemplary.

2 The rise of modern philosophy

Boethius's *Consolation of Philosophy* is available in the Loeb Classical Library (bilingual, Latin and English), ed. H. F. Stewart and E. K. Rand, London and New York, 1918. There is an interesting translation by Chaucer, entitled *Boece*.

St Thomas Aquinas's *Summa Theologica* has been re-issued, in a scholarly bilingual edition, by Blackfriars in association with Eyre & Spottiswoode and McGraw-Hill, London and New York. The best short commentary is Anthony Kenny's *Aquinas*, in the Past Masters series, ed. Keith Thomas, Oxford, 1980.

For the other figures mentioned, see F. C. Copleston, *Medieval Philosophy*, London, 1952. The principal texts can be found in A. Hyman and J. J. Walsh (eds), *Philosophy in the Middle Ages*, New York, Evanston and London, 1967, which contains extracts from Aquinas as well as from the Arabic, Jewish and Christian philosophers of the pre-Thomist period.

Bacon's philosophical writings are most accessibly presented in F. H. Anderson (ed.), *The New Organon and Related Writings*, New York, 1960.

3 Descartes

The standard edition of Descartes' works is *Œuvres de Descartes*, 12 vols plus supplement, edited by Charles Adam and Paul Tannery, and published in Paris by Leopold Cerf, 1897–1913. English editions often quote the page numbering of this edition in the margins of the translated text.

The following English editions are acceptable: *The Philosophical Works of Descartes*, translated by E. S. Haldane and G. R. T. Ross, 2 vols, Cambridge, 1911–12, paperback edition New York, 1955. *Descartes: Philosophical Writings*, a selection translated and edited by Elizabeth Anscombe and P. T. Geach, Sunbury-on-Thames, 1954, revised edition 1970. *The Philosophical Writings of Descartes*, translated and edited by John Cottingham, Robert Stoothoff and Dugald Murdoch, 2 vols, Cambridge, 1985. This will no doubt become the standard English edition and should be read in preference to the above if possible. There is also a selection from the same edition, published in one volume, Cambridge, 1988. This contains everything that a newcomer to Descartes will need and has been brilliantly edited to meet the demands of today's student.

Commentaries are legion, but the following have had considerable impact on recent scholarship: Anthony Kenny, *Descartes: A Study of his Philosophy*, New York, 1968; Bernard Williams, *Descartes: The Project of Pure Enquiry*, an imaginative and insightful work, which conveys an unmatched sense of the intellectual importance of Descartes and his project; Margaret Wilson, *Descartes*, London, 1983, a thorough and careful guide to the argument. For the immediate background to Descartes' thought, see R. H. Popkin, *The History of Scepticism from Erasmus to Descartes*, New York, 1968. There is also a *Cambridge Companion to Descartes*, edited by John Cottingham, Cambridge, 1992, which contains interesting articles on all aspects of Descartes' philosophy.

4 The Cartesian revolution

Father Mersenne's collection of objections to Descartes, and Descartes' replies, can be found in E. S. Haldane and G. R. T. Ross (eds), *The Philosophical Works of Descartes*, 2 vols, 1911–12, paperback edition New York, 1955, and also in the edition of Descartes' philosophical writings, edited by J. Cottingham et al., Cambridge, 1985. The Port-Royal logic is available in a recent edition, tr. James Dickoff and Patricia James as *The Art of Thinking*, Indianapolis and New York, 1964. For Petrus Ramus, see

W. and M. Kneale, *The Development of Logic*, Oxford, 1962, pp. 301f. Pascal's *Pensées* are available in translations by Martin Turnell, London, 1962, and W. F. Trotter, New York, 1958, with an introduction by T. S. Eliot. Nicolas Malebranche's *Dialogues on Metaphysics and Religion* are available in a translation by Morris Ginsberg, London, 1923.

For the history of ideas covering the period from the Cartesians to the *philosophes*, see Paul Hazard, *The European Mind: 1680–1715*, tr. J. L. May, reissued London, 1973. For Diderot, Voltaire, d'Alembert and the *philosophes* in general, see Diderot, *Rameau's Nephew and Other Works*, tr. Barzun and Bowen, New York, 1956; Voltaire, *Philosophical Dictionary*, 2 vols, tr. Gray, New York, 1963 and Norman L. Torrey, *The Spirit of Voltaire*, Oxford, 1962. There is also a useful article on the movement in D. J. O'Connor (ed.), *A Critical History of Western Philosophy*, London, 1964, by E. A. Gellner, entitled 'French Eighteenth Century Materialism'.

5 Spinoza

The standard edition of the works of Spinoza in the original Latin is that edited by C. Gebhardt, *Spinoza Opera*, 4 vols, Heidelberg, 1925.

There are several translations of the major metaphysical works available. Undeniably the best, in what will surely become the standard English-language edition of Spinoza, is that by Edwin Curley: *The Collected Works of Spinoza*, vol. 1, Princeton, 1985. (Vol. 2, containing the political works and the remainder of Spinoza's correspondence, has yet to appear.) This magisterial edition, containing all that the student needs, is complete with glossary, index and editorial apparatus, and makes the works fully accessible in English for the first time.

Unfortunately Curley's edition is expensive and not very easy to obtain. The cheap and acceptable alternative is the translation of the *Ethics* by Samuel Shirley, edited with a useful and lively introduction by Seymour Feldman, and published by the Hackett Publishing Co., Indianapolis, 1992. This also contains the *Treatise on the Emendation of the Intellect*, and a selection from the correspondence, both of which are of considerable importance.

The complete correspondence of Spinoza is obtainable in a translation edited by A. Wolf, London 1928, reissued 1962. The correspondence relating to the metaphysical works also occurs in Curley, where it is illuminatingly introduced by the translator. The correspondence should not be neglected, since it contains Spinoza's own attempts to make his system clear and accessible to puzzled or sceptical readers.

Among commentaries, the following might prove useful: R. Scruton, *Spinoza*, Oxford, 1986: a very short introduction, which is intended as a map of the territory; Stuart Hampshire, *Spinoza*, Harmondsworth, 1951, reprinted 1981: a path-breaking book, though now somewhat dated; Jonathan Bennett, *A Study of Spinoza's Ethics*, Cambridge, 1984: a difficult and strenuous book, which is relentlessly combative towards its subject matter; Edwin Curley, *Behind the Geometrical Method: A Reading of Spinoza's Ethics*, Princeton, 1988: a reworking of a previous commentary, intended in part as a response to Bennett – perhaps the most readable and accessible of the shorter commentaries; Henry Allison, *Benedict de Spinoza: An Introduction*, New Haven, 1987: also very accessible, and frequently illuminating.

Among the collections of articles now available, that edited by S. Paul Kashap, entitled *Studies in Spinoza: Critical and Interpretive Essays*, Los Angeles, 1972, is perhaps the most useful. It contains the important essay 'Spinoza and the Idea of Freedom', by Stuart Hampshire, and an essay by G. H. R. Parkinson, which is an adequate substitute for the same author's *Spinoza's Theory of Knowledge*, Oxford, 1954. The interested student would also gain much from the following two articles: Thomas Carson Mark, 'The Spinozistic Attributes', *Philosophia* 7, 1977; and Ralph Walker, 'Spinoza and the Coherence Theory of Truth', *Mind* 94, 1985.

6 Leibniz

Leibniz's works (most of them unpublished in his lifetime) are being issued in scholarly editions by the German Academy of Sciences, descendant of the Prussian Academy which Leibniz himself founded. Moving with exemplary slowness (due in part to the political division of Germany in recent times), the Academy has done little to replace the previous standard edition in German, edited by C. I. Gerhardt, published between 1875 and 1890. As a result, the Gerhardt edition is still widely referred to as the leading text.

There is also a famous collection of Leibniz's unpublished writings put together by the French mathematician Louis Couturat, *Opuscules et fragments inédits de Leibniz*, Paris, 1903. This was highly influential in emphasising the role that logical theory played in shaping Leibniz's metaphysics.

There have been two widely used English-language editions of the more important works: Leroy E. Loemker (ed.), *Leibniz: Philosophical Papers and Letters*, 2nd edition, Dordrecht, 1969; Philip P. Wiener (ed.), *Leibniz Selections*, New York, 2nd edn, 1986. (The first edition of this work is unreliable.)

More useful than either of those to the student, however, is: G. W. Leibniz, *Philosophical Essays*, tr. and ed. Roger Ariew and Daniel Garber, Indianapolis and Cambridge, 1989. This contains the crucial metaphysical works, in lucid and elegant translations.

Among other important works, the following are well worth reading: *The Leibniz–Arnauld Correspondence*, tr. H. T. Mason, Manchester, 1967; *The Leibniz–Clarke Correspondence*, tr. Samuel Clarke, ed. H. G. Alexander, Manchester, 1956; G. W. Leibniz, *New Essays on Human Understanding*, abridged, translated and edited by Peter Remnant and Jonathan Bennett, Cambridge, 1982. This last is an extremely useful and inexpensive book, with a marvellously succinct introduction containing a brief biography of Leibniz, a summary of several of his important theories, and a map of the *New Essays*. It has an up-to-date and lucid bibliography.

Commentaries include the following: G. H. R. Parkinson, *Logic and Reality in Leibniz's Metaphysics*, Oxford, 1965: dry, scholarly and reliable; Benson Mates, *The Philosophy of Leibniz: Logic and Language*, Oxford, 1986: accessible, interesting, occasionally misleading; C. D. Broad, *Leibniz: An Introduction*, Cambridge, 1975: posthumously published lectures – thorough, comprehensive, and a trifle out of date; Hide Ishiguro, *Leibniz's Philosophy of Logic and Language*, London, 1972: difficult, tortuous, but worth the effort. There is also a famous book by Bertrand Russell, *A Critical Exposition of the Philosophy of Leibniz*, 2nd edn, London, 1937. This tried to show that Leibniz's metaphysics (which Russell did not admire) was motivated by his logic (which he did). The interpretation offered was very influential, though now largely rejected.

Among collections of articles, the following can be recommended: Michael Hooker (ed.), *Leibniz: Critical and Interpretative Essays*, Minneapolis, 1983; R. S. Woolhouse (ed.), *Leibniz: Metaphysics and Philosophy of Science*, Oxford, 1981: contains a good, if undiscriminating, bibliography; Nicholas Jolley (ed.), *The Cambridge Companion to Leibniz*, Cambridge, 1994.

For the place of both Spinoza and Leibniz in the history of ideas, see A. Lovejoy's classic study, *The Great Chain of Being*, London, 1936.

7 Locke and Berkeley

Thomas Hobbes, *Leviathan*, ed. with an introduction by Michael Oakeshott, Oxford, 1947.

Editions of Locke's *Essay on the Human Understanding* are of varying quality; by far the best is that edited by Peter H. Nidditch, Oxford, 1975. This contains a useful foreword by the editor.

Because the *Essay* is so diffuse and repetitious, various abridgements have been attempted, among which the most popular has been that by A. S. Pringle-Pattison, Oxford, 1924.

Good introductory commentaries include Stephen Priest, *The British Empiricists*, London, 1990, and R. I. Aaron, *John Locke*, 3rd edn., Oxford, 1971. More challenging are: Jonathan Bennett, *Locke, Berkeley and Hume: Central Themes*, Oxford, 1971, especially useful on the theory of meaning and ideas; J. L. Mackie, *Problems from Locke*, Oxford, 1976, which relates Locke's concerns to modern debates in metaphysics and the philosophy of science; Michael Ayers, *Locke: Epistemology and Ontology*, London, 1991: in many ways a model of scholarly research, which is also an impressive philosophical statement in its own right.

Among collections of articles, the most useful is probably V. C. Chappell (ed.), *The Cambridge Companion to Locke*, Cambridge, 1994.

The most useful edition of Berkeley is that edited by G. J. Warnock, entitled *The Principles of Human Knowledge and Other Writings*, London, 1977. There are several useful commentaries available, including that by Bennett mentioned above, together with A. C. Grayling, *Berkeley: The Central Arguments*, London, 1986, and J. O. Urmson, *Berkeley*, Oxford, 1982.

8 The idea of a moral science

L. A. Selby-Bigge (ed.), *British Moralists*, vol. 1, Oxford, 1897, contains principal works by the writers mentioned.

Other sources worth consulting are Shaftesbury, *Characteristics*, ed. J. M. Robertson, London, 1900, and W. E. Gladstone (ed.), *The Works of Joseph Butler*, 2 vols, Oxford, 1897. No satisfactory commentary on the British moralists seems to exist at present, although the chapter on Butler in C. D. Broad's *Five Types of Ethical Theory*, London, 1930, remains helpful.

For standard editions of the works of the individual writers, the reader should consult the *Encyclopedia of Philosophy*, edited by Paul S. Edwards, London and New York, 1967.

9 Hume

The standard editions of the *Treatise* and *Enquiries* are those edited by L. A. Selby-Bigge and P. H. Nidditch, Oxford, 1978 and 1975 respectively.

Many editions exist of Hume's *Essays, Moral and Political* (1741–2), and recent editions have been enlarged to include most of Hume's incidental writings. The *Dialogues Concerning Natural Religion* (1779) are also widely available in reliable editions.

Among commentaries, the following deserve special mention: Norman Kemp Smith, *The Philosophy of David Hume*, London, 1949: a path-breaking study which initiated the modern emphasis on Hume's 'naturalism'. Its gist can be obtained from reading: Barry Stroud, *Hume*, London, 1977, which gives what is fast becoming the orthodox reading of Hume, as the exponent of a 'natural philosophy' of the mind. David Pears's *Hume's System*, Oxford, 1990, is a highly sophisticated work along the same lines, which also contains an interesting defence of Hume against the charge that his system leads to an irreversible scepticism.

Among collections of articles that edited by V. C. Chappell (*Hume*, New York, 1966) is as readable as any.

10 Kant I: The *Critique of Pure Reason*

To date there is no acceptable edition of the *Critique of Pure Reason* in English, apart from the translation by Norman Kemp Smith, London, 1929. This translates and collates both editions, and contains marginal references to the original page numberings of each of them.

There is a standard German edition of Kant, published as *Gesammelte Schriften* by the Prussian (subsequently German) Academy of Sciences between 1902 and 1968. This provides standard page numberings for many translations. More useful, because cheaper and more readily available is the twelve-volume Suhrkamp edition of Kant, which is, however, incomplete.

Kant himself wrote a kind of introduction to his metaphysical views in the *Prolegomena to any Future Metaphysics*, tr. P. G. Lucas, Manchester, 1953. There is also available in English a useful selection from Kant's 'pre-critical' writings (those written before the first *Critique*): G. B. Kerferd, D. K. E. Walford and P. G. Lucas (eds), *Kant: Selected Pre-critical Writings*, Manchester, 1968.

A complete translation of the works of Kant, in conformity with the latest scholarship, is projected by Cambridge University Press; so far, however, the major works have not been retranslated for this edition.

Among recent commentaries, the following are especially important: Jonathan Bennett, *Kant's Analytic*, Cambridge, 1966; Jonathan Bennett, *Kant's Dialectic*, Cambridge, 1974; P. F. Strawson, *The Bounds of Sense*, London, 1966; Ralph Walker, *Kant*, London, 1978; Henry E. Allison, *Kant's Transcendental Idealism: An Interpretation and Defense*, New Haven, 1983.

Among collections of articles, the most useful are: L. W. Beck (ed.), *Kant's Theory of Knowledge*, Boston, 1974; Ralph Walker (ed.), *Kant on Pure Reason*, Oxford, 1987; Paul Guyer (ed.), *The Cambridge Companion to Kant*, Cambridge, 1994.

11 Kant II: Ethics and aesthetics

Kant wrote a number of works on ethics, of which the most important are: *Critique of Practical Reason*, tr. L. W. Beck, New York, 1965; *Groundwork of the Metaphysic of Morals*, tr. H. J. Paton, New York, 1964; *Lectures on Ethics*, tr. L. Infield, New York, 1973; *Die Metaphysik der Sitten*, translated in two parts: (i) *The Metaphysical Elements of Justice*, tr. J. Ladd, New York, 1965; (ii) *The Doctrine of Virtue*, tr. Mary J. Gregor, New York, 1964.

Kant's aesthetic theory is contained in the third *Critique: Critique of Judgement*, tr. with an extensive introduction by Werner S. Pluhar, Indianapolis, 1987. (Two older translations exist – both inadequate.)

Commentaries include: Roger Scruton, *Kant*, Oxford, 1982: a short commentary on the whole of Kant's philosophy, which tries to show the place of the ethical and aesthetic theories within it; L. W. Beck, *A Commentary on Kant's 'Critique of Practical Reason'*, Chicago, 1960; Henry E. Allison, *Kant's Theory of Freedom*, New Haven, 1991; Anthony Savile, *Aesthetic Reconstructions: The Seminal Writings of Lessing, Kant and Schiller*, Oxford, 1987.

The English-language sources for post-Kantian idealism include the following:

Fichte
The Science of Knowledge, with the first and second introductions, ed. and tr. Peter Heath and John Lacks, Cambridge, 1982. This gives the *Wissenschaftslehre* in its most complete form, with useful addenda and commentary, in an up-to-date translation. The student should beware of nineteenth-century translations of this work.

Schelling
System of Transcendental Idealism, tr. Peter Heath, with an introduction by Michael Vater, Charlottesville, Va., 1978. This is the principal source for Schelling's philosophical ideas. In addition the reader might consult: *Of Human Freedom*, tr. James Gutman, Chicago, 1936, and *The Ages of the World*, tr. F. de Wolfe Bolman Jr., New York, 1942, which expounds Schelling's influential theory of history.

Schiller
On the Aesthetic Education of Man in a Series of Letters, ed. and tr. Elizabeth M. Wilkerson and L. A. Willoughby, Oxford, 1982.

12 Hegel

Hegel translations and editions were hastily put together in the last century, and the hitherto authoritative English-language versions finally published by T. M. Knox are now themselves giving way to newer versions, incorporating the more sober hopes entertained towards the Hegelian system by modern scholars. Technical terms are translated differently by different authors, but a certain standardisation is gradually emerging. The confusion is partially dispelled by: Michael Inwood, *A Hegel Dictionary*, Oxford, 1992.

The works of Hegel that are important for the argument of this chapter are: *Hegel's Science of Logic*, tr. A. V. Miller, with a foreword by J. N. Findlay,

London, 1969; *Hegel's Logic: Part of the Encyclopedia*, tr. William Wallace, 3rd edn, Oxford, 1975; *The Phenomenology of Spirit*, tr. A. V. Miller, with a foreword by J. N. Findlay, Oxford, 1977.

Commentaries on Hegel are appearing with increasing frequency. Charles Taylor's *Hegel*, Oxford, 1975, was a pioneering attempt to look at Hegel through the eyes of analytical philosophy. More useful for the student, however, is Robert Solomon's attempt to reconstruct the argument of the *Phenomenology*, entitled *In the Spirit of Hegel*, Oxford, 1983. More sober and succinct is Stephen Houlgate, *Freedom, Truth and History: An Introduction to Hegel's Philosophy*, London, 1991.

The most useful collection of articles is: Frederick C. Baiser, *The Cambridge Companion to Hegel*, Cambridge, 1993.

I merely touch on the aspect of Hegel's thinking which has been most widely influential – namely, the philosophy of history, and the theory of the *Zeitgeist*. This is contained in: *Lectures on the Philosophy of History*, tr. J. Sibree, London, 1890, reissued New York, 1956.

13 Reactions: Schopenhauer, Kierkegaard and Nietzsche

Schopenhauer

There are two translations of Schopenhauer's major work, with two different terms ('idea' and 'representation') used to translate Schopenhauer's '*Vorstellung*'. 'Representation' is to be preferred, since Schopenhauer has another use for the term 'Idea'. *The World as Will and Idea*, tr. R. B. Haldane and J. Kemp, London, 1906; *The World as Will and Representation*, tr. E. F. J. Payne, India Hills, Colo., 1958.

There are many editions of Schopenhauer's shorter essays. Perhaps the best is: *Parerga and Paralipomena: Short Philosophical Essays*, tr. E. F. J. Payne, Oxford, 1974.

Commentaries are for the most part unexciting. Perhaps the most reliable, from the point of view of philosophical history, is that by Christopher Janaway: *Schopenhauer*, Oxford 1994.

Kierkegaard

It is almost impossible to distinguish the central from the peripheral among Kierkegaard's many and varied writings. However, I have drawn on the following: *Either/Or: A Fragment of Life*, tr. David F. and Lillian Marvin Swenson, Oxford, 1944; *'Fear and Trembling' and 'Repetition'*, ed. and tr. H. V. and E. H. Hong, Princeton, N.J., 1983; *The Concept of Dread*, tr. with an introduction by Walter Lowrie, Princeton, N.J., 1944; *The Sickness unto Death*, tr. W. Lowrie, Princeton, N.J., 1941; *Concluding Unscientific Postscript*, tr. David F. Swenson, completed by Walter Lowrie, Princeton, N.J., 1941.

Among the commentaries on Kierkegaard, that by W. Lowrie, *Kierkegaard*, New York, 1938, remains illuminating.

Nietzsche
Nietzsche is most accessible through well-edited selections, such as: *The Portable Nietzsche*, tr. and ed. Walter Kaufmann, New York, 1954, 1968; *Basic Writings*, tr. and ed. Walter Kaufmann, New York, 1992; *A Nietzsche Reader*, tr. and ed. R. J. Hollingdale, Harmondsworth, 1977.

For the specific works referred to, see: *'Twilight of the Idols' and 'The Antichrist'*, tr. R. J. Hollingdale, with an introduction by Michael Tanner, London, 1990; *Beyond Good and Evil: Prelude to a Philosophy of the Future*, tr. with an introduction by R. J. Hollingdale, Harmondsworth, 1973; *Thus Spake Zarathustra*, tr. with an introduction by R. J. Hollingdale, Harmondsworth, 1969; *'The Birth of Tragedy' and 'The Case of Wagner'*, tr. with commentary by Walter Kaufmann, New York, 1967; *The Gay Science*, tr. Walter Kaufmann, New York, 1974; *The Will to Power*, tr. Walter Kaufmann and R. J. Hollingdale, New York, 1967. This last contains Nietzsche's posthumous writings, with some of his most abstract and philosophical ideas.

Nietzsche attracts commentators from many disciplines, and with many aims. The following are readable: Arthur Danto, *Nietzsche as Philosopher*, New York, 1965: a book which draws the teeth of Nietzsche the moralist; Michael Tanner, *Nietzsche*, Oxford, 1994: a lively survey and introduction, which tries to save Nietzsche from the charge of nihilism; Erich Heller, *The Importance of Nietzsche*, Chicago, 1988: a work that explores the real Nietzsche and his relation to the literary tradition that created him: a necessary antidote to the laboured attempts to recast Nietzsche as a metaphysician. Alexander Nehemas, *Nietzsche: Life as Literature*, Harvard, 1985: a distinctly modern, maybe post-modern, interpretation.

For Max Stirner, see *The Ego and His Own*, ed. and abridged by John Carroll, New York, 1971.

14 Political philosophy from Hobbes to Hegel

Hobbes, *Leviathan*, ed. with introduction by Michael Oakeshott, Oxford, 1947.

Spinoza, *Political Works*, tr. and ed. A. G. Wernham, Oxford, 1958.

Locke, *Two Treatises of Government*, critical edn, ed. P. Laslett, London, 1960.

Richard Hooker, *The Laws of Ecclesiastical Polity*, Everyman edn.

Montesquieu, *Spirit of the Laws*, tr. T. Nugent, New York, 1949.

J. J. Rousseau, *Political Writings*, tr. and ed. C. A. Vaughan, 2 vols, Cambridge, 1915.

G. W. F. Hegel, *Elements of the Philosophy of Right*, tr. H. B. Nisbet, ed. Allen W. Wood, Cambridge, 1991.

Commentaries: It is difficult to provide a guide to the literature that has accumulated in this area of philosophical history. One of the most interesting of the commentaries on Hegel's *Philosophy of Right* remains that of Karl Marx (Cambridge, 1970). For Locke, see J. W. Gough, *John Locke's Political Philosophy: Eight Studies*, Oxford, 1950. The introduction by M. Oakeshott to the edition cited of the *Leviathan* is one of the liveliest and most adventurous commentaries on that work. Perhaps the best way to acquire a modern understanding of these complementary political philosophies is to compare modern works which defend some Lockean or neo-Lockean doctrine of the 'natural right' (e.g. Robert Nozick, *Anarchy, State and Utopia*, Oxford, 1974) with those which regard allegiance, in the manner of Hegel, as prior to the recognition of individual rights (e.g. Roger Scruton, *The Meaning of Conservatism*, 2nd edn, London, 1984).

15 Marx

Confusion in the texts of Marx's principal works, while less than that which still prevails in the case of Leibniz, is great enough to cause me not to give a proper bibliography. There is another reason for this, namely that many of the writings are fragmentary, and almost all stand in need of an editor. The task of editor has been ably accomplished by David McLellan, in *Karl Marx: Selected Writings*, Oxford, 1977, and by Allen W. Wood, *Marx: Selections*, London, 1988. Both contain all the important philosophical writings, together with a guide to *Capital*, selections from which they reprint.

Commentaries: Elementary – Peter Singer, *Marx*, Past Masters series, Oxford, 1980. Advanced – G. A. Cohen, *Karl Marx's Theory of History*, Oxford, 1979 . Both of those concentrate on the mature theories of Marx; the second is unique in Marxian scholarship, in that it treats its subject matter entirely from the methodological standpoint of analytical philosophy. The best short commentary on Marx's immediate predecessors is W. T. Brazill: *The Young Hegelians*, New Haven and London, 1970. For the latter-day followers of the early Marx see George Lukács: *History and Class Consciousness*, tr. R. Livingstone, London, 1971, in which the theory of alienation and the later theory of 'false consciousness' are combined to form the idea of 'reification'; and also the writings of philosophers of the 'Frankfurt School', in particular Herbert Marcuse, *Reason and Revolution*, Oxford, 1941; and Jürgen Habermas, *Theory and Practice*, tr. J. Viertel, London, 1974.

16 Utilitarianism and after

A new standard edition of Bentham's works is in the course of preparation. Meanwhile the basic text is J. Bowring (ed.), *The Works of Jeremy Bentham*, 11 vols, Edinburgh, 1838–43 (incomplete). *The Fragment on Government* and *Introduction* exist in several reliable popular editions, as does Adam Smith's *Wealth of Nations*.

J. S. Mill, *A System of Logic*, London, 1843; *Utilitarianism*, *On Liberty* and the *Autobiography* exist in many popular editions.

F. H. Bradley, *Ethical Studies*, Oxford, 1876; *The Principles of Logic*, Oxford, 1883; *Appearance and Reality*, Oxford, 1893.

R. L. Nettleship, *The Works of Thomas Hill Green*, London, 1885–8.

On utilitarianism in general the best modern commentary is by J. J. C. Smart and Bernard Williams, *Utilitarianism: For and Against*, Cambridge, 1973.

On Bradley the most interesting commentary is that by Richard Wollheim, Harmondsworth, 1959; see also A. Manser and G. Stock (eds), *The Philosophy of F. H. Bradley*, Oxford, 1984.

17 Frege

Frege, *The Foundations of Arithmetic*, tr. J. L. Austin, Oxford, 1950; *Philosophical Writings*, ed. M. Black and P. T. Geach, Oxford, 1952, 3rd edn 1980.

Commentaries: W. and M. Kneale, *The Development of Logic*, Oxford, 1962, chapter 8. (This book provides an unsurpassed history of the subject of logic, and makes the revolutionary character of Frege's logic easy to grasp.) Also M. Dummett, *Frege: Philosophy of Language*, London, 1973: a diffuse and difficult work, which nevertheless has done much to impress on the philosophical public the importance of Frege. The *Begriffsschrift* is translated in Frege, *Philosophical Writings*. Michael Dummett has continued his commentaries on Frege with *Frege and Other Philosophers*, Oxford, 1991, and *Frege: Philosophy of Mathematics*, Oxford, 1991.

18 Phenomenology and existentialism

F. Brentano, *Psychology from an Empirical Standpoint*, tr. L. McAlister et al., London, 1973.

E. Husserl, *Logical Investigations*, tr. J. N. Findlay, 2 vols, London, 1970; *Ideas for a Pure Phenomenology*, tr. W. R. Boyce Gibson, London, 1931; *Cartesian Meditations*, tr. D. Cairns, The Hague, 1960; *Phenomenology of Internal Time Consciousness*, tr. J. S. Churchill, ed. M. Heidegger, The Hague, 1964.

M. Heidegger, *Being and Time*, tr. J. Macquarrie and E. S. Robinson, New York, 1962.

J. P. Sartre, *The Psychology of Imagination*, tr. B. Frechtman, New York, 1948; *Being and Nothingness*, tr. Hazel E. Barnes, New York, 1956.

M. Merleau-Ponty, *Phenomenology of Perception*, tr. Colin Smith, London, 1962; *Signs*, tr. R. C. McCleary, Evanston, 1964.

A general, but uncritical and obscure, survey is contained in H. Spiegelberg, *The Phenomenological Movement*, 2 vols, The Hague, 1960. There is an excellent introduction to Husserl by David Bell: *Husserl*, London, 1990. On Heidegger it is worth reading the famous paper by Rudolf Carnap: 'The Elimination of Metaphysics Through the Logical Analysis of Language' (1932), published in A. J. Ayer (ed.), *Logical Positivism*, Chicago,

1959. There is, however, no balanced commentary, to my knowledge, on this philosopher. Sartre has the benefit of Mary Warnock's *The Philosophy of Sartre*, London, 1965, and also Iris Murdoch's *Sartre: Romantic Rationalist*, New Haven, 1953, and Arthur Danto's *Sartre*, London, 1975 (Modern Masters Series, Fontana). Perhaps the best account, however, is that by David Cooper, *Existentialism*, Oxford, 1990. There is also a *Cambridge Companion to Sartre*, ed. C. Howells, Cambridge, 1992. On Wilhelm Dilthey, see H. P. Rickmann (ed.), *Wilhelm Dilthey: Selected Writings*, London, 1980.

19 Wittgenstein

Bertrand Russell, 'On Denoting', the article which presents the theory of descriptions, is collected together with other expressions of Russell's logical atomism in *Logic and Knowledge*, ed. R. C. Marsh, London, 1956.

Wittgenstein, *Tractatus Logico-Philosophicus*, German text with translation by D. F. Pears and B. F. McGuiness, London, 1961; *Philosophical Investigations*, tr. G. E. M. Anscombe, Oxford, 1953; *Remarks on the Foundations of Mathematics*, tr. G. E. M. Anscombe, Oxford, 1956.

Commentaries: On atomism and positivism generally see J. O. Urmson, *Philosophical Analysis*, Oxford, 1956, a lucid but dated book, written from the standpoint of Oxford linguistic philosophy. See also D. F. Pears, *Bertrand Russell*, London, 1967. On Wittgenstein see Anthony Kenny, *Wittgenstein*, London, Penguin, 1973, which is perhaps the least misleading among the short commentaries on the later work. Among more advanced commentaries, the following deserve mention: Saul Kripke, *Wittgenstein on Rules and Private Language*, Oxford, 1982, and David Pears, *The False Prison*, 2 vols, Oxford, 1987.

INDEX